Mastering Credit
Derivatives

FT Prentice Hall
FINANCIAL TIMES

In an increasingly competitive world, we believe it's quality of thinking that gives you the edge – an idea that opens new doors, a technique that solves a problem, or an insight that simply makes sense of it all. The more you know, the smarter and faster you can go.

That's why we work with the best minds in business and finance to bring cutting-edge thinking and best learning practice to a global market.

Under a range of leading imprints, including *Financial Times Prentice Hall*, we create world-class print publications and electronic products bringing our readers knowledge, skills and understanding, which can be applied whether studying or at work.

To find out more about Pearson Education publications, or tell us about the books you'd like to find, you can visit us at **www.pearsoned.co.uk**

Mastering Credit Derivatives

A step-by-step guide to credit derivatives and structured credit

Second Edition

ANDREW KASAPIS

FT Prentice Hall
FINANCIAL TIMES

An imprint of **Pearson Education**

Harlow, England • London • New York • Boston • San Francisco • Toronto • Sydney • Singapore • Hong Kong
Tokyo • Seoul • Taipei • New Delhi • Cape Town • Madrid • Mexico City • Amsterdam • Munich • Paris • Milan

PEARSON EDUCATION LIMITED

Edinburgh Gate
Harlow CM20 2JE
Tel: +44 (0)1279 623623
Fax: +44 (0)1279 431059
Website: www.pearsoned.co.uk

First published in Great Britain in 1999
Second edition published 2008

© Pearson Education Limited 1999
© Credit Hedge Limited 2008

The right of Andrew Kasapis to be identified as author of this work has been asserted
by him in accordance with the Copyright, Designs and Patents Act 1988.

ISBN: 978-0-273-71485-9

British Library Cataloguing in Publication Data
A catalogue record for this book is available from the British Library

Library of Congress Cataloging-in-Publication Data

Kasapis, Andrew.
    Mastering credit derivatives : a step-by-step guide to credit
derivatives and structured credit / Andrew Kasapis. -- 2nd ed.
        p. cm.
    "First published in Great Britain in 1999."
    Includes bibliographical reference and index.
    ISBN 978-0-273-71485-9 (pbk.)
    1.   Credit derivatives. 2. Credit--Management. I. Title.
    HG6024.A3K376 2008
    332.7--dc22
                                                                    2008041027

10 9 8 7 6 5 4 3 2 1
11 10 09 08

Typeset in 11.5pt Garamond by 30
Printed by Ashford Colour Press Ltd., Gosport

The publisher's policy is to use paper manufactured from sustainable forests.

About the author

Andrew Kasapis is a consultant in market risk management methodology and a expert on most derivative products across all asset classes, in particular structured credit-driven products. He has worked for NatWest Markets, BZW, IBM Trading and Risk, and is a consultant on market risk projects for Tier 1 banks in London. Andrew is currently director of Credit Hedge Ltd.

Contents

Preface   xi
Publisher's acknowledgements   xiv

1 Introduction   1
What's in a name?   2
What are credit derivatives?   3
How big is the market?   3
Who is involved?   6
Evolution of the market   10

2 Credit derivative instruments and applications   13
Credit derivatives products   14
Trades using credit derivatives   20
Risk measures for CDS   23
Comparing bond spreads and CDS prices   24
Basket default swaps   29
Synthetic CDOs   35
Summary: application of credit derivatives   41

3 Pricing a CDS and the cash bond basis   43
Credit modelling   44
Calibrating recovery rates   47
A practical approach to pricing a CDS   49
Using default swaps to make a credit curve   55
Linking the credit default swap and cash markets   56
Cash and CDS basis   60
Bond spread measures and the CDS–bond basis definition   62
Basis drivers   67
Summary: credit default swaps compared with bonds   74

4 Credit derivative documentation and regulations   **79**

Documentation   80

Infrastructure and ISDA's role   81

Restructuring: the 2003 definitions   83

Other considerations   87

Bank regulation of credit derivatives   89

5 Tranched indices   **97**

Credit default swap indices   98

Determining the upfront payment   103

Impact of defaults on index cashflows   103

Tranches of standard default swap indices   104

Characteristics of benchmark tranches   105

Investment strategies with credit derivative indices   108

Investors   112

6 What is correlation?   **113**

What do we mean by correlation?   114

Correlation in structured credit markets   115

Observing default correlation   117

Valuation in structured credit markets   120

Getting to a portfolio loss distribution   121

Copula functions   122

Correlation as a relative value metric (base correlation)   123

Base correlation   125

Practical use of correlation   126

Analysing a portfolio of credit risk   129

Modelling correlated defaults   129

Simulating correlated defaults with a copula   131

What is correlation missing?   136

A summary of CDO pricing   137

Correlation trading rules of thumb   138

Copula drawbacks   138

7 First-to-default (FTD) baskets   **141**

Basket default swap mechanics   142

Investor motivation   144

Mergers and FTD baskets   145

Second-through-fifth default baskets   148

Funded baskets   149

8   Cash CDOs   **151**

CDO terminology   153

Assets, tranches, purposes and credit structures   153

The à la carte CDO menu   157

How do cash CDOs work in practice?   160

Cash CDOs: a taxonomy   165

Structural features and performance tests in cash CDOs   167

Understanding CDO equity returns   174

Understanding CDO debt returns   174

Details of a cash CDO's structure   175

9   Synthetic CDOs   **179**

What are synthetic CDOs?   180

Example of a fully unfunded synthetic CDO   185

Example of an AAA reference portfolio CDO   187

Case studies of managed synthetic CDOs   188

Single-tranche CDOs (STCDOs)   190

CSO trade opportunities   200

Synthetic CDO structures   201

Analytical challenges in modelling synthetic CDOs   209

The ABCs of CDOs – squared   211

10   Understanding tranche sensitivity   **215**

Introduction   216

Tranches as options on default   217

Sensitivity to spread changes ('delta')   218

'I – Gamma': sensitivity to spread distribution changes   219

Delta migration   221

'M – Gamma': convexity   224

Jump-to-default sensitivity   226

'Theta': time decay   228

'Rho': sensitivity to correlation changes   229

Conclusion   232

11 Innovation, the credit crisis and the future   233

Innovation outstrips risk management   234

Subprime mortgage crisis of 2007   234

Credit crisis events in context   244

Action taken   251

Subprime credit crunch: a summary   251

Subprime and credit crunch debate   252

How regulators and banks improve risk management   257

Notes and references   259
Glossary   263
Index   269

Preface

The credit derivatives business is at a crossroads. This is a market that has enjoyed a phenomenal growth rate over the past ten years or so. Credit events such as Enron, WorldCom, the subprime crisis and the resulting credit crunch have brought down institutions of the calibre of Bear Sterns in the US and Northern Rock in the UK.

Greater liquidity in credit derivatives markets has enabled the development of more sophisticated credit structures, such as complex collateralized debt obligations (CDOs), but the volatility of credit markets has also revealed a fundamental weakness in the way in which most financial firms manage their credit risk.

The lack of prudent house loan lending (not a credit derivative, I may add), combined with the lack of structured credit product transparency and an unexpected housing market crash in the US has damaged structures such as synthetic corporate CDOs and other structured credit products that had sub-prime second home loans and first mortgages underpinning them. The increase in expected defaults on these loans because of the fall in house prices has essentially been the trigger for the current credit crunch problems. The mark-to-market values of positions in these structured credit products have plummeted. This has highlighted the catastrophic losses incurred by many banks. In hindsight, the ratings on these tranches were unrealistic

All of the above, coupled with a short-term credit crisis in which banks were reluctant to lend to each other for fear of the unknown losses each financial institution might be exposed to, have created a watershed for the structured credit market.

Nevertheless, structured credit products are an integral part of the set of asset classes and instruments in the financial world. All parties to this market have benefited and will continue to benefit differently but equally from the market's growth and development. The future may look problematic but, historically, I believe the lessons learned in other crisis situations are that the structured credit derivatives market's future is secure. It will simply evolve and cope, as it has in the past, to survive.

Central banks are stepping in to provide cheap funds to banks to alleviate the current credit situation. The rating agencies have acted to re-rate a number of corporate synthetic CDOs by introducing more realistic stress tests in their rating models. Credit derivatives are here to stay and structured credit products will become more robust.

In this text, I cover the numerous structured credit derivatives products as well as giving an overview on the more flow-like instruments.

This book is dedicated to David Moore & Maria Kasapis

Publisher's acknowledgements

The publishers are grateful to the following for permission to reproduce copyright material:

Figure 1.1 BusinessWeek; Table 1.1 reprinted from ISDA Market Survey by permission of International Swaps and Derivatives Assocation, Inc. © 2008 International Swaps and Derivatives Association, Inc.; Table 1.2 Creditflux Data+; Table 8.3 © Moody's Investor Service, Inc. and/or its affiliates. Reprinted with permission. All Rights Reserved.

In some instances we have been unable to trace the owners of copyright material, and would appreciate any information that would enable us to do so.

Introduction

'Everything should be as simple as possible, but no simpler'

Albert Einstein

When approaching the structured credit market in a strategic way, one of the most daunting tasks is balancing complexity and simplicity. As in the physical sciences, expressing concepts in the simplest form is appealing. Yet, the state-of-the-art in financial engineering, combined with increasing demand for complexity from credit investors, can make this process a challenge. Thinking about concepts intuitively and strategically in a straightforward manner will remain one of the goals for this introduction to structured credit products.

'Structured credit' means different things to different people, but I tend to think of it literally. Structured credit is the process of taking ordinary credit instruments and 'structuring' them to meet certain goals, which can include diversification, loss or payment redistribution, hedging, principal protection, achieving rating targets or stability, and altering a portfolio's sensitivity to spread movements and defaults. Structured credit instruments can be focused on single names or portfolios, but for purpose of this book, Chapters 1 and 2 address flow credit derivatives from single issuers as an introduction to credit derivatives. The rest of the book covers structured credit in portfolio form and is focused on corporate credit risk.

Tranched credit, by far the largest portion of the structured credit business today, is really two markets that share a common lineage, one in which underlying collateral is cash assets (bonds and loans) and the other in which it is synthetic (credit default swaps). In my view, the two markets are conceptually more similar than they are different, but for many reasons that we shall discuss throughout this book, they have important structural differences and can be culturally disparate as well. Nevertheless, I have tried to discuss the differences from several perspectives and also try to comment on how they might converge again in the future.

WHAT'S IN A NAME?

Perhaps one of the most confusing aspects of the tranched credit market is the plethora of names used to describe what is essentially a single idea. The French word *tranche* means slice, as in *tranche de pain* (slice of bread). If one thinks of the full loaf as being a blended credit portfolio, then the slices are the pieces that investors can use to gain exposure to the portfolio, although these slices can differ in terms of thickness, exposure to portfolio losses and cashflows.

WHAT ARE CREDIT DERIVATIVES?

Credit derivatives were first traded sporadically at the end of the 1980s but it was not until the early 1990s that a market for these products began to emerge. In the late 1990s and the first half of the next decade, credit derivatives grew rapidly to achieve a central role in the financial markets.

The purpose of a credit derivative is to transfer only the credit risk of a borrower and not the associated interest rate risk. The fact that credit risk can be traded in isolation makes credit derivatives a powerful tool.

The main types of credit derivative products are: single-name credit default swaps; credit derivative indices; index tranches; synthetic CDOs; CPDO (Constant Proportion Debt Obligation) and CPPI (Constant Proportion Portfolio Insurance).

Unlike bonds and loans, which are financial contracts between a borrower and a lender, credit derivatives are contracts between any two counterparties that reference a specific borrower (the 'reference entity'). Often, neither counterparty is a lender to the reference entity. The reference entity is rarely involved in the trade and usually has no reason to know that the credit derivative contract exists.

All credit derivatives traded by mid-2006 were over-the-counter (OTC) derivatives. Unlike many equity or commodity options and futures, they are not traded on an exchange but are simply private contracts between two counterparties – one of which is usually a dealer (also called a market maker).

HOW BIG IS THE MARKET?

Because credit derivatives are private contracts, it is difficult to calculate the size of the market with any accuracy. The task is also complicated by the ways volumes are measured, problems of double-counting and doubts about whether or not certain products should be considered as credit derivatives.

As a result, estimates of the size of the market vary greatly. But the various surveys agree that volumes have grown very rapidly since 2000.

The International Swaps and Derivatives Association (ISDA), the trade association for dealers and users of over-the-counter derivatives, carries out a twice-yearly survey of the size of the market. It asks its members to calculate the total notional amount of all the derivatives they have outstanding. (In 2006, eighty-six firms provided information on their credit derivative positions, indicating that most big market participants were included in the survey.) In summary:

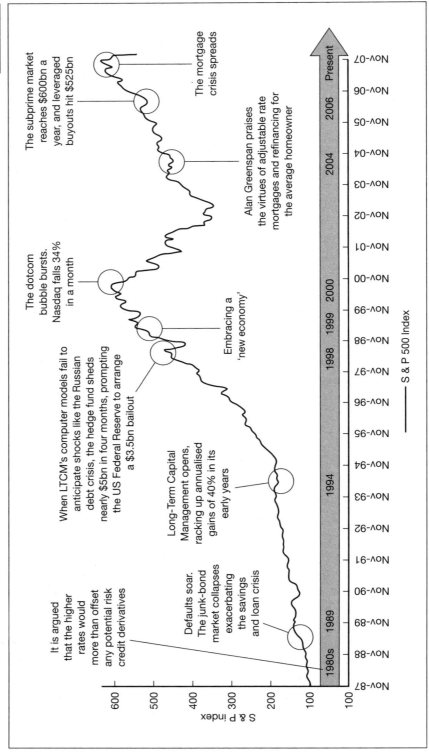

Figure 1.1

Timeline of growth of US credit derivatives market

It is argued that the higher rates would more than offset any potential risk credit derivatives

Defaults soar. The junk-bond market collapses exacerbating the savings and loan crisis

Long-Term Capital Management opens, racking up annualised gains of 40% in its early years

When LTCM's computer models fail to anticipate shocks like the Russian debt crisis, the hedge fund sheds nearly $5bn in four months, prompting the US Federal Reserve to arrange a $3.5bn bailout

The dotcom bubble bursts. Nasdaq falls 34% in a month

Embracing a 'new economy'

Alan Greenspan praises the virtues of adjustable rate mortgages and refinancing for the average homeowner

The subprime market reaches $600bn a year, and leveraged buyouts hit $525bn

The mortgage crisis spreads

S & P index

600
500
400
300
200
100

Nov-87 Nov-88 Nov-89 Nov-90 Nov-91 Nov-92 Nov-93 Nov-94 Nov-95 Nov-96 Nov-97 Nov-98 Nov-99 Nov-00 Nov-01 Nov-02 Nov-03 Nov-04 Nov-05 Nov-06 Nov-07

1980s 1989 1994 1998 1999 2000 2004 2006 Present

100

—— S & P 500 Index

Source: DCT, 2008/Bloomberg, Business Week

- The value of outstanding credit derivatives grew from less than $1,000bn in 2001 to $62,000bn in 2007 according to ISDA (see Table 1.1).

- The value of outstanding cash CDOs stood at $986bn at the start of 2007, according to Creditflux Data+ (see Table 1.2).

- The value of synthetic CDO tranches traded in 2004–07 was $739bn, according to Creditflux Data+.

- The largest category of cash CDOs is formed by those backed by asset-backed securities (CDOs of ABS), closely followed by those collateralized by leveraged loans (collateralized loan obligations or CLOs).

National amounts outstanding, semi annual data, all surveyed contracts (adjusted for double counting)

Table 1.1

Year	Credit default swaps outstanding ($bn)
2001	918.87
2002	2,191.57
2003	3,779.40
2004	8,422.26
2005	17,096.14
2006	34,422.80
2007	62,173.20

Source: ISDA Market Survey. Reprinted with permission of International Swaps and Derivatives Association. © 2008 International Swaps and Derivatives Association, Inc.

Cash CDO outstanding (January 2007)

Table 1.2

	$bn	%
Structured finance	492	50
Corporate	412	42
Trups	26	3
Other	56	6
Total	986	100

Source: Creditflux Data+

The most liquid credit derivative products are credit indices. The main indices are the investment-grade indices iTraxx Europe and CDX NA IG, the CDX NA HY North American high-yield index, and the North American and European Xover and HiVol indices.

Credit derivatives are over-the-counter contracts almost always documented using standard templates and definitions drawn up by the International Swaps and Derivatives Association (ISDA).

One of the fastest growing areas of credit derivatives is the market for credit index tranches. Volumes of this 'correlation' business are expected to have surpassed $5,000bn in 2006, according to Creditflux Data+.

WHO IS INVOLVED?

The credit derivatives business has been dominated by banks and investment banks. This is not surprising when you consider the roles that banks and investment banks play in the credit business. Commercial banks are the main type of institution involved in lending money to companies using loans. Meanwhile, investment banks (also known as securities houses) underwrite and distribute the bonds that governments, financial institutions and corporates (non-financial companies) issue to the broader investment community.

According to figures compiled by the British Bankers' Association for the global market in 2003, banks were the most important group of buyers of protection – that is, counterparties using credit derivatives to offload credit risk (Figure 1.2). They were also the biggest group of protection sellers – that is, counterparties using derivatives to invest in credit.

Figure 1.2

Traders in credit protection (2003)

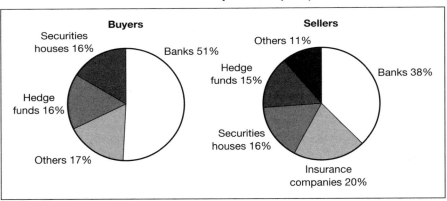

Source: British Bankers' Association

Banks

There is a common perception that banks use credit derivatives mainly to reduce their exposure to credits they do not like. While this may be true for many banks, it is by no means the whole story.

All banks are regulated indirectly by the BIS (under regulations called the Basel Accord, which is being updated to Basel II) to reserve a certain amount of capital against the assets they hold. This is called the bank's regulatory capital requirement and it depends on factors such as the credit risk and maturity of the assets it holds. Regulatory capital is a measure designed to preserve bank capital, since the riskier a bank's assets the more capital it has to reserve against those assets. The credit portfolio management function of a typical commercial bank looks at the profitability of the assets on its balance sheet, taking into account the regulatory cost of holding those assets. The credit portfolio manager may choose to sell an asset that does not provide enough of a return over its regulatory capital charge or does not fit with its portfolio strategy. Alternatively, in many cases, the credit portfolio manager will hedge the risk using a credit derivative, which allows the bank to release regulatory capital.

In addition, banks of all types make use of credit derivatives as an investment tool. Many banks have a proprietary trading desk that makes short- or medium-term bets on credit in much the same way that a hedge fund does. In addition, many commercial banks invest in single-name credit or in synthetic CDO tranches on a longer-term basis. They may also be a dealer (see below). Many regional banks act as a dealer within a certain niche, for example, repackaging synthetic CDOs for smaller banks and investors in their own country.

Dealers (market makers)

Dealers or market makers provide a service allowing market participants such as banks, insurance companies, corporates and hedge funds to buy and sell credit derivatives, making money from the difference between the buying and selling price (known as the bid and the offer). They can be commercial banks such as Citigroup or investment banks such as Morgan Stanley.

Large credit derivative dealers typically offer a wide range of credit derivative instruments and make a market on a range of reference entities. In almost all cases they also trade credit derivatives for their own book, though sometimes this proprietary trading business is kept at arm's length from the market-making function. Most credit derivative dealers have dealing desks in New York and London, and some also trade from Hong Kong, Singapore, Sydney or Tokyo.

The biggest credit derivative dealers have been JPMorgan and Deutsche Bank, two large universal banks (offering both commercial banking and investment banking). In recent years, the business has become less concentrated and around a dozen firms can be thought of as full-blown credit derivative dealers. The list of institutions signed up as dealers on the main credit derivative indices in Europe and in North America (see Table 1.3) gives an indication of which banks are involved as credit derivative dealers.

Table 1.3	Big users of credit derivatives

Licensed index dealers (CDX)

ABN Amro	Goldman Sachs
Bank of America	HSBC
Barclays Capital	JP Morgan
Bear Stearns	Lehman Brothers
BNP Paribas	Merrill Lynch
Citigroup	Morgan Stanley
Credit Suisse	UBS
Deutsche Bank	Wachovia

Licensed index dealers (iTraxx Europe)

ABN Amro	HypoVereinsbank
Bank of America	ING
Bank of Montreal	Ixis Corporate & Investment Bank
Barclays Capital	JP Morgan
Bayerische Landesbank	Lehman Brothers
BBVA	Merrill Lynch
Bear Stearns	Morgan Stanley
BNP Paribas	Natexis Banques Populaires
Calyon	Nomura
Citigroup	Nordea
Commerzbank	Royal Bank of Scotland
Credit Suisse	Santander
Deutsche Bank	Société Générale
Dresdner Kleinwort	TD Securities
Goldman Sachs	UBS
HSBC	

Hedge funds

Hedge funds are investment management vehicles designed to produce positive returns regardless of the direction of the market and are typically short-term investors. One of their biggest concerns is to ensure that they will be able to get out of – or unwind – a position when they need to. (This ability is known as 'liquidity'.)

For a long time, few hedge funds traded credit derivatives, regarding the market as too illiquid. That changed in around 2003, with the launch of the liquid credit derivative indices that later evolved into iTraxx and CDX. This meant that for the first time, hedge funds could trade in and out of credit in large amounts without losing large sums of money on the difference between the buying and selling price (the bid–offer spread) on each trade.

Since then, hedge funds have become important users of the credit derivatives market. Anecdotal evidence suggests their share of the market in terms of outstanding trades has grown substantially since 2003, when the British Banker's Association (BBA) survey put this figure at 15 per cent. In fact, because they are active buyers and sellers, hedge funds can often dominate daily trading volumes.

Some of the biggest multi-strategy hedge funds such as Amaranth, Citadel Investment, Moore Capital and Tudor Investment use the credit market. Other big hedge fund players are credit specialists, typically set up by former credit derivative traders at investment banks. These include BlueMountain Capital, Cairn Capital, Cheyne Capital Management, Solent Capital and Tricadia Capital. Most credit hedge fund managers are based in London or in the US. The funds themselves are usually domiciled offshore.

Asset managers

Asset managers that look after institutional money are fairly active in credit derivatives, especially those that manage CDOs. Traditional long-only funds such as mutual funds are much less involved. However, their involvement is thought to be increasing, and many funds became members of the DTCC DerivServ settlement system for credit default swaps in 2005 and 2006.

Insurance companies

Insurance companies are involved in credit derivatives in two ways. Life assurers and US property and casualty insurers hold large investment port-folios to match their liabilities. Some have invested a small portion of these funds in credit derivatives, generally using credit-linked notes.

The other way insurance companies use the credit derivatives market is by writing insurance policies. In economic terms, this is similar to selling protection on credit default swaps and these insurance policies are usually converted into credit derivative contracts through a special insurance vehicle known as a transformer. The insurance companies that are involved in this business include both specialist bond insurers, known as monoline insurers, and reinsurers.

Pension funds

Pension funds are not big users of credit derivatives, though some have invested in CDOs and their involvement is growing. Pension funds often face compliance issues in trading credit derivatives, because their invest-ment management guidelines often prevent the use of derivatives.

Retail investors

Credit derivatives are wholesale financial products that can almost never be traded directly by individual investors. Not only are the minimum trade sizes too large for most investors, banks are usually prohibited from offering these products to retail customers.

However, funded credit derivative products such as CDOs and credit CPPI products, which more easily lend themselves to being highly rated or principal protected, are an exception. These products are commonly sold to rich individuals, and in certain countries (notably Australia, Canada and the Netherlands) have been sold to ordinary retail customers.

Corporates

Despite the best efforts of many credit derivative salespeople, big corporates have not taken to using credit derivatives in the same way that they routinely hedge their currency or commodity price exposures.

Interdealer brokers

Interdealer brokers do not trade credit derivatives themselves. They act as agents when credit derivative dealers trade with each other. As in other derivatives markets, almost all credit derivative trades between dealers are brokered by one of the small number of these specialist firms. The biggest include Creditex, Creditrade, Garban, GFI and Tullett Prebon.

EVOLUTION OF THE MARKET

The timeline below outlines the way the market for credit derivatives developed, from the late 1980s to 2008. The final two years of that period were marked by the US subprime housing loan crisis and the credit crunch. The unfolding of these related crises is analysed in Chapter 11.

Highlights in the evolution of the credit derivatives market

Late 1980s
First cashflow CDOs issued

First credit derivatives begin to be traded, often swaps on specific bonds created for tax or regulatory purposes

Mid to late 1990s
Issuance of large balance sheet synthetic CDOs for the purpose of achieving regulatory capital relief

1996
The International Swaps and Derivatives Association (ISDA) publishes the first credit derivative definitions

July 1999
ISDA publishes the second credit derivative definitions, which bring greater standardization and acceptance to the market

September 2000
Bank of America extends the maturity of a loan to Conseco, triggering a controversy that eventually leads the market to change its definition of restructuring as a credit event

December 2001
Default of Enron, the biggest company default by volume of debt outstanding

Default of Argentina, the biggest sovereign default by volume of debt outstanding, triggering a controversy on the definition of repudiation/moratorium, the main credit event for sovereigns

April 2002
Morgan Stanley launches Synthetic Tracers, which becomes the market standard index for North American investment-grade credit

Dealers launch the reference entity database (Red) in response to high-profile cases in which counterparties had disagreed over which was the intended reference entity in a credit default swap. The project is later taken over by data company Markit

December 2002
North American dealers begin trading credit derivatives with standard maturity and payment dates in an effort to increase liquidity. European dealers later also adopt this practice

March 2003
ISDA publishes 2003 credit derivative definitions, which significantly revise the 1999 short-form documentation in areas such as restructuring, successor events and guarantees

April 2003
JP Morgan and Morgan Stanley kick-start credit index trading in Europe by merging their proprietary indices to form Trac-x

October 2003
North American dealers launch CDX NA IG, which takes over as the standard credit index for North American investment grade ▶

April 2004	Credit derivative dealers agree to merge various indices to form a single index in each market
April/May 2005	A sudden repricing of credit index tranches causes losses to banks and hedge funds
May 2005	Default of Collins & Aikman, the first credit event to be settled using an auction
June 2005	ISDA launches standard documentation for credit default swaps on asset-backed securities
September 2005	The New York Federal Reserve hosts a meeting between top credit derivative dealers and regulators from around the world, who are concerned about the operational weaknesses of the credit derivatives market. Dealers agree to take steps to cut the time it takes to settle trades
October 2005	Default of Delphi, thought to be the biggest default to date in terms of credit derivatives outstanding
October 2007	Start of the subprime mortgage crisis that triggered the credit crunch
March 2008	Bear Sterns said it obtained short-term financing from JP Morgan Chase and the Federal Reserve Bank of New York, stating that its liquidity position had 'significantly deteriorated'. The news sent the market into a freefall, with the Dow Jones Industrial Average declining more than 300 points in a day before stabilising

2

Credit derivative instruments and applications

CREDIT DERIVATIVES PRODUCTS

The credit default swap is the basic building block for most 'exotic' credit derivatives and hence, for the sake of completeness, this chapter sets out a short description before exploring more exotic products. A credit default swap (CDS) is used to transfer the credit risk of a reference entity (corporate or sovereign) from one party to another. In a standard CDS contract, one party purchases credit protection from the other party, to cover the loss of the face value of an asset following a credit event. A credit event is a legally defined event that typically includes bankruptcy, failure to pay and restructuring.

Key point	**Credit protection**

Buying credit protection is economically equivalent to shorting the credit risk. Equally, selling credit protection is equivalent to going long the credit risk.

This protection lasts until some specified maturity date. For this protection, the protection buyer makes quarterly payments to the protection seller, as shown in Figure 2.1, until a credit event or maturity, whichever occurs first. This is known as the premium leg. The actual payment amounts on the premium leg are determined by the CDS spread adjusted for the frequency using a basis convention (usually Actual 360).

Figure 2.1	**Mechanics of a credit default swap (CDS)**

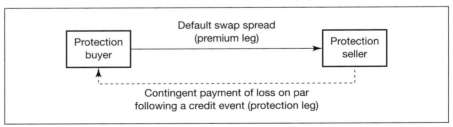

If a credit event does occur before the maturity date of the contract, there is a payment by the protection seller to the protection buyer. This is called the protection leg of the CDS. This payment equals the difference between par and the price of the assets of the reference entity on the face value of the protection, and compensates the protection buyer for the loss. There are two ways to settle the payment of the protection leg, the choice being made at the initiation of the contract. They are:

■ Physical settlement – This is the most widely used settlement procedure. It requires the protection buyer to deliver the notional amount of deliverable obligations of the reference entity to the protection seller in return for the notional amount paid in cash. In general, there are several deliverable obligations from which the protection buyer can choose that satisfy a number of characteristics. Typically, they include restrictions on the maturity and the requirement that they be *pari passu* – most CDS are linked to senior unsecured debt. If the deliverable obligations trade with different prices following a credit event, which they are most likely to do if the credit event is a restructuring, the protection buyer can take advantage of this situation by buying and delivering the cheapest asset. The protection buyer is therefore long a cheapest-to-deliver option.

Cash settlement   **Key point**

This is the alternative to physical settlement and is used less frequently in standard CDS but overwhelmingly in tranched CDOs, as discussed later. In cash settlement, a cash payment is made by the protection seller to the protection buyer equal to par minus the recovery rate of the reference asset. The recovery rate is calculated by referencing dealer quotes or observable market prices over some period after default has occurred.

Suppose a protection buyer takes five-year protection on a company at a CDS spread of 300bp. The face value of the protection is $10m. The protection buyer therefore makes quarterly payments approximately equal to $10m \times 0.03 \times 0.25 = \$75,000$ (ignore calendars and day count conventions). After a short period, the reference entity suffers a credit event. Assuming that the cheapest deliverable asset of the reference entity has a recovery price of $45 per $100 of face value, the payments are as follows:

■ The protection seller compensates the protection buyer for the loss on the face value of the asset received by the protection buyer. This is equal to $5.5m.

■ The protection buyer pays the accrued premium from the previous premium payment date to the time of the credit event.

For example, if the credit event occurs after a month, the protection buyer pays approximately $10m × 300bp × 1/12 = $25,000 of premium accrued. Note that this is the standard for corporate reference entity linked CDS.

For severely distressed reference entities, the CDS contract trades in an upfront format where the protection buyer makes a cash payment at trade initiation which purchases protection to some specified maturity – there are no subsequent payments unless there is a credit event in which the protection leg is settled, as in a standard CDS.

Liquidity in the CDS market differs from the cash credit market. For a start, a wider range of credits trade in the CDS market than in cash. In terms of maturity, the most liquid CDS is the five-year contract, followed by the three-year, seven-year and ten-year. The fact that a physical asset does not need to be sourced means that it is generally easier to trade in large round sizes with CDS.

CDS description

The credit default swap is a bilateral contract whereby the buyer of protection pays a periodical premium in a swap-format to the protection seller. In return, the protection buyer (known in the contract as the 'fixed rate payer') receives a contingent payment from the protection seller (the 'floating rate payer') if a pre-agreed credit event occurs.

The underlying company can be one company but could as well be a basket of different entities (reference portfolio). The credit default swap is an off-balance-sheet product that is traded in the over-the-counter (OTC) market. A typical tenure is three to five years. Furthermore, a credit default swap is standardized and is part of the 1999–2003 ISDA credit derivatives definitions.

If the CDS reference entity defaults (that is, it undergoes one of the 'credit events' defined in the contract):

- bankruptcy;
- failure to pay;
- restructuring;

the protection buyer stops paying premiums and receives a one-off payment from the protection seller. This compensates the protection buyer for the loss experienced as a result of the default.

(Note, however, that a credit default swap is not an insurance contract. There are important legal and economic differences between the two products. For example, the buyer of an insurance policy can normally only insure itself against an event that would cause it a loss – that is, it must have an insurable interest in the risk – whereas a buyer of credit protection does not need to own debt issued by the reference entity.)

In the event of a default, the credit default swap terminates and settlement takes place with the protection seller making a payment to the protection buyer. Depending on the terms agreed upfront by the counterparties, settlement can be either physical (current market standard) or cash. In either case, the settlement amount is intended to compensate the protection buyer for the loss that it would have incurred had it owned the notional amount of the reference entity's debt.

CDS settlement examples

The settlement of a credit default swap in case of a credit event is based on either cash or physical asset:

- Physical settlement (70–85 per cent of all deals): the protection buyer transfers an asset or a portfolio of pre-specified obligations to the protection seller and receives the face amount.
- Cash settlement (25–10 per cent of all deals): the protection buyer receives the difference or the fall in price of a reference obligation below par value. The method of pricing pre-agreed to the contract.
- Fixed recovery (less than 5 per cent of all deals): a pre-agreed fixed amount is received by the protection buyer. The underlying company can be one company but could as well be a basket of different entities (reference portfolio).

Physical settlement

The standard form of settlement for credit derivatives is physical settlement. After the protection buyer has triggered a credit event, with the delivery of a 'notice of physical settlement', the protection buyer delivers to the protection seller bonds or loans ('deliverable obligations') with a notional amount identical to the notional amount of the credit default swap. The protection seller then pays the protection buyer the notional amount of the credit default swap.

For example, for a standard $10m contract on IBM, if IBM defaulted, the protection buyer would deliver defaulted bonds with a $10m face value and receive $10m from the protection seller. If the defaulted bonds were worth $4m (40 per cent of their face value, called the recovery rate), the protection buyer has effectively saved $6m as a result of buying protection (Figure 2.2). The seller of protection could choose to sell the defaulted bonds, so achieving their recovery value.

Figure 2.2

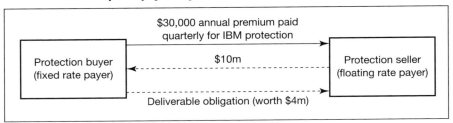

Example of physically-settled credit default swap (CDS)

Source: Credit Hedge Ltd

Deliverable obligations

Credit default swap contracts define the 'deliverable obligations' – that is, which of the issuer's bonds or loans can be delivered by the protection buyer following a credit event. This 'pool of deliverables' is usually defined as bonds or loans issued by the reference entity that are not subordinated to the reference obligation.

However, certain types of debt instruments – such as those denominated in minor currencies, those that are not fully transferable, and those whose payment is contingent on particular circumstances – are usually excluded from this pool and may not be delivered.

In a standard credit default swap, the pool of deliverables includes all the entity's conventional senior debt (bonds and loans, secured and unsecured), but it excludes subordinated (junior) debt, preference shares, trade debts and obligations with certain non-standard features.

The reference obligation is simply a specific bond or loan issued by the reference entity which is agreed to at the start of the trade to 'characterize' the deliverable obligations.

Cheapest-to-deliver option

If the protection buyer can access more than one deliverable obligation, it has the option of delivering the cheapest one available. Thus the protection buyer owns a cheapest-to-deliver option, which is one of the main reasons that credit default swap spreads are usually wider than bond spreads for the same reference entity.

Physical settlement has the advantage that it is not subject to manipulation by either party. But it has severe drawbacks. As a result, many credit derivatives are settled in cash.

Cash settlement

In a cash-settled credit default swap, no bonds or loans are delivered. Instead, the protection seller simply pays the protection buyer an amount of money calculated as the notional value of the contract minus the recovery rate (Figure 2.3). The recovery rate is based on a dealer poll, where the calculation agent obtains quotes from several firms that are active market makers in the reference obligation to determine its market value. For example, if the $10m IBM contract were to be settled in cash, the protection seller would pay the protection buyer $6m, based on the 40 per cent market value (recovery rate) of IBM's reference obligation.

Example of cash-settled credit default swap (CDS)   Figure 2.3

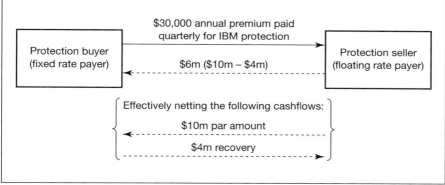

Source: Credit Hedge Ltd

Binary or digital settlement

In 'binary' or 'digital' credit default swaps, the recovery rate is fixed. For example, if two counterparties trade a $10m credit default swap on IBM with a 40 per cent fixed recovery rate, the protection seller will simply pay the protection buyer $6m in the event of a default by IBM.

This approach has the advantage of simplicity, but the disadvantage that the protection buyer does not know if it has bought enough protection to cover its losses. For this reason, binary credit derivatives are relatively rare.

Uses of a CDS

A CDS is generally used when a customer has a credit exposure and expects this risk to increase over time or expects the underlying company to go into default during the lifetime of the contract.

The most common type of CDS is one where there is a single reference entity. This is called a single-name credit default swap. The reference entity can be any borrower, whether corporate, financial or government (sovereign).

The CDS can do almost everything that cash can do and more. Some of the main applications of CDS are:

■ The CDS has revolutionized credit markets by making it easy to short credit. This can be done for long periods without assuming any repo risk. This is very useful for those wishing to hedge current credit exposures or those wishing to take a bearish credit view.

■ CDS are unfunded so leverage is possible. This is also an advantage for those who have high funding costs, because CDS implicitly lock in Libor funding to maturity.

■ CDS are customizable, although deviation from the standard may incur a liquidity cost.

■ CDS can be used to take a spread view on a credit, as with a bond.

■ Dislocations between cash and CDS present relative value opportunities. This is known as trading the default swap basis.

TRADES USING CREDIT DERIVATIVES

This section is all about putting on trades to try to take advantage of changes in credit spreads. These trades are not free of risk; if credit spreads do not move as anticipated, you lose money. Various strategies are discussed.

Trading the credit spread

Suppose a trader anticipates the credit spread on an entity to tighten (narrow). How can the trader take advantage of this view?

Consider five-year Fiat risk trading at 300bp. The trader sells protection on €10m. This means that, provided there is no credit event, the trader will earn just over €100,000 a year in carry income (the trader gains if credit spreads tighten and loses if they widen).

The profit and loss that arises from a 1bp change in the credit spreads is approximately €4,380. The loss in the event of default could be estimated using the anticipated recovery rate of, say, 40 per cent, giving a loss given default (LGD) of €6m.

This trade benefits from ease of execution. It does not require a principal outlay and only requires an ISDA master agreement between the counter-parties. The main disadvantages of this trade are counterparty credit exposure on the trade and the loss that arises if a credit event occurs (the trader is also short a delivery option).

Relative value trades

Suppose our trader considers that Fiat credit spreads will tighten but BMW credit spreads will widen. The trader can 'put on' a relative value trade. He could sell protection on Fiat and buy protection on BMW.

Let's assume both trades are €10m, five year with the Fiat spread at 300bp and the BMW spread at 45bp. The income and risk on the trades are shown in Table 2.1.

Income and risk example

Table 2.1

Credit	Nominal	Maturity (years)	Premium pa	Income pa (€)	Delta –0.01 %	Recovery rate	LGD (€)
Fiat	10,000,000	5	3.00%	304,167	4379	40%	6,000,000
BMW	10,000,000	5	–0.45%	–45,625	–4379	40%	6,000,000
			2.55%	258,54	0.00%		

This trade benefits from a narrowing of the credit spread between Fiat and BMW. However, if the credit spreads widen the trade loses money. There is also a net positive carry because the premium received for selling protection exceeds that paid to buy protection.

One of the main risks of this trade is how closely the two credits are linked. If you sell protection on Fiat and there was a credit event you would lose a substantial sum. But would the BMW trade hedge you? The value of the BMW trade would probably move in your favour (as auto spreads widened), but it is very unlikely to recoup your Fiat loss (unless BMW also experienced a credit event).

Negative basis trade

Negative basis trades involve being long the bond and long (buying) credit protection. They benefit the trader when the asset swap spread of the bond exceeds the cost of buying protection. The return of the transaction can be enhanced if the repo rate (funding cost) is relatively low.

This type of trade is relatively easy to execute. The trader also benefits from a positive carry and any tightening in the basis. And if there is a credit event the trader is long any delivery option. The disadvantage of this trade is credit exposure to the CDS counterparty and mark-to-marker profit and loss (P&L) adjustments arising from any change in the basis.

Positive basis trades

When the default swap premium is greater than the asset swap spread the trader may decide to ensure a positive basis trade.

This trade really is a substitution. To benefit, the dealer already needs to own the bond that has the relatively low asset swap spread. The dealer sells the bond and invests the proceeds in a money market deposit. The dealer then replaces the credit exposure by selling credit protection on the same entity. Because the premium received on the CDS is greater than the asset swap the dealer benefits from a higher return.

Credit curve trades

Credit curve steepening trade

This trade benefits from anticipation in a steepening of the credit curve for a particular credit. This trade works as follows: suppose VW credit risk trades at 50bp for five years and 68bp for ten years.

The trader sells credit protection on VW for five years and buys credit protection on VW for ten years.

This trade can be executed on a basis point value basis. This means the size of the five-year trade is significantly larger than the size of the ten-year trade.

Where are the benefits and risks?

The trader benefits if the credit curve for VW steepens. But the trader has the risk that the credit curve could flatten, leading to a mark-to-market risk.

There is another significant risk. If there is a credit event and the trade is weighted, by basis point value the trader has sold more credit protection on VW than he has purchased. The result would be a substantial credit loss.

Senior versus subordinated trades

Subordinated credit risk trades with a wider credit spread than the senior credit risk. This is because subordinated credit, as the name suggests, ranks after senior debt in a recovery situation. Therefore, if you own subordinated debt you can lose more money.

However, the market does not evaluate the relative risk between senior and subordinate debt as being constant. When credit spreads are narrowing (improving), the spread between subordinated debt and senior debt also tends to narrow. In other words, subordinate debt becomes relatively more expensive. And when credit spreads widen, subordinate debt tends to be more adversely affected than senior debt.

Traders can take advantage of anticipated changes in the relative spread between senior and subordinate debts using credit default swaps.

Suppose five-year Barclays Bank senior trades at 5bp and the subordinate trades at 15bp. How can a trade be constructed?

The trader may decide that the credit spread differential between the senior and subordinate debt could narrow. The trader would buy protection on the senior debt and sell protection on the subordinate debt. And provided the credit spread did in fact narrow the trader would gain. But if there were a credit event, the trader would have sold protection on the more risky subordinate debt. The trader would therefore lose money because the recovery rate on the subordinate debt would be lower than the senior debt.

The trader could therefore weight the original position to protect against this risk. The weighting could be based on estimated recovery rates of the senior and subordinate positions.

For example, if the estimated recovery rate for the senior debt is 65 per cent and the subordinate debt 40 per cent, the loss given default (LGD) for each position is:

100% – 65% = 35%

and

100% – 40% = 60%

If the probability of a credit event is identical for both senior and subordinate debt a simple hedge ratio is 60/35 = 1.71.

This means that, using these assumptions, a €10m subordinate CDS is hedged with €17m senior CDS.

If the trader sold protection on the subordinate risk then he would benefit if the senior to subordinated spread narrows. If the spread widens, there would be a mark-to-market loss. If there is a credit event and the recovery rates were not as anticipated, the trader would have a windfall gain or loss on the trade.

RISK MEASURES FOR CDS

By measuring the risks associated with CDS trades, it is possible to control and monitor the exposure being taken. Risk measures are also useful for constructing trades and hedge ratios.

There are several risk measures.

Jump-to-default (JTD) risk

JTD is the loss a trader incurs if there is a credit event under the CDS. This means it equates to the nominal amount less the recovery rate:

1 – recovery rate

Understanding the JTD is helpful. It is a measure of how much could be lost after a credit event.

Products based on the same underlying credit can have different JTDs. For example, a CDS with a recovery rate of 40 per cent has a JTD of 60 per cent. A bond issued by the same reference entity priced at 101.50 with the same recovery rate would have a JTD of 61.50 per cent. The difference occurs because the bond investor would obtain a recovery based on par.

Spread PV01

Spread PV01 (SPV01) is similar to the traditional interest rate PV01, sometimes referred to as DV01 or delta. SPV01 indicates how much would be made or lost for a small change in the credit spread (typically a 0.01 per cent change).

This is a very helpful figure. It gives estimates of how much a small change in credit spreads could cost. It may also be used to develop small hedge ratios.

When one looks at the SPV01 in more detail, you can see exactly why the mark-to-market (MTM) of a CDS changes with changes in market prices. Suppose you sold protection for 100bp and now the market prices of the CDS is 101bp. You have lost 1bp.

The rise in the CDS price indicates that the market considers there is more risk. So the probability of default has increased and/or recovery rates have fallen.

COMPARING BOND SPREADS AND CDS PRICES

Traders make comparisons between bond prices and CDS spreads. The purpose of this comparison is one of relative value. The relative value is normally assessed as a spread or yield differential. The calculation is sometimes called the basis. We may anticipate the basis to be zero. This means the bond credit spread and the CDS premium are the same, but frequently this is not the case. There are many reasons for this, which are covered in Chapter 3 on the CDS bond basis.

But how can we calculate the basis? There are several methods; here are two:

- Compare the CDS premium with the par asset swap spread.
- Compare the CDS premium with an asset swap spread based on the bond price (non-par structure).

There is a third option. This uses the bond's current market price and an assumed recovery rate.

This works by taking the current market price of the bond. You apply a recovery rate to derive the implied default probabilities. (The implied default probabilities when used to calculate the PV of the bond cashflows will reconcile with the current market price.)

You can now calculate the default probabilities and use them to find the implied CDS premium.

To do this you take a CDS with the same recovery rate assumption as the bond and solve to find what CDS spread will give you a net present value (NPV) of nil for the CDS.

This calculated CDS spread can then be used as a comparison. You compare it with market prices for CDS on the reference entity. If the market CDS spreads are greater than the CDS price implied from the bond price, the bond is relatively expensive in comparison with the CDS.

It is important to note that the default swap buyer has a short position in the credit quality of the reference obligation. If the credit quality and the price of the bond decrease, the present value (the premium, if paid upfront) of the default swap will increase. Thus the premium that the default swap buyer paid in the original contract is lower than the market premium after the bond price decrease. If desired, the default swap buyer can sell the default swap at the higher market premium with a profit.

Example of a single-name credit default swap

An investor who wants to take a view on France Telecom might sell credit default swap protection. Dealers might quote five-year credit default swap spreads on France Telecom at 37/39 basis points. This means the dealer quotes 37bp for a trade where the investor sells five-year protection and the dealer buys protection, and 39bp for a trade where the investor buys protection. (The difference between the two quotes is the 'bid–offer spread'.)

On a typical trade size of €10 million, the protection seller would receive €37,000 a year, usually in four quarterly payments. Conversely, the investor could buy protection for 39bp, paying €39,000 a year.

If France Telecom defaulted during the life of the trade and, following the default, the value of the company's debt fell to 40 per cent of face value, the protection seller would compensate the protection buyer for the €6m loss.

Credit default swap: Wal-Mart example

To buy protection over three years an investor has to pay a 30bp premium on Wal-Mart. Based on a notional deal of €25m, the quarterly payment to the protection seller is:

Premium × Notional × 90/360

As illustrated by the cashflow scheme (Figure 2.4), two outcomes are possible:

- Wal-Mart enters into a credit event during the maturity of the credit default swap. Based on the pre-agreed terms, the protection buyer receives the credit default swap amount of €25m or the face amount of a reference portfolio and the contract matures early.

- Wal-Mart does not enter into a credit event during the maturity of the credit default swap. The protection buyer pays a premium each quarter to the protection seller until the end date of the credit default swap.

Figure 2.4

Cashflow scheme for Wal-Mart

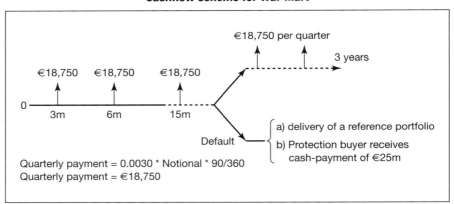

Practical credit default swap application

Consider Wessanen, a US food supplier. It could use a credit default swap to protect Wessanen itself against a credit event on the part of one of its major customers. The customers are equally weighted.

The notional protection is €20m. The customers might have credit ratings as follows:

- Safeway Baa2/BBB;
- Wal-Mart Aa2/AA;
- Albertson's Baa1/BBB+;
- Kroger BBB.

Table 2.2 offers an overview of the pricing on a three- and five-year base.

Pricing overview
Table 2.2

Customer	3-year	5-year
Safeway	120	125
Wal-Mart	30	30
Albertson's	115	120
Kroger	145	147

Summary

Wessanen purchases protection for each company. By entering into four swaps, Wessanen is protected on each customer but has to invest on average 102.5bp in the three-year and 105.5bp in the five-year period.

To overcome this cost, Wessanen could also enter into a credit default swap based on the basket of these four companies on a *first to default* base. The advantage would be a lower premium investment, but the contract would end if one of the four companies entered into a credit event. Wessanen would then be left without credit protection and would have to enter into a new hedge.

CDS definitions
Key features

Reference entity: this is the exact name of the entity for which the protection buyer is seeking protection.

Premium: the default swap premium that has to be paid for the protection. If the company enters into a credit event, the periodic payment ends.

Credit event: this event is defined in the ISDA 1999 or 2003 contract. The three standard events are:

- bankruptcy;
- failure to pay; and
- restructuring.

Credit event triggering: the event can be triggered by the buyer as well as the seller of protection.

Settlement: a credit default swap can be settled in cash or on a physical base. The settlement as well as the calculation method is predetermined.

Cash determining the CDS spread

The premium payments in a CDS are defined in terms of a CDS spread, which is paid periodically on the protected notional until maturity or a credit event. It is possible to show that the CDS spread can, to a first approximation, be proxied by either:

- a par floater bond spread (the spread to Libor at which the reference entity can issue a floating-rate note of the same maturity at a price of par); or
- the asset swap spread of a bond of the same maturity provided it trades close to par.

Demonstrating these relationships relies on several assumptions that break down in practice. For example, by assuming a common market-wide funding level of Libor, we ignore accrued coupons on default, we ignore the delivery option in the CDS, and we ignore counterparty risk. Despite these assumptions, cash market spreads usually provide the starting point for where CDS spreads should trade. The difference between where CDS spreads and cash Libor spreads trade is known as the default swap basis, defined as:

Basis = CDS spread – Cash libor spread

(A full discussion of the drivers behind the CDS basis is provided in Chapter 3.)

Many investors now exploit the basis as a relative value play. Determining the CDS spread is not the same as valuing an existing CDS contract. For that, we need a model. A discussion of the valuation of CDS is provided in Chapter 3.

Funded versus unfunded credit derivatives, including CDS, can be traded in a number of formats. The most commonly used is known as swap format, and this is the standard for CDS. This format is also termed 'unfunded' format because the investor makes no upfront payment. Subsequent payments are simply payments of spread and there is no principal payment at maturity. Losses require payments to be made by the protection seller to the protection buyer, and this has counterparty risk implications. The other format is to trade the risk in the form of a credit-linked note. This format is known as 'funded' because the investor has to fund an initial payment, typically par.

This par is used by the protection buyer to purchase high-quality collateral. In return, the protection seller receives a coupon, which may be floating rate, ie, Libor plus a spread, or may be fixed at a rate above the same maturity swap rate. At maturity, if no default has occurred the collateral matures and the investor is returned par. Any default before maturity results in the collateral being sold, the protection buyer covering his loss and the investor receiving par minus the loss.

The protection buyer is exposed to the default risk of the collateral rather than the counterparty.

BASKET DEFAULT SWAPS

Correlation products are based on redistributing the credit risk of a portfolio of single-name credits across a number of securities. The portfolio may be as small as five credits or as large as 200 or more. (See Chapter 7 for a full description of first-to-default baskets.)

The redistribution mechanism is based on the idea of assigning losses on the credit portfolio to the securities in a specified order, with some securities taking the first losses and others taking later losses. This exposes the investor to the tendency of assets in the portfolio to default together, i.e., default correlation. The simplest correlation product is the basket default swap.

A basket default swap is similar to a CDS, the difference being that the trigger is the nth credit event in a specified basket of reference entities. Typical baskets contain five to ten reference entities. In the case of a first-to-default (FTD) basket, $n=1$, and it is the first credit in a basket of reference credits whose default triggers a payment to the protection buyer. As with a CDS, the contingent payment typically involves physical delivery of the defaulted asset in return for a payment of the par amount in cash. In return for assuming the nth-to-default risk, the protection seller receives a spread paid on the notional of the position as a series of regular cashflows until maturity or the nth credit event, whichever is sooner.

Advantage of FTD basket

Key point

The advantage of an FTD basket is that it enables an investor to earn a higher yield than any of the credits in the basket. This is because the seller of FTD protection is leveraging their credit risk.

To see this, consider that the fair-value spread paid by a credit-risky asset is determined by the probability of a default multiplied by the size of the loss given default. FTD baskets leverage the credit risk by increasing the probability of a loss by conditioning the pay-off on the first default among several credits.

The size of the potential loss does not increase relative to buying any of the assets in the basket. The most an investor can lose is par minus the recovery value of the FTD asset on the face value of the basket.

The advantage is that the basket spread paid can be a multiple of the spread paid by the individual assets in the basket.

This is shown in Figure 2.5 where a basket of five investment-grade credits pays an average spread of about 28bp. The FTD basket pays a spread of 120bp.

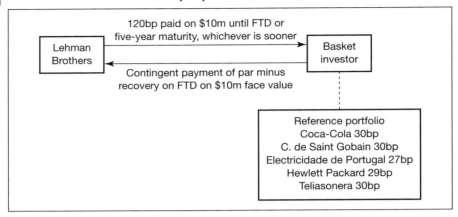

Figure 2.5 **Five default (FTD) on a basket of five credits**

More risk-averse investors can use default baskets to construct lower-risk assets: second-to-default (STD) baskets, where $n=2$, trigger a credit event after two or more assets have defaulted. As such, they are lower-risk second-loss exposure products that will pay a lower spread than an FTD basket.

One way to view an FTD basket is as a trade in which the investor sells protection on all of the credits in the basket with the condition that all the other CDS cancel at no cost following a credit event. Such a trade cannot be replicated using existing instruments.

Valuation therefore requires a pricing model. The model inputs to determine the nth-to-default basket spread are:

- Value of n. An FTD ($n=1$) is riskier than an STD ($n=2$) and so commands a higher spread.

- Number of credits. The greater the number of credits in the basket, the greater the likelihood of a credit event, so the higher the spread.

- Credit quality. The lower the credit quality of the credits in the basket, in terms of spread and rating, the higher the spread.

- Maturity. The effect of maturity depends on the shape of the individual credit curves.

- Recovery rate. This is the expected recovery rate of the nth-to-default asset following its credit event. This has only a small effect on pricing because a higher expected recovery rate is offset by a higher implied default probability for a given spread. However, if there is a default, the investor will certainly prefer a higher realized recovery rate.

- Default correlation. Increasing default correlation increases the likelihood of assets to default or survive together. The effect of default correlation is subtle and significant in terms of pricing. We now discuss this is more detail.

Baskets and default correlation

See Chapter 6 for a fuller explanation of default correlation in the credit markets.

Baskets are essentially a default correlation product. This means that the basket spread depends on the tendency of the reference assets in the basket to default together. It is natural to assume that assets issued by companies within the same country and industrial sector should have a higher default correlation than those within different industrial sectors. After all, they share the same market, the same interest rates and are exposed to the same costs. At a global level, all companies are affected by the performance of the world economy. These systemic sector risks far outweigh idiosyncratic effects so we expect that default correlation is usually positive.

There are several ways to explain how default correlation affects the pricing of default baskets. Confusion is usually caused by the term 'default correlation'. The fact is that if two assets are correlated, they will not only tend to default together, they will also tend to survive together. There are two correlation limits in which an FTD basket can be priced without resorting to a model – independence and maximum correlation.

- Independence. Consider a five-credit basket where all of the underlying credits have flat credit curves. If the credits are all independent and never become correlated during the life of the trade, the natural hedge is for the basket investor to buy CDS protection on each of the individual names to the full notional. If a credit event occurs, the CDS hedge covers the loss on the basket and all of the other CDS hedges can be unwound at no cost, since they should on average have rolled down their flat credit curves. This implies that the basket spread for independent assets should be equal to the sum of the spreads of the names in the basket.

- Maximum correlation. Consider the same FTD basket but this time where the default correlation is at its maximum. In practice, this means that when any asset defaults, the asset with the widest spread will always default too. As a result, the risk of one default is the same as the risk of the widest spread asset defaulting. Because an FTD is triggered by only one credit event, it will be as risky as the riskiest asset and the FTD basket spread should be the widest spread of the credits in the basket. The best way to understand the behaviour of default baskets between these two correlation limits is to study the loss distribution for the basket portfolio. See Chapter 3 for a discussion of how to model the loss distribution for correlation products.

Consider a basket of five credits with spreads of 100bp and an assumed recovery rate for all of 40 per cent. We have plotted the loss distribution for correlations of 0 per cent, 20 per cent, and 50 per cent in Figure 2.6. The spread for a first-to-default basket depends on the probability of one or more defaults, which equals one minus the probability of no defaults. We see that the probability of no defaults increases with increasing correlation – the probability of credits surviving together increases – and the FTD spread should fall.

| Figure 2.6 | Loss distribution for a five-credit basket, with 0%, 20% and 50% correlation |

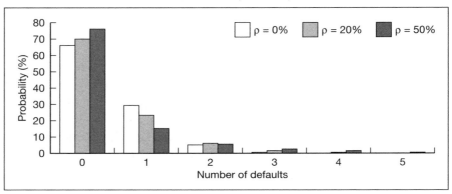

The risk of a second-to-default (STD) basket depends on the probability of two or more defaults. As correlation goes up from 0 per cent to 20 per cent, the probability of two, three, four and five defaults increases. This makes the STD spread increase.

The process for translating these loss distributions into a fair-value spread requires a model of the type described in Chapter 3.

Essentially, the basket spread has to be found for which the present value of the protection payments equals the present value of the premium payments. It should not be forgotten that in addition to the protection leg, the premium leg of the default basket also has correlation sensitivity because it is only paid for as long as the nth default does not occur. Using a model, the correlation sensitivity of the FTD and STD spread for the five-credit basket can be calculated (Figure 2.7). At low correlation, the FTD spread is close to 146bp, which is the sum of the spreads. At high correlation, the basket has the risk of the widest spread asset and so is at 30bp.

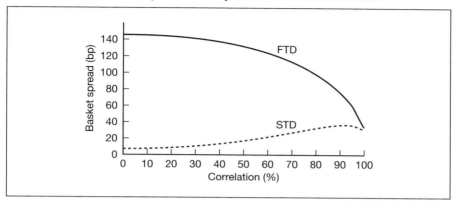

Correlation dependence of spread for FTD and STD basket

Figure 2.7

The STD spread is lowest at zero correlation because the probability of two assets defaulting is low if the assets are independent. At maximum correlation, the STD spread tends towards the spread of the second-widest asset in the basket[1], which is also 30bp.

The basket can be customized to the investor's exact view regarding size, maturity, number of credits, credit selection, FTD or STD.

Applications

Baskets have a range of applications. The reference entities in the basket are all typically investment grade and so are familiar to most credit analysts.

- Investors can use default baskets to leverage their credit exposure and so earn a higher yield without increasing their notional at risk.
- Buy-and-hold investors can enjoy the leveraging of the spread premium. This is discussed in more detail later.
- Credit investors can use default baskets to hedge a blow-up in a portfolio of credits more cheaply than buying protection on the individual credits.
- Default baskets can be used to express a view on default correlation. If the investor's view is that the implied correlation is too low then the investor should sell FTD protection. If implied correlation is too high they should sell STD protection.

Hedging default baskets

The issuers of default baskets need to hedge their risks. Spread risk is hedged by selling protection dynamically in the CDS market on all of the credits in the default basket. Determining how much to sell, known as the delta, requires a pricing model to calculate the sensitivity of the basket value to changes in the spread curve of the underlying credit.

Delta hedging

Although this delta hedging should immunize the dealer's portfolio against small changes in spreads, it is not guaranteed to be a full hedge against a sudden default.

For example, a dealer hedging an FTD basket where a credit defaults with a recovery rate of R would receive a payment of $(1-R)F$ from the protection seller, and will pay $D(1-R)F$ on the hedged protection, where F is the basket face value and D is the delta in terms of percentage of face value. The net payment to the protection buyer is therefore $(1-D)(1-R)F$.

There will also probably be a loss on the other CDS hedges. The expected spread widening on default on the other credits in the basket due to their positive correlation with the defaulted asset will result in a loss when they are unwound. The greater unwind losses for baskets with higher correlations will be factored into the basket spread.

One way for a default basket dealer to reduce his correlation risk is by selling protection on the same or similar default baskets. However, it is usually difficult to find protection buyers who select the exact same basket as an investor. The other hedging approach is for the dealer to buy protection using default baskets on other orders of protection.

This is based on the observation that a dealer who is long first, second, third up to mth order protection on an m-credit basket has almost no correlation risk, because this position is almost economically equivalent to buying full face value protection using CDS on all m credits in the basket.

Table 2.3 shows an example basket with the delta and spread for each of the five credits. Note that the deltas are very similar. This reflects the fact that all of the assets have a similar spread. Differences are mainly due to our different correlation assumptions.

Table 2.3 **Default basket deltas for a €10m notional five-year FTD basket on five credits. The FTD spread is 246bp**

Reference entity	CDS spread	Delta
Walt Disney	62bp	6.26m
Rolls-Royce	60bp	6.55m
Sun Microsystems	60bp	6.87
Eastman Chemical	60bp	7.16m
France Telecom	64bp	7.57m

Hedgers of long protection FTD baskets are also long gamma. This means that as the spread of an asset widens, the delta will increase and so the hedger will be selling protection at a wider spread. If the spread tightens, then the delta will fall and the hedger will be buying back hedges at a tighter level. So spread volatility can be beneficial.

This effect helps to offset the negative carry associated with hedged FTD baskets. This is clear in the example of Table 2.3 where the income from the hedges is 211bp, lower than the 246bp paid to the FTD basket investor. Different rating agencies have developed their own model-based approaches for the rating of default baskets. (See Chapter 7.)

SYNTHETIC CDOs

Synthetic collateralized debt obligations (synthetic CDOs) were conceived in 1997 as a flexible and low-cost mechanism for transferring credit risk off bank balance sheets. The primary motivation was for banks to reduce their regulatory capital. More recently, the fusion of credit derivatives modelling techniques and derivatives trading have led to a new type of synthetic CDO, which we call a customized CDO, which can be tailored to the exact risk appetites of different classes of investors. As a result, the synthetic CDO has become an investor-driven product. Overall, these synthetic CDOs have a market size estimated by the Risk 2003 survey to be close to $500bn. What is also of interest is that the dealer-hedging of these products in the CDS market has generated a substantial demand to sell protection, balancing the traditional protection-buying demand coming from bank loan book managers. See Chapter 9 for a full breakdown of synthetic CDOs.

> **The CDO redistribution of risk**　　　　　　　　　　　　　**Key point**
>
> The performance of a synthetic CDO is linked to the incidence of default in a portfolio of CDS. The CDO redistributes this risk by allowing different tranches to take these default losses in a specific order. To see this, consider the synthetic CDO in Figure 2.8. It is based on a reference pool of 100 CDS, each with a €10m notional.

This risk is redistributed into three tranches:

(i)　an equity tranche, which assumes the first €50m of losses;

(ii)　a mezzanine tranche, which takes the next €100m of losses;

(iii)　the senior tranche with a notional value of €850m takes all remaining losses.

The equity tranche has the greatest risk and is paid the widest spread. It is typically unrated. Next is the mezzanine tranche, which is lower risk and so is paid a lower spread. Finally, there is the senior tranche, which is protected by €150m of subordination. To get a sense of the risk of the senior tranche, note that it would require more than twenty-five of the assets in the one hundred credit portfolio to default with a recovery rate of 40 per cent before the senior tranche would take a principal loss. Consequently, the senior tranche is typically paid a very low spread.

Figure 2.8

A standard synthetic CDO

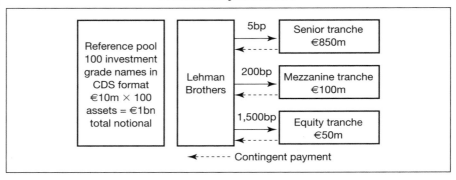

The advantage of CDOs is that by changing the details of the tranche in terms of its attachment point (this is the amount of sub subordination below the tranche) and width, it is possible to customize the risk profile of a tranche to the investor's specific profile.

Full capital structure synthetics in the typical synthetic CDO, structured using securitization technology – the sponsoring institution, typically a bank, enters into a portfolio default swap with a special purpose vehicle (SPV). This is shown in Figure 2.9. The SPV typically provides credit protection for 10 per cent or less of the losses on the reference portfolio. The SPV in turn issues notes in the capital markets to cash collateralize the portfolio default swap with the originating entity. The notes issued can include a non-rated 'equity' piece, mezzanine debt and senior debt, creating cash liabilities.

Figure 2.9

Full capital structure of a synthetic CDO

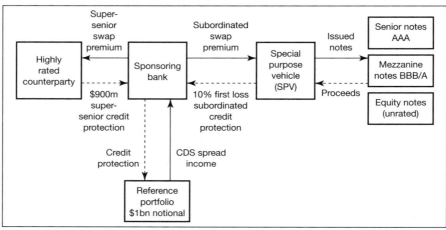

The remainder of the risk, 90 per cent or more, is generally distributed via a senior swap to a highly rated counterparty in an unfunded format. Reinsurers, who typically have AAA/AA ratings, have traditionally had a healthy appetite for this type of senior risk, and are the largest participants in this part of the capital structure – often referred to as super-senior AAAs or super-senior swaps. The initial proceeds from the sale of the equity and notes are invested in highly rated, liquid assets.

If an entity in the reference pool defaults, the trust liquidates investments in the trust and makes payments to the originating entity to cover default losses. This payment is offset by a successive reduction in the equity tranche, then the mezzanine and, finally, the super-seniors are called to make up losses. See Chapters 8 and 9 for more details.

Mechanics of a synthetic CDO

When nothing defaults in the reference portfolio of the CDO, the investor simply receives the Libor spread until maturity and nothing else changes. Using the synthetic CDO shown in Figure 2.9, consider what happens if one of the reference entities in the reference portfolio undergoes the first credit event with a 30 per cent recovery, causing a €7m loss.

The equity investor takes the first loss of €7m, which is immediately paid to the originator. The tranche notional falls from €50m to €43m and the equity coupon, set at 1.500bp, is now paid on this smaller notional. These coupon payments therefore fall from €7.5m to 15 per cent times €43m = €6.45m. If traded in a funded format, the €3m recovered on the defaulted asset is either reinvested in the portfolio or used to reduce the exposure of the most-senior tranche (similar to early amortization of senior tranches in cashflow CDOs). The senior tranche notional is decreased by €3m to €847m, so that the sum of protected notional equals the sum of the collateral notionals which is now €990m. This has no effect on the other tranches.

This process repeats following each credit event. If the losses exceed €50m then the mezzanine investor must bear the subsequent losses with the corresponding reduction in the mezzanine notional. If the losses exceed €150m, then it is the senior investor who takes the principal losses.

Synthetic CDOs are simple   **Key point**

The mechanics of a standard synthetic CDO are therefore simple, especially compared with traditional cashflow CDO 'waterfalls'. This also makes them easier to model and price.

The CDO tranche spread

The synthetic CDO spread depends on several factors. These include:

- **Attachment point.** This is the amount of subordination below the tranche. The higher the attachment point, the more defaults are required to cause tranche principal losses and the lower the tranche spread.
- **Tranche width.** The wider the tranche for a fixed attachment point, the more losses to which the tranche is exposed. However, the incremental risk ascending the capital structure is usually declining and so the spread falls.
- **Portfolio credit quality.** The lower the quality of the asset portfolio, measured by spread or rating, the greater the risk of all tranches due to the higher default probability and the higher the spread.
- **Portfolio recovery rates.** The expected recovery rate assumptions have only a secondary effect on tranche pricing. This is because higher recovery rates imply higher default probabilities if the spread is fixed. These effects offset each other to first order.
- **Swap maturity.** This depends on the shapes of the credit curves. For upward-sloping credit curves, the tranche curve will generally be upward-sloping and so the longer the maturity, the higher the tranche spread.
- **Default correlation.** If default correlation is high, assets tend to default together and this makes senior tranches more risky. Assets also tend to survive together, making the equity safer. To understand this more fully, we need to better understand the portfolio loss distribution.

The portfolio loss distribution

No matter what approach is used to generate it, the loss distribution of the reference portfolio is crucial for understanding the risk and value of correlation products. The portfolio loss is clearly not symmetrically distributed: it is therefore informative to look at the entire loss distribution, rather than summarizing it in terms of expected value and standard deviation. Models of the type discussed in Chapter 3 can be used to calculate the portfolio loss distribution. We can expect to observe one of the two shapes:

- a skewed bell curve; or
- a monotonically decreasing curve.

The skewed bell curve applies to the case when the correlation is at or close to zero. In this limit, the distribution is binomial and the peak is at a loss only slightly less than the expected loss.

As correlation increases, the peak of the distribution falls and the high quantiles increase: the curves become monotonically decreasing. We see that the probability of larger losses increases and, at the same time, the probability of smaller losses also increases, thereby preserving the expected loss, which is correlation independent (for further discussion on correlation see Chapter 6).

For very high levels of asset correlations (hardly ever observed in practice), the distribution becomes U-shaped. At maximum default correlation, all the probability mass is located at the two ends of the distribution. The portfolio either all survives or it all defaults. It resembles the loss distribution of a single asset.

How then does the shape of the portfolio loss distribution affect the pricing of tranches?

To see this we must study the tranche loss distribution.

The tranche loss distribution

Figures 2.10, 2.11 and 2.12 show the loss distributions for a CDO with a 5 per cent equity, 10 per cent mezzanine and 85 per cent senior tranche for correlation values of 20 per cent and 50 per cent.

Portfolio loss distribution for a large portfolio at 0%, 20% and 95% correlation

Figure 2.10

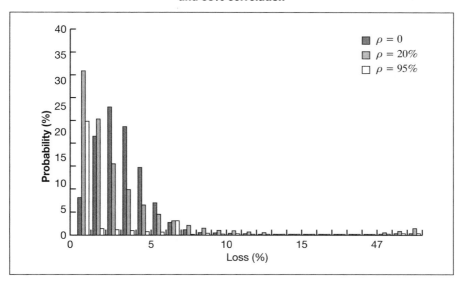

Figure 2.11   **Equity tranche loss distribution for correlations of 20% and 50%**

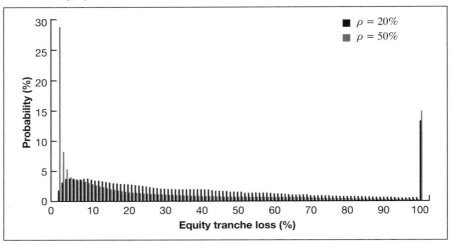

Figure 2.12   **Mezzanine tranche loss distribution for correlation of 20% and 50%. The zero loss peak, which is about 86% in both cases, has been eliminated**

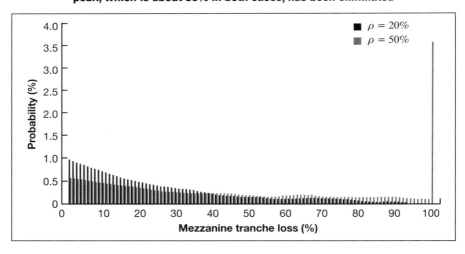

At 20 per cent correlation, most of the portfolio loss distribution (Figure 2.10) is inside the equity tranche, with about 14 per cent beyond, as represented by the peak at 100 per cent loss. As correlation goes to 50 per cent the probability of small losses increases while the probability of 100 per cent losses increases only marginally.

Clearly, equity investors benefit from increasing correlation. The mezzanine tranche becomes more risky at 50 per cent correlation. As shown in Figure 2.12, the 100 per cent loss probability jumps from 0.50 per cent to 3.5 per cent. In most cases, mezzanine investors benefit from falling correlation – they are short correlation.

However, the correlation directionality of a mezzanine tranche depends upon the collateral and the tranche. In certain cases a mezzanine tranche with a very low attachment point may be a long correlation position.

SUMMARY: APPLICATION OF CREDIT DERIVATIVES

The application of credit derivatives in trading can be divided into arbitrage of mispricing in defaultable bonds and the possibility to trade a view on the credit quality of a reference credit.

In general, banks use credit derivatives to

- manage credit lines;
- manage loan exposure without needing the consent of the debtor;
- manage (or arbitrage) regulatory capital or exploit comparative advantages in costs of funding;
- reduce the regulatory capital (securitization).

Why use credit default swaps ?

The broad reasons are:

- Reducing various types of risk such as default risk, credit deterioration risk, and also other types of risk such as market risk and operational risk.
- Yield enhancement: usually assuming credit risk on a reference obligation.
- Convenience and cost reduction: a default swap allows a lender to eliminate the credit exposure to a debtor without knowledge of the debtor, thus maintaining a good bank debt or relationship.
- Arbitrage: since default swaps (and other credit derivatives) can be replicated with other financial instruments, arbitrage opportunities may exist.
- Regulatory capital relief: default swaps can help reduce the amount of regulatory capital.

Clearly, the main application of default swaps is hedging against default of a reference obligation. Default swaps are usually purchased if the default swap buyer owns the reference obligation and wants to protect against default of this obligation. Hence, when owning the underlying reference obligation, the default swap functions as an insurance against default.

Does a default swap hedge credit deterioration risk?

A default swap protects against default risk; if the reference obligation of the reference credit defaults, the default swap buyer receives a payment from the default swap seller. A crucial question remains: does a default swap hedge credit deterioration risk (i.e. the risk that the credit quality of the reference entity decreases and thus the obligation of the reference entity decreases in price)? The answer to the question is a clear 'That depends!' It depends whether the default swap is marked-to-market or not.

If the default swap is not marked-to-market, an obligation will decrease in price if the credit quality of the reference entity decreases with no compensating effect of the default swap. In this case, the default swap does not protect against credit deterioration risk.

However, if the default swap is marked-to-market, a default swap does protect against credit deterioration risk. This will be demonstrated by the following arbitrage argument: in an arbitrage-free environment, the returns of two portfolios must be identical if the risk is identical. Assuming the notional and maturity of the risk-free bond, the risky bond and the default swap are identical, we get the equation:

Key point Long a risk-free bond = Long a risky bond + Long a default swap

3

Pricing a CDS and the cash bond basis

CREDIT MODELLING

To price and manage the risk of credit derivatives, a framework is needed for valuing credit risk to a single issuer and to many issuers. The growth of the credit derivatives market has created a need for more powerful models and for a better understanding of the empirical evidence needed to calibrate these models. This section presents an overview of modelling approaches from a practical perspective, in terms of models, implementation and calibration.

Single credit modelling

Credit modelling uses two main approaches: structural and reduced form. In the structural approach, the default is characterized as the consequence of some event such as a company's asset value being insufficient to cover a repayment of debt. Such models are usually extensions of Merton's 1974 model[1] that used a contingent claims analysis for modelling default.

Structural models are generally used to say at what spread corporate bonds should trade based on the internal structure of the company. They therefore require information about the balance sheet of the company and can be used to establish a link between pricing in the equity and debt markets. However, they are limited in a number of ways including the fact that they generally lack the flexibility to fit exactly a given term structure of spreads; and they cannot be extended easily to price complex credit derivatives. In the reduced-form approach, the credit process is modelled directly via the probability of the credit event itself. Reduced-form models also generally have the flexibility to refit the prices of a variety of credit instruments of different maturities. They can also be extended to price more exotic credit derivatives. It is for these reasons that reduced-form models are used for credit derivatives pricing.

The hazard rate approach

The most widely used reduced-form approach is based on the work of Jarrow and Turnbull (1995)[2], who characterize a credit event as the first event of a Poisson counting process that occurs at some time t with a probability defined as:

$$\Pr[\tau \leq t + dt | \tau > t] = \lambda(t)dt$$

i.e., the probability of a default occurring within the time interval $[t, t+dt)$, conditional on surviving to time t, is proportional to some time-dependent function $\lambda(t)$, known as the hazard rate, and the length of the time interval dt.

Over a finite time period T, it is possible to show that the probability of surviving is given by:

$$Q(0,T) = E^Q\left[\exp\left(-\int_0^T \lambda(s)ds\right)\right]$$

The expectation is taken under the risk-neutral measure. A common assumption is that the hazard rate process is deterministic. By extension, this assumption also implies that the hazard rate is independent of interest rates and recovery rates.

Pricing model for CDS

The breakeven spread in a CDS is the spread at which the present values (PV) of premium and protection legs are equal, i.e:

Premium PV = Protection PV

To determine the spread, it is necessary to value the protection and premium legs. It is important to take into account the timing of the credit event because this can have a significant effect on the present value of the protection leg and also the amount of premium paid on the premium leg. Within the hazard rate approach, this timing problem can be solved by conditioning on the probability of defaulting within each small time interval $[s,s+ds]$, given by $Q(0,s)\lambda(s)ds$, then paying $(1-R)$ and discounting this back to today at the risk-free rate.

Assuming that the hazard rate and risk-free rate term structures are flat, the value for the protection leg can be written as:

$$(1-R)\int_0^T \lambda e^{-(r+\lambda)s}ds = \frac{\lambda(1-R)(1-e^{-(r+\lambda)T})}{r+\lambda}$$

The value of the premium leg is the PV of the spread payments, which are made to default or maturity. If we assume that the spread S on the premium leg is paid continuously, we can write the present value of the premium leg as:

$$S\int_0^T e^{-(r+\lambda)s}ds = \frac{S(1-e^{-(r+\lambda)T})}{r+\lambda}$$

Equating the protection and premium legs and solving for the breakeven spread gives:

$$S = \lambda(1-R)$$

This relationship is known as the credit triangle because it is a relationship between three variables where knowledge of any two is sufficient to calculate the third. It basically states that the spread paid for each small time interval exactly compensates the investor for the risk of default for that interval.

Within this model, the interest rate dependency drops out. Given a CDS that has a flat spread curve at 150bp, and assuming a 50 per cent recovery rate, the implied hazard rate is 0.015 divided by 0.5, or 3 per cent. The implied one-year survival probability is therefore exp(−0.03)=97.04 per cent. For two years it is exp(−0.06)=94.18 per cent, and so on.

Valuation of a CDS position

The value of a CDS position at time t following initiation at time 0 is the difference between the market implied value of the protection and the cost of the premium payments, which have been set contractually at SC.

We therefore write MTM(t) = ± (Protection PV − Premium PV), where the sign is positive for a long protection position and negative for a short protection position.

If the current market spread is given by $S(t)$ then the mark-to-market can be written as:

$$MTM(t) = (S(t) - S(0)) \times RPV01$$

where the $RPV01$ is the risky PV01, which is given by:

$$RPV01(t) = \frac{(1 - e^{-(r+\lambda)(\tau-t)})}{(r + \lambda)}$$

And where:

$$\lambda = \frac{S(t)}{1 - R}$$

As an example, an investor buys \$10m of five-year protection at 100bp. One year later, the credit trades at 250bp. Assuming a recovery rate of 40 per cent, the value is given by substituting $r=3.0$ per cent, $R=40$ per cent, $S(t)=0.025$, $S(0)=0.01$ and $t=4$ into the above equation to give $\lambda=4.17$ per cent and an MTM value of \$521,661.

This is a simple yet fairly accurate model that works well when the interest rate and credit curves are flat. When this is not the case, it becomes necessary to use bootstrapping techniques to build a full-term structure of hazard rates. This may be assumed to be piecewise flat or piecewise linear. For a description of such a model see O'Kane and Turnbull (2003)[3].

Default probabilities

The default probabilities calculated for pricing purposes can be quite different from those calculated from historical default rates of assets with the same rating. These real-world default probabilities are generally much lower. The reason for this is that the credit spread of an asset contains not just a compensation for pure default risk; it also depends on the market's risk aversion expressed through a risk premium, as well as on supply and demand imbalances.

As for the market's use of Libor as a risk-free rate in pricing, theory shows that the price of a derivative is the cost of replicating it in a risk-free portfolio using other securities. Since most market dealers are banks, which fund close to Libor, the cost of funding these other securities is also close to Libor. As a consequence, it is the effective risk-free rate for the derivatives market.

CALIBRATING RECOVERY RATES

The calibration of recovery rates presents a number of complications for credit derivatives.

Recovery rates   **Key point**

Strictly speaking, the recovery rate used in the pricing of credit derivatives is the expected recovery rate following a credit event where the expectation is under the risk-neutral measure.

Such expectations are only available from price information, and the problem in credit is that given one price, it is difficult to separate the probability of default from the recovery rate expectation.

The market standard is therefore to revert to rating agency default studies for estimates of recovery rates. These typically show the average recovery rate by seniority and type of credit instrument, and usually focus on a US corporate bond universe. Adjustments may be made for non-US corporate credits and for certain industrial sectors. Problems with rating agency recovery statistics include the fact that they look backward and that they only include the default and bankruptcy credit events – restructuring is not included. In their favour, they represent the price of the defaulted asset as a fraction of par some thirty days after the default event, so they are similar to the definition of the recovery value in a CDS. Recent work (Altman et al. 2001)[4] shows there is a significant negative correlation between default and recovery rates. One way to incorporate this effect is to assume that recovery rates are stochastic. The standard approach is to use a beta distribution.

Modelling default correlation

By modelling correlation products, we mean modelling products whose pricing depends upon the joint behaviour of a set of credit assets. These include default baskets and synthetic CDOs. As a result of the growth in use of these products, this is an area of pricing that has recently gained a lot of attention, and in which there have been significant modelling developments.

This section describes some of these current models, shows how they can be applied to the valuation of baskets and CDOs, and towards the end discusses model calibration issues.

Modelling joint defaults

The valuation of default-contingent instruments calls for the modelling of default mechanisms. As discussed earlier, a classical dichotomy in credit models distinguishes between a 'structural approach', where default is triggered by the market value of the borrower's assets (in terms of debt plus equity) falling below its liabilities, and a 'reduced-form approach', where the default event is directly modelled as an unexpected arrival.

Although both the structural and the reduced-form approaches can in principle be extended to the multivariate case, structural models calibrated to market-implied default probabilities (often called 'hybrid' models) have gained favour among practitioners because of their tractability using many assets.

If defaults are considered as being generated by asset values falling below a given boundary, then the probabilities of joint defaults over a specified horizon must follow from the joint dynamics of asset values: consistent with their descriptive approach of the default mechanism, multivariate structural models rely on the dependence of asset returns to generate dependent default events.

This is shown in Figure 3.1, which simulates 1,000 pairs of asset returns modelled as normally distributed random variables, for two firms i and j for two different asset return correlations of 10 per cent and 90 per cent. The vertical and horizontal lines represent default thresholds for firms i and j respectively. Clearly, the probability of both i and j defaulting, represented by the number of points in the bottom left area defined by the default thresholds, increases as the asset return correlation increases.

So, asset correlation leads to default correlation.

Although the pay-offs for multi-credit default-contingent instruments such as nth-to-default baskets and synthetic loss tranches cannot be statically replicated by trading in a set of single-credit contracts, current market practice is to value correlation products using standard no-arbitrage arguments. It follows that the valuation of these multi-credit exposures boils down to the computation of (risk-neutral) expectations over all possible default scenarios.

Scatterplot of 1,000 simulated asset returns with 0 per cent and 90 per cent correlation. Default thresholds are also shown

Figure 3.1

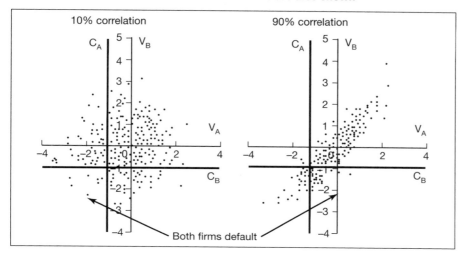

Several hybrid frameworks have been proposed for modelling correlated defaults and pricing multi-name credit derivatives. Hull and White (2001)[5] generate dependent default times by diffusing correlated asset values and calibrating default thresholds to replicate a set of given marginal default probabilities. Multi-period extensions of JPMorgan's one-period Credit Metrics framework are also commonly used, even if they produce the undesirable serial independence of the realized default rate. JPMorgan's model, CreditMetrics[6], is a framework for quantifying credit risk in portfolios of traditional credit products (loans, commitments to lend, financial letters of credit), fixed income instruments, and market-driven instruments subject to conterparty default (swaps, forwards, etc.).While most multi-credit models require simulation, the need for accurate and fast computation of changes in delta and gamma has pushed researchers to look for different models. Such models are beyond the scope of this book.

A PRACTICAL APPROACH TO PRICING A CDS

Predictive or theoretical pricing models of credit swaps

A common question when considering the use of credit swaps as an investment or a risk management tool is how they should be priced. Credit risk has for many years been thought of as a form of deep out-of-the-money put option on the assets of a firm. To the extent that this approach to pricing could be applied to a credit swap, it could also be applied to any traditional credit instrument. In fact, option pricing models have already been applied to credit derivatives for the purpose of proprietary 'predictive' or 'forecasting' modelling of the term structure of credit spreads.

A model that prices default risk as an option will require, directly or implicitly, as parameter inputs both default probability and severity of loss given default, net of recovery rates, in each period to compute both an expected value and a standard deviation or 'volatility' of value.

These are the analogues of the forward price and implied volatility in a standard Black–Scholes model. However, in a practical environment, irrespective of the computational or theoretical characteristics of a pricing model, that model must be parameterized using either market data or proprietary assumptions.

A predictive model using a sophisticated option-like approach might postulate that loss given default is 50 per cent and default probability is 1 per cent and derive that the credit swap price should be, say, 20bp. A less sophisticated model might value a credit derivative based on comparison with pricing observed in other credit markets (e.g. if the undrawn loan pays 20bp and bonds trade at Libor + 15 bp, then, adjusting for liquidity and balance sheet effects, the credit swap should trade at around 25 bp).

Yet the more sophisticated model will be no more powerful than the simpler model if it uses as its source data the same market information.

Key point	**Observation problem**
	Ultimately, the only rigorous independent check of the assumptions made in the sophisticated predictive model can be market data. Yet, in a sense, market credit spread data presents a classic example of a joint observation problem.

Credit spreads imply loss severity given default, but this can only be derived if one is prepared to make an assumption as to what they are simultaneously implying about default likelihoods (or vice versa).

Thus, rather than encouraging more sophisticated theoretical analysis of credit risk, the most important contribution that credit derivatives will make to the pricing of credit will be in improving liquidity and transferability of credit risk and hence in making market pricing more transparent, more readily available, and more reliable.

Mark-to-market and valuation methodologies for credit awaps

Another question that often arises is whether credit swaps require the development of sophisticated risk modelling techniques to be marked-to-market.

It is important in this context to stress the distinction between a user's ability to mark a position to market (its 'valuation' methodology) and its ability to formulate a proprietary view on the correct theoretical value of a position, based on a sophisticated risk model (its 'predictive' or 'forecasting' methodology).

Interestingly, this distinction is recognized in the bank regulatory capital framework: while eligibility for trading book treatment of, for example, interest rate swaps depends on a bank's ability to demonstrate a credible valuation methodology, it does not require any predictive modelling expertise.

Fortunately, given that a number of institutions make markets in credit swaps, valuation may be directly derived from dealer bids, offers or mid-market prices (as appropriate depending on the direction of the position and the purpose of the valuation).

Without the availability of dealer prices, valuation of credit swaps by proxy to other credit instruments is relatively straightforward. Validation is related to an assessment of the market credit spreads prevailing for obligations of the reference entity that can be substituted *pari passu* with the reference obligation, or similar credits, with the point in time matching that of the credit swap, rather than that of the reference obligation itself.

For example, a five-year credit swap on XYZ in a predictive modelling framework may be evaluated on the basis of a postulated default probability and recovery rate. However, it should be marked-to-market based on prevailing market credit spreads (which as discussed above provide a joint observation of implied market default probabilities and recovery rates) for five-year XYZ obligations substantially similar to the reference obligation (whose maturity could exceed five years).

If there are no such five-year obligations, a market spread can be interpolated or extrapolated from longer- and/or shorter-term assets. If there is no prevailing market price for similar rank obligations to the reference obligation, adjustments for relative seniority can be made to market prices of assets with different priority in liquidation.

If there are no currently traded assets issued by the reference entity, comparable instruments issued by similar credit types may be used, with appropriately conservative adjustments. Hence, it should be possible, based on available market data, to derive or bootstrap a credit curve for any reference entity.

Constructing a credit curve from bond prices

To price any financial instrument, it is important to model the underlying risks on the instrument in a realistic manner. In any credit-linked product, the primary risk lies in the potential default of the reference entity: without any default in the reference entity, the expected cashflows will be received in full, whereas if a default event occurs the investor will receive some recovery amount. It is therefore natural to model a risky cashflow as a portfolio of contingent cashflows corresponding to these default scenarios weighted by the probability of these scenarios occurring.

Example: risky zero-coupon bond with one year to maturity

In this case, at the end of the year there are two possible scenarios:

- The bond redeems at par; or
- The bond defaults, paying some recovery value, *RV*.

The decomposition of the zero-coupon bond into a portfolio of contingent cashflows is therefore clear (Figure 3.2).

| Figure 3.2 | Probable value scenario |

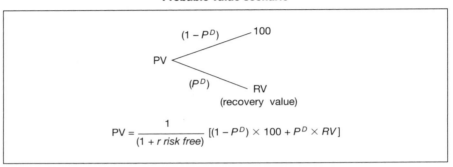

$$PV = \frac{1}{(1 + r \text{ risk free})} [(1 - P^D) \times 100 + P^D \times RV]$$

This approach to pricing risky cashflows by Jarrow and Turnbull can be extended to give a consistent valuation framework for the pricing of many risky products. The idea is the same as that applied in fixed-income markets: to value the product by splitting it into its component cashflows; to price these individual cashflows using the above method; and then sum the values to get a price for the product.

This framework can be used to value more than just risky instruments. It enables the pricing of any combination of risky and risk-free cashflows, such as capital guaranteed notes (we shall return to the capital guaranteed note later in this section, as an example of pricing a more complex product). This pricing framework can also be used to highlight relative value opportunities in the market. For a given set of probabilities, it is possible to see which products are trading above or below their theoretical value and hence use this framework for taking a position on relative value.

Calibrating the probability of default

The pricing approach described above hinges on being able to provide a value for the probability of default on the reference credit. In theory, we could simply enter probabilities based on our appreciation of the reference name's creditworthiness and price the product using these numbers. This would value the product based on our view of the credit and would give a good basis for proprietary positioning. However, this approach would give no guarantee that the price thus obtained could not be arbitraged against other traded instruments holding the same credit risk and it would make it impossible to manage the risk of the position using other credit instruments. In practice, the probability of default is found from the market prices of traded market instruments.

The idea is simple: given a probability of default and recovery value, it is possible to price a risky cashflow. Therefore, the (risk neutral) probability of default for the reference credit can be derived from the price and recovery value of this risky cashflow.

For example, suppose that a one-year risky zero-coupon bond trades at 92.46 and the risk-free rate is 5 per cent. This represents a multiplicative spread of 3 per cent over the risk-free rate, because:

$$100/(1 + 0.05)(1 + 0.03) = 92.46$$

If the bond had a recovery value of zero, from the pricing equation:

$$92.46 = 1/(1.05) \times [(1 - P^D) \times 100 + P^D \times 0]$$

and so:

$$P^D = 1 - (1.03)1$$

So the implied probability of default on the bond is 2.91 per cent. Note that under the zero recovery assumption there is a direct link between the spread on the bond and the probability of default. Indeed, the two numbers are the same to the first order.

With a non-zero recovery, the equations are not as straightforward, but there is still a strong link between the bond spread (s) and the default probability:

$$P^D = \frac{100}{1 - \dfrac{1}{(1+5)}} = \frac{s}{1 - \dfrac{RV}{100}}$$

This useful formula provides a 'back-of-the-envelope' value for the probability of default on an asset given its spread over the risk-free rate. Such approximation must, of course, be used with caution, because there may be term structure effects or convexity effects causing inaccuracies.

Fundamental link   **Key point**
This link between credit spread and probability of default is a fundamental one, and is analogous to the link between interest rates and discount factors in fixed-income markets.

Indeed, most credit market participants think in terms of spreads rather than in terms of default probabilities, and analyse the shape and movements of the spread curve rather than the change in default probabilities.

However, it is important to remember that the spreads quoted in the market need to be adjusted for the effects of recovery before default probabilities can be computed. Extra care must be taken when dealing with emerging market debt, where bonds often have guaranteed principals or rolling guaranteed coupons.

The effect of these features needs to be stripped out before the spread is computed as, otherwise, an artificially low spread will be derived.

Problems encountered in practice

In practice, it is rare to find risky zero-coupon bonds from which to extract default probabilities and so one has to work with coupon bonds. Also, the bonds linked to a particular name will typically not have evenly spaced maturities. As a result, it becomes necessary to make interpolation assumptions for the spread curve, in the same manner as zero rates are bootstrapped from bond prices. Naturally, the spread curve and hence the default probabilities will be sensitive to the interpolation method selected and this will affect the pricing of any subsequent products.

Assumptions need to be made with respect to the recovery value because it is impossible, in practice, to have an accurate recovery value for the assets. It is clear from the equations above that the default probability will depend substantially on the assumed recovery value, and so this parameter will also affect any future prices taken from a spread curve.

A more theoretical problem worth mentioning relates to the meaning of the recovery assumption itself.

The equations above assume that each individual cashflow has some recovery value, RV, which will be paid in the event of default. This allows a risky asset to be priced as a portfolio of risky cashflows without worrying about when the default event occurred.

If this assumption held, higher coupon bonds should trade higher than lower coupon bonds in the event of default (because they would be expected to recover a greater amount). The reason this does not occur in practice is that, while accrued interest up until the default is generally a valid claim, interest due post default is generally not a viable claim in work-out. As a result, when defaults do occur, assets tend to trade like commodities and the prices of different assets are only distinguished based on perceived seniority rather than coupon rate.

A different assumption is that a bond recovers a fixed percentage of outstanding notional plus accrued interest at the time of default. While this is more consistent with the observed clustering of asset prices during default, it makes splitting a bond into a portfolio of risky zeros much harder. This is because the recovery on a cashflow coming from a coupon payment will now depend on when the default event occurred, whereas the recovery on a cashflow coming from a principal repayment will not.

USING DEFAULT SWAPS TO MAKE A CREDIT CURVE

For many credits, an active credit default swap (CDS) market has been established. The spreads quoted in the CDS market make it possible to construct a credit curve in the same way that swap rates make it possible to construct a zero-coupon curve.

Like swap rates, CDS spreads have the advantage that quotes are available at evenly spaced maturities, so avoiding many of the concerns about interpolation. The recovery rate remains the unknown and has to be estimated based on experience and market knowledge.

Strictly speaking, to extract a credit curve from CDS spreads, the cashflows in the default and no-default states should be diligently modelled and bootstrapped to obtain the credit spreads. However, for relatively flat spread curves, approximations exist.

To convert market CDS spreads into default probabilities, the first step is to strip out the effect of recovery.

A standard CDS will pay out par minus recovery on the occurrence of a default event. This effectively means that the protection seller is only risking $(100 - \text{recovery})$. So the real question is how much does an investor risking 100 expect to be paid? To compute this, an approximation can be used (where S is the bond spread):

$$S_{RV} = O = S_{Market}/(1 - RV/100)$$

Note the similarity between this equation and the earlier one derived for risky zero-coupon bonds. Here, the resulting zero-recovery CDS spread is still a running spread. However, as an approximation it can be treated as a credit spread, and therefore:

$$\text{Default probability} = 1 - 1/(1 + S_{RV} = 0)^t$$

This approximation is analogous to using a swap rate as a proxy for a zero-coupon rate. Although it is really only suitable for flat curves, it is still useful for providing a quick indication of what the default probability is. Combining the two equations above:

$$\text{Default probability} = 1 - 1/[1 + S_{Market}/(1 - RV/100)]^t$$

LINKING THE CREDIT DEFAULT SWAP AND CASH MARKETS

An interesting area for discussion is that of the link between the bond market and the CDS market. To the extent that both markets are trading the same credit risk, the prices of assets in the two markets should be related. This idea is reinforced by the observation that selling protection via a CDS exactly replicates the cash position of being long a risky floating-rate note paying Libor plus spread and being short a riskless floating-rate note paying Libor flat1 (i.e. Libor with no additional spread). Because of this, it would be natural to expect a CDS to trade at the same level as an asset swap of similar maturity on the same credit.

However, in practice we observe a basis between the CDS market and the asset swap market, with the CDS market typically – but not always – trading at a higher spread than the equivalent asset swap. The normal explanations given for this basis are liquidity premiums and market segmentation. Currently, the bond market holds more liquidity than the CDS market and investors are prepared to pay a premium for this liquidity and accept a lower spread. Market segmentation often occurs because of regulatory constraints that prevent certain institutions from participating in the default swap market even though they are allowed to source similar risk via bonds. However, there are also participants who are more inclined to use the CDS market. For example, banks with high funding costs can effectively achieve Libor funding by sourcing risk through a CDS when they might pay above Libor to use their own balance sheet.

Another more technical reason for a difference in the spreads on bonds and default swaps lies in the definition of the CDS contract. In a default swap contract there is a list of obligations that may trigger a credit event and a list of deliverable obligations that can be delivered against the swap in the case of such an event. In Latin American markets the obligations are typically all public external debt, whereas outside of Latin America the obligations are normally all borrowed money. If the obligations are all borrowed money this means that if the reference entity defaults on any outstanding bond or loan a default event is triggered. In this case the CDS spread will be based on the spread of the widest obligation. Since less liquid deliverable instruments will often trade at a different level to the bond market this can result in a CDS spread that differs from the spreads in the bond market.

For contracts where the obligations are public external debt there is an arbitrage relation that ties the two markets and ought to keep the basis within certain limits.

Unfortunately, it is not a cheap arbitrage to perform, which explains why the basis can sometimes be substantial. Arbitraging a high CDS spread involves selling protection via the CDS and then selling short the bond in the cash market.

Locking in the difference in spreads involves running this short position until the maturity of the bond. If this is done through the repo market, the cost of funding this position is uncertain and so the position has risk, including the risk of a short squeeze if the cash paper is in short supply. However, obtaining funding for term at a good rate is not always easy. Even if the funding is achieved, the counterparty on the CDS still has a credit exposure to the arbitrageur. It will clearly cost money to hedge out this risk and so the basis has to be big enough to cover this additional cost. Once both of these things are done the arbitrage is complete and the basis has been locked in.

However, even then, on a mark-to-market basis the position could still lose money over the short term if the basis widens. So, ideally, it is better to account for this position on an accrual basis.

Using the credit curve

As an example of pricing a more complex structure off the credit curve, consider the example of pricing a five-year, fixed-coupon, capital-guaranteed, credit-linked note. This is a structure where the notional on the note is guaranteed to be repaid at maturity (i.e. is not subject to credit risk) but all coupon payments will terminate in the event of a default of the reference credit. The note is typically issued at par and the unknown is the coupon paid to the investor. For this example, assume that the credit default spreads and risk-free rates are as given in Table 3.1.

Cumulative default probabilities

Table 3.1

Year	Risk-free (%)	CDS spread (%)	Cumulative default probability (%)
1	5.00	7.00	7.22
2	5.00	7.00	13.91
3	5.00	7.00	20.13
4	5.00	7.00	25.89
5	5.00	7.00	31.24

The capital guaranteed note can be decomposed into a risk-free, zero-coupon bond and a zero-recovery risky annuity, with the zero-coupon bond representing the notional on the note and the annuity representing the coupon stream. Because the zero-coupon bond carries no credit risk, it is priced off the risk-free curve. In this case:

Zero price = $100/(1.05)^5 = 78.35$

So all that remains is to price the risky annuity. As the note is to be issued at par, the annuity component must be worth $100 - 78.35 = 21.65$. But what coupon rate does this correspond to?

Suppose the fixed payment on the annuity is some amount, C. Each coupon payment can be thought of as a risky zero-coupon bond with zero recovery. So we can value each payment as a probability-weighted average of its value in the default and no default states (Table 3.2).

Table 3.2

Coupon paid under a capital protection structure

Year	Discount factor	Forward value	PV
1	0.9524	C'0.9278 + 0'0.0722	C'0.8837
2	0.9070	C'0.6609 + 0'0.1391	C'0.7808
3	0.6638	C'0.7988 + 0'0.02013	C'0.6900
4	0.8227	C'0.0741 + 0'0.02589	C'0.6097
5	0.7835	C'0.6876 + 0'0.3124	C'0.5388

So the payment on the annuity should be:

$$C = 21.65 / (0.8837 + 0.7808 + 0.6900 + 0.6097 + 0.5388)$$

$$C = 6.18$$

Figure 3.3

Valuing a fixed coupon guaranteed note

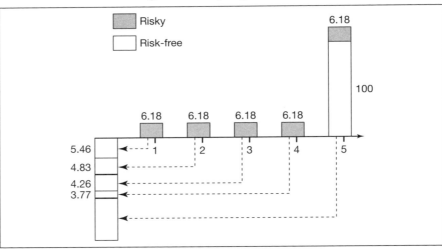

Cashflow 1: $5.46 = 6.18 \times 0.8837$

Cashflow 2: $4.83 = 6.18 \times 0.7808$

Cashflow 3: $4.26 = 6.18 \times 0.6900$

Cashflow 4: $3.77 = 6.18 \times 0.6097$

Cashflow 5: $57.20978 = 106.18 \times 0.5388$

Counterparty considerations: pricing the two-name exposure in a credit default swap

In a credit swap the protection buyer has credit exposure to the protection seller related to the performance of the reference entity. If the protection seller defaults, the buyer must find other protection and will be exposed to changes in replacement cost due to changes in credit spreads since the inception of the original swap. More seriously, if the seller defaults and the reference entity defaults, the buyer is unlikely to recover the full default payment due, although the final recovery rate on the position will benefit from any positive recovery rate on obligations of both the reference entity and the seller.

Counterparty risk consequently affects the pricing of credit derivative transactions. Protection bought from higher-rated counterparties will command a higher premium. Furthermore, a higher credit quality premium protection purchased from a counterparty against a reference entity is less valuable if a simultaneous default on the two names has a higher probability.

The problem of how to compute and charge for counterparty credit exposure is in large part an empirical one, for it depends on computing the joint likelihood of arriving in different credit states, which will in turn depend on an estimate of credit quality correlation between the seller and reference entity, which cannot be observed directly.

Fortunately, significant efforts have been undertaken in the area of default correlation estimation in connection with the development of credit portfolio models such as CreditMetrics.

The following expression describes a simple methodology for computing a 'counterparty credit charge' (CCC), as the sum of expected losses due to counterparty (CP) default across N different time periods, t, and states of credit quality (R) of the reference entity (RE) from default through to AAA. Given an estimate of credit quality correlation, it is possible to estimate the joint likelihood of the reference entity being in each state, given a counterparty default, from the respective individual likelihoods of arriving in each state of credit quality. Since loss can only occur given a default of the counterparty, we are interested only in the default likelihood of the counterparty.

However, since loss can occur due to changes in the mark-to-market (MTM) of the credit swap caused by credit spread fluctuations across different states of the reference entity, we are interested in the full matrix of credit quality migration likelihoods of the reference entity.

Typically, the counterparty credit charge is subtracted from the premium paid to the protection seller and accounted for by the buyer as a reserve against counterparty credit losses.

$$CCC = (100\% - \text{Recovery Rate}_{CP}) \sum_{t=t_0}^{tN} \sum_{R=Def}^{AAA} \text{Prob}_{Joint} \left\{ CP_{in\ default} RE_{Rating=R} \right\} Op_{Rating=R}$$

CP = Counterparty

RE = Reference entity

N = Number of time periods, t

R = Rating of the reference entity in time t

Op = Price of an option to replace a risky exposure to *RE* in state *R* at time *t* with a riskless exposure, i.e. when *RE* has defaulted, value is (100% – Recovery Rate *RE*) When *RE* has not defaulted, value is (100% – MTM of credit swap, based on credit spreads)

CASH AND CDS BASIS

No-arbitrage assumptions have a key role in the pricing of financial instruments, and in finance theory more generally.

Derivative markets for credit risk transfer have experienced tremendous growth over the past decade because of contract standardization efforts, increasing market transparency and the introduction of tradable indices, so it is worthwhile examining to what extent theoretical no-arbitrage relationships have held in this recently established segment of the global finance industry.

The worldwide market for credit derivatives expanded more than fivefold in the space of two years, and amounted to $17,300bn by the end of 2005. It is thus the fastest growing part of the $285,000bn global financial derivatives market (BIS 2006). Also, single-name credit default swaps (CDS) are the most important product, accounting for more than two-thirds of all outstanding credit derivatives.

CDS are also the main building blocks for many structured credit products. The number of reference entities, mostly corporations but also sovereign issuers, has been steadily increasing. Also, the investor base has been broadening, and includes banks, brokerage firms, insurance companies, pension funds, financial guarantors, hedge funds and asset managers.

As more dealer/brokers have developed their credit skills, market liquidity has improved and CDS bid–ask spreads have narrowed.

In some cases, both outstanding volumes of credit derivatives and daily trading activity have even outgrown the comparable cash bond market, imposing challenges on the credit community.

Flow of funds statistics from the US Federal Reserve (2006) show that, at the end of 2005, outstanding amounts of aggregate US non-financial corporations' balance sheets exceeded $10,000bn and that corporate bonds accounted for 30 per cent of the liability side. Comparable European data (ECB 2006)[7] showed corporate bonds representing only 7 per cent of euro-zone non-financial corporations' aggregate balance sheets, confirming the thesis that public markets for corporate debt were more developed in the US, while European corporate financing remained more focused on bank loans. Nevertheless, markets for credit derivatives have known comparable growth on both sides of the Atlantic.

A credit default swap is an agreement between two parties to exchange the credit risk of a reference entity. The buyer of the CDS is said to buy protection, has a similar credit risk position to selling a bond short and investing the proceeds in a risk-free asset, usually pays a periodic fee, and profits if the reference entity has a credit event, or if the credit worsens while the swap is outstanding. A credit event triggers a contingent payment on the CDS and includes bankruptcy, failure to pay outstanding debt obligations, and in some CDS contracts a restructuring of a bond or loan (ISDA 2003). Conversely, the seller of the CDS is said to sell protection, collects the periodic fee, and profits if the credit of the reference entity remains stable or improves while the swap is outstanding.

Versions of restructuring

Key features

However, several versions of the restructuring credit event are used in different market segments:

- So-called 'modified restructuring', which considers only certain types of restructuring as a default event and under which the maturity of the debt instruments eligible for delivery is restricted, is common in US investment-grade markets (rated Baa3/BBB− and better).
- European CDS contracts are usually drafted with 'modified modified restructuring', which imposes different limits on the bonds that can be delivered upon restructuring.
- US high-yield markets (rated Ba1/BB+ and worse) do not include restructuring at all under standard documentation.

Selling protection has a similar credit risk profile to maintaining a long position in a bond or a loan. If a credit event occurs, the compensation is to be paid by the protection seller to the buyer via either physical settlement or cash settlement, as specified in the contract. Physical settlement is the most common form of settlement in the CDS market, and normally takes place within thirty days after the credit event.

Delivery option

Key point

Under physical settlement, the protection buyer holds a delivery option, as in the event of default he is free to choose from a basket of deliverable bonds.

The premium paid by the protection buyer to the seller, often called the 'spread', is quoted in basis points per annum of the contract's notional value, is usually paid quarterly, and is not based on any specific risk-free bond or benchmark interest rate.

Therefore, a CDS is like a put option written on a bond, as the protection buyer is protected from losses incurred by a decline in the value of the bond as a result of a credit event.

Like CDS premia, bond spreads over a risk-free benchmark mainly compensate investors for default risk embedded in credit-risky assets. Both corporate bond and CDS spread levels and changes are influenced by micro- and macroeconomic determinants such as:

- default rates;
- corporate soundness (leverage, profitability, and liquidity);
- ratings;
- equity volatility;
- the economic cycle;
- risk-free interest rates or the slope of the yield curve.

Besides fundamental factors, technical drivers are also important, as prices for a specific bond and CDS are determined by supply and demand and may include a varying liquidity premium. Credit spread modelling for both cash and derivative instruments has focused on two types of frameworks.

Structural models of credit risk build on Merton's original idea (1974) that both debt and equity can be modelled as options on the firm's assets. Reduced-form models of credit risk, also called intensity-based models, look upon defaults as exogenous rare events that can be modelled by a jump process.

It can be shown that, under certain assumptions, investing in a floating-rate note or investing in a credit-risky bond together with buying a fixed-to-floating interest rate swap (combined position known as an asset swap) has the same economic risk profile as selling protection in a CDS. As a result, no-arbitrage arguments imply that the CDS premium should reflect the Libor spread on an equivalent asset swap.

While evidence is thin, analysis of lead–lag relationships has shown that CDS tends to lead cash bond markets, hence indicating that some price discovery exists. The next section describes the economic determinants of the CDS–bond basis (hereinafter also denoted as the 'basis').

BOND SPREAD MEASURES AND THE CDS–BOND BASIS DEFINITION

Spread measures for fixed-rate bonds

An appropriate definition of the CDS–bond basis starts with the observation that the trading and valuation of credit-risky bonds in the cash market is based on a spread quotation. Ignoring the risk premium, tax and liquidity aspects, credit spreads are designed to compensate investors for expected loss from default. Explaining the basis requires an understanding of the inherent characteristics of the spread measures used to compare cash and CDS markets.

A CDS premium is a relatively straightforward measure, which tends to reflect the perceived credit risk of the reference entity in a pure way. However, different bond spread concepts exist, depending on the choice of the risk-free benchmark and the computational complexity. This complexity is a function of the accuracy by which maturity matching is accomplished, and depends on whether timing of cashflows is considered, by explicitly taking into account the shape of the benchmark term structure. It can be argued that asset swap spreads are the appropriate spread measure against which to compare CDS premia, but it is useful to first review concepts of other, often more intuitive, widely used spread measures.

Bond spreads

Originally, bond spreads were mostly calculated as the simple yield-to-maturity differential between a credit-risky bond and a credit-risk-free benchmark bond. The closest on-the-run Treasury bond, in terms of maturity, was commonly chosen as the risk-free benchmark. This concept of a *spread to a benchmark Treasury bond* can be refined by interpolating the Treasury curve to match exactly the risky bond's maturity. Interpolation to obtain a *spread to the interpolated Treasury curve* may be carried out roughly by drawing a straight line between the yields of the closest longer and shorter Treasury issues, or, alternatively, may result from yield curve estimation procedures, providing a smooth curve shape.

Traditionally, Treasury bonds were used mostly as a risk-free benchmark by bond traders, but nowadays interest rate swap rates are the most common reference, certainly for derivative traders, because

- the swap curve is a more liquid curve in many developed markets;
- the swap curve does not suffer from temporary humps due to repo specialness, as on-the-run Treasuries do;
- the swap curve is less influenced by regulatory and taxation issues;
- Libor/swap rates correspond closely to the funding cost of many market participants. Also, academics seem to have adopted swap instead of Treasury benchmark curves.

Previous approaches on the pricing of CDS, on the analysis of the CDS–bond basis, have built their analysis using swap benchmark curves.

I-spread

The yield-to-maturity differential between a credit-risky fixed-rate bond and the interpolated swap rate is denoted as the *I-spread* (I from interpolated). It may be noted that the difference between the spread to the interpolated Treasury curve and the I-spread is equal to the swap spread.

Z-spread

A more refined measure that takes into account the full term structure of the benchmark swap curve for discounting each of the cashflows at its own rate is denoted as *Z-spread* (zero volatility spread), sometimes also called stripped spread. *Z-spread* is defined as the spread that must be added to a given benchmark zero swap curve so that the sum of the bond's discounted cashflows equals its price, with each cashflow discounted at its own rate.

Asset swap spreads

While the above spread concepts were developed for calculating spreads on fixed-rate securities, in terms of cashflow profile, a CDS is most readily comparable with a par floating-rate note funded at Libor or with an asset-swapped fixed-rate bond financed in the repo market.

Floating rate notes are much less commonly traded securities than fixed-rate bonds, so this chapter will focus on the asset swap structure. Through an asset swap an investor can separate interest rate risk from credit risk, transforming fixed payments into a floater.

Key features

Asset swap spread

Such a fixed-to-floating asset swap is an over-the-counter package product consisting of two simultaneous trades: buying a fixed-rate bond and entering into a fixed-to-floating interest rate swap (IRS) of the same maturity. The fixed leg of the IRS is the bond's coupon, while the floating leg is Libor augmented by an agreed amount (in bp), denoted the *asset swap spread* (ASW-spread).

Par asset swap

In a par asset swap, a buyer effectively buys the package from the asset swap seller at par, regardless of the cash price of the bond, and the notional amount of the swap is equal to the face value of the underlying bond. A par asset swap is the most commonly traded asset swap package.

It should be noted that neither of the above spread measures is able to account for options that might be embedded in a bond (e.g. callable or putable securities). In a so-called *option-adjusted spread* (OAS), appropriate adjustments have been made.

When the deal is initiated, the present value of all cashflows must be zero, so that any upfront difference due to the bond trading away from par will be accounted for in the asset swap spread. Consequently, the *market asset swap spread* equals the par asset swap spread divided by the dirty price of the bond on a percentage basis.

The CDS–bond basis

Figure 3.4 shows how, for an investor who funds himself at Libor, a combined position of buying protection in a CDS and entering into an asset swap in which the fixed-coupon payments of a bond that trades at par are swapped against a

The theoretical no-arbitrage relationship between credit default swaps and asset swaps   Figure 3.4

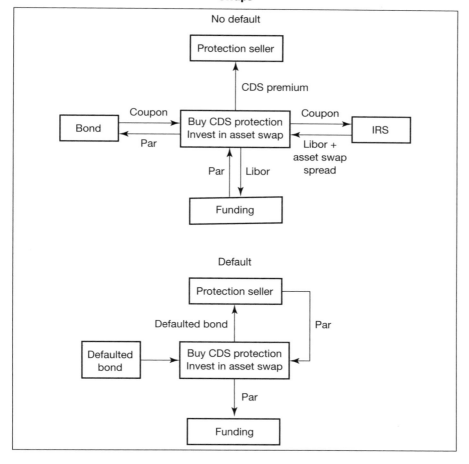

stream of floating rates is fully hedged in any state of the world. Before maturity, there are two possibilities: no default (top) and default (bottom, assuming physical delivery and unwinding of the IRS).

In both cases, the combined position is free of credit risk. Therefore, the CDS premium should match the asset swap spread. If the difference between the CDS premium and the asset swap spread were to diverge from zero, that would constitute a theoretical arbitrage opportunity.

■ Comparison of asset swap spreads with CDS premia requires fulfilment of one important condition: the two credit-risk-sensitive instruments need to have the same remaining maturity.

■ As the bond and the CDS will rarely trade at exactly the same remaining maturity, some calculation will be needed to match maturities. Both interpolation and yield curve estimation techniques may be considered to avoid maturity mismatches.

■ Even if the par asset swap spread is an appropriate bond spread measure with which to compare CDS premiums, there may be room for refinement.

In quantifying the CDS–bond basis to express an outright rich/cheap judgement, both probability of default, which may vary through a bond's lifecycle, and recovery on default must be considered. Also, when a credit event occurs, the interest rate swap of an asset swap package persists, unless the investor has opted to enter into an extinguishable IRS. However, that is an illiquid instrument, so allowance should also be made for the potential cost of unwinding the IRS in an asset swap.

Many financial institutions have built their own models to reflect these issues in their in-house assessment of the CDS–bond basis. Nevertheless, the biases of using asset swap spreads instead of those more refined spread concepts are small and negligible, certainly for low-spread securities. The *true* credit risk is reported to be very close to the asset swap spread, the interest rate risk is almost perfectly hedged, and an asset swap is said to be a very convenient structure to trade as a package.

For relative value considerations in the high-grade market, assessing asset swaps versus CDS may be sufficient to extract value from the basis between the two, and for most investment-grade bonds, the difference in relation to par equivalent CDS spreads will be within a few basis points.

In *any* case the appropriate spread measure for comparing cash bonds with CDS is the asset swap spread.

The CDS–bond basis is the CDS premium minus the asset swap spread. In this chapter, the CDS–bond basis (the basis) is defined as the difference between the CDS premium and the maturity matched par asset swap spread. If this difference is higher (lower) than zero, we say that the basis is positive (negative). The CDS premium for a given CDS ticker n at time t is denoted as

CDSn,t, and the corresponding maturity matched par asset swap spread as *ASWn,t*. Then the basis *Bn,t* can be written as the simple difference:

$$B_{n,t} = CDS_{n,t} - ASW_{n,t}$$

A basis that diverges from zero may present an arbitrage opportunity. In the case of a positive (negative) basis, a positive (negative) basis trade can be set up, in which the cash bond is sold (bought) in an asset swap and CDS protection is sold (bought) at the same time.

However, an investor should be aware that not every apparently attractive basis trade will necessarily be a free lunch, as transaction costs (bid–ask spreads) are significant in credit markets and the basis is determined by a complex set of factors, some of which cannot be controlled in a quantitative manner. The following section examines these economic basis drivers.

BASIS DRIVERS

Although the no-arbitrage condition between CDS premiums and asset swap spreads predicts the basis to be equal to zero, this relation does not always hold in practice. Indeed, market data show that the basis can be either positive or negative, and that its value is both firm-specific and time-dependent. A smorgasbord of factors determines both the direction and the amplitude of the basis. This section will outline the basis determinants that have been described by both academic and market sources.

Table 3.3 shows that basis drivers can be ordered across two different axes. First, factors can be grouped according to their expected effect, as they can either cause the basis to become positive or negative, or even have a mixed effect depending on the precise situation. Second, factors can be grouped

Basis drivers

Table 3.3

		Basis		
		Positive	Negative	Undecided
Factors	Fundamental	CDS cheapest to deliver option CDS premia are floored at zero CDS restructuring clause – technical default Bond trading below par Profit realization	Funding issues Counterparty default risk Accrued interest differences on default Bond trading above par	Coupon specificities
	Technical	Demand for protection – difficulties in shorting cash Issuance patterns	Synthetic CDO issuance	Relative liquidity in segmented markets

according to whether they are more fundamental or technical in nature. Fundamental factors are reasons that relate to the precise specification of a CDS contract and can make it behave differently from a cash bond, while technical factors refer to the nature of the markets in which both contracts are traded.

Key point	**Risk factors**
	In general terms, factors that add risk to the CDS relative to the asset swap tend to increase the basis, while factors that add risk to the asset swap relative to the CDS tend to decrease the basis.

Also, factors that tend to increase the return of an asset swap relative to a CDS drive the basis upwards, while factors that tend to increase the return of a CDS relative to an asset swap have the effect of depressing the basis. It is clear that not all features are equally powerful and that, depending on the specific reference entity and moment in time, some factors can outweigh others, while some determinants may even be irrelevant under certain conditions.

Of the 14 drivers identified below, the four main determinants of the CDS-bond basis are:

- the CDS cheapest-to-deliver option;
- difficulties in shorting cash bonds in a context of structural demand for protection;
- relative liquidity in segmented markets;
- synthetic CDO issuance.

Knowing that it is difficult to quantify, or even find a proxy for, the assumed effect of some factors, it need hardly be said that assessing the combined effect of all determinants on the basis of a specific CDS–asset swap combination is a very challenging task for a credit trader.

Arbitrage opportunities

When faced with an apparently attractive arbitrage opportunity, one should always question to what extent all relevant basis drivers are reflected in the observed basis measure. If this measure is judged to be appropriate, then the issue is whether sufficient liquidity is available in both market segments (CDS and bonds) to permit the profitable execution of arbitrage trades, after having accounted for transaction costs.

Factors that make the basis positive

Fundamental determinants

CDS cheapest-to-deliver option

In the case of physical delivery after a credit event, a protection buyer holds a delivery option, as he is free to choose the cheapest from a basket of deliverable bonds. Since it is likely that protection sellers will end up owning the least favourable option if different deliverable bonds are trading at different spreads, they should receive a higher premium to compensate for this risk.

As a result, the cheapest-to-deliver option tends to increase the basis.

Depending on the type of credit event and the composition of the basket of deliverables, this ability to switch out of one asset into a cheaper one to deliver into the contract can be of significant value. The higher the likelihood of occurrence of a credit event and the wider the spectrum of deliverable bonds and loans in terms of covenants, maturities and coupons, the more valuable this delivery option may be, though it is difficult to quantify its exact value. Given the exponential growth of outstanding derivative contracts, following a default there can be heavy demand from protection buyers for the cheaper cash bonds, which can lead to a market squeeze on the deliverable obligations, with the paradoxical effect of their price rising. This phenomenon has been observed on several occasions, e.g. in case of defaults by US car parts maker Delphi and Calpine, the US energy company, in October 2005 and December 2005, respectively. It tends to reduce the value of the cheapest-to-deliver option, and has revived market participants' interest in developing standardized cash settlement procedures.

CDS premia are floored at zero

Asset swap spreads for high quality issuers (e.g. AAA/Aaa names) may well trade at levels below Libor, given that markets for interbank lending and interest rate swaps are generally populated by institutions that carry an AA−/Aa3 rating. Conversely, default swap premiums cannot be negative since these are insurance-like contracts, in which no protection seller would accept a negative premium.

The basis for reference entities that are perceived to be very creditworthy tends to be positive.

CDS restructuring clause – technical default

The risk of technical default is the risk that the definitions or the legal structure used in the default protection documentation of the CDS differ from those that would constitute default on the cash bond.

If, under specific circumstances, protection sellers in a CDS are forced to pay out on an event that is not a full default, a higher CDS premium will be required, thereby increasing the basis.

More specifically, CDS contracts that include the restructuring credit event are vulnerable to divergence from bond documentation, despite improvements by ISDA in standardizing and harmonizing CDS legal documentation.

Bond trading below par

A seller of protection in a CDS is exposed to the par amount following a credit event, while fixed-rate bonds can trade significantly below par as a result of an increase in risk-free rates or credit spreads after the security has been issued to the market.

In such a case, the seller of a CDS contract guarantees the par amount will require a higher spread than the comparable bond investor who is exposed to lower risk, increasing the basis.

Contrary to many other basis determinants, in the case of a bond price that diverges from 100, the change in the basis can be mathematically estimated, even if an assumption about the expected recovery rate is required.

Profit realization

Locking in a profit on a CDS position requires entering into an offsetting transaction, in which a lower premium is paid. Hence the full mark-to-market can only be monetized by waiting until both trades mature. However, if default occurs during the remaining lifetime, both contracts will trigger a credit event, remaining spread payments will terminate, and any further anticipated gain is lost.

As a compensation for this risk, an investor would require a higher premium when selling a CDS contract, which should widen the basis.

However, two caveats apply. First, while selling a bond enables gains to be locked in immediately, it can be argued that terminating an asset swap also requires entering into an offsetting interest rate swap. However, the credit risk involved in an outstanding IRS is perceived to be lower than for an outstanding CDS, at least for lower-rated reference entities. Second, while locking in profit on a CDS for an end-investor does indeed require entering into another CDS contract, early termination services exist, which organize 'novation' of outstanding default swaps between dealer/brokers participating in the system.

Technical determinants

Demand for protection – difficulties in shorting cash bonds

Banks constantly shed credit risk, as they often hedge exposure of the loan book to maintain a client relationship within all applicable risk limits, including concentration constraints. For these hedging purposes, banks tend to buy protection in CDS markets, as shorting in the cash bond markets is less convenient.

Key point	**Shorting**

Shorting

Shorting the cash market tends to be difficult, because the bond needs to be sourced in an illiquid and short-dated repo market in which bonds additionally might trade on special, making it expensive to borrow the bond. This drives out the CDS premium relative to cash bond spreads, hence widening the basis.

This is all the more the case for reference entities that experience a negative market sentiment because of deteriorating credit quality.

Furthermore, a long bond investor can fund his position in the repo market at a rate that is close to Libor, as it constitutes a collateralized loan. However, if the asset becomes special and its repo yield decreases, the investor would be able to roll over the funding at a cheaper level.

Since such repo optionality is not present in a CDS, it tends to further increase the basis.

Issuance patterns

CDS spreads are often driven wider by market flows during and following the issuance of a convertible bond. Hedge funds specialized in convertible arbitrage strategies are frequently reported to provide a strong bid to the new issue as a means of acquiring a cheap source of equity volatility. At the same time, they hedge out the credit risk by buying protection in the CDS market, hence driving default swap spreads up and the basis wider.

Also, bond syndication desks that hedge forthcoming straight issuance, and banks participating in syndicated loans, will usually buy protection in the CDS markets, causing the basis to widen. Conversely, new bond issues are often launched in the primary market at a somewhat higher spread to provide attractive levels for investors to step in, driving the CDS–bond basis back down.

Factors that make the basis negative

Fundamental determinants
Funding issues

The supposed equality between CDS premia and asset swap spreads is derived under the assumption that cash investors can fund themselves at Libor. However, many market participants only obtain funding above Libor, prompting them to obtain credit exposure by selling CDS rather than by acquiring asset swaps, driving the CDS–bond basis down.

On balance, the greater the ratio of lower-rated versus higher-rated market participants, the more negative the basis should be.

In addition, investors are exposed to future changes in the cost of funding (relative versus Libor), while a default swap locks in an effective funding rate of Libor flat, reinforcing the effect.

The fact that different investors may fund themselves at different rates implies that the actual no-arbitrage level of a CDS versus asset swap trade varies for different market participants.

Counterparty default risk

The two contractors in a CDS bear exposure to each other's ability to fulfil their respective obligations throughout the life of the trade. While the protection seller's counterparty risk is fairly contained, the buyer of protection faces greater uncertainty since, following a credit event, the difference between par and the recovery value of the defaulted asset is at stake, should the protection seller default on the back of the reference entity's credit event.

Protection buyers will, as a form of compensation, tend to be only willing to pay a lower premium, reducing the basis.

Buying a cash bond is a straightforward transaction that involves no additional layer of counterparty risk. However, entering into an asset swap also involves an interest rate swap that overlays the reference bond, and funding of the purchase of the bond often takes place through repo. These additional transactions create additional counterparty risks. However, both of these risks are considered as being minimal.

Accrued interest differentials on default

In the event of default, in most cases a bond does not pay accrued interest as issuers rarely compensate investors for any coupons owed. In contrast, under standard CDS documentation, protection buyers must pay the accrued premium up to the credit event.

While the expected present value of this contractual difference, which is a function of the coupon size and the probability of default, is typically small, it tends to drive the CDS–bond basis more negative.

Bond trading above par

As argued above, a bond trading below par makes the basis positive.

As a corollary a bond trading above par causes the basis to be negative. Indeed, if a bond trades at a price above 100, the seller of a CDS contract who guarantees the par amount will settle for a correspondingly lower spread.

Technical determinant
Synthetic CDO issuance

Issuance in structured credit markets, and in markets for synthetic collateralized debt obligations in particular, has been rising exponentially over the past few years and is expected to continue to grow.

At the same time, this is a factor that has been driving CDS spreads tighter and, as a result, depressing the CDS–bond basis.

Indeed, to be able to sell synthetic credit risk to investors via these structures, the originators will typically have to take an offsetting long credit risk position by selling protection to hedge the transaction. The impact may vary significantly among individual credits, as it is a function of the relative liquidity of a reference name in the CDS and cash bond markets.

Factors that make the basis either positive or negative

Fundamental determinant

Coupon specificities

Some bonds carry clauses triggering a coupon step-up in the event of a ratings downgrade, which adds another layer of protection for bondholders that is not reflected in a similar default swap position.

As a result, the CDS should trade wider than this bond, i.e. the basis should be positive and widening in case of a negative rating trend or weakening market sentiment for the issuer. Alternatively, coupon step-down clauses in the wake of a rating upgrade are also sometimes included in a bond structure, and these should imply a negative basis.

Coupon payment conventions also play a role; e.g. in case of US corporate bonds, coupon payments are made semi-annually on a 30/360 day-count convention, while CDS premia are due quarterly and accrue using an actual/360 convention. It is of course possible to control for this factor, but the investor who is considering a basis trade should be aware.

Technical determinant

Relative liquidity in segmented markets

Prices in both cash bond and CDS markets are a function of their specific supply and demand dynamics, which tend to exhibit diverging characteristics in these two, segmented markets. Despite integration of global financial markets, blurring of frontiers, and the existence of arbitrageurs, who are technically able to exploit price discrepancies between the two markets, this is still one of the main reasons for the existence of the CDS–bond basis.

The basis will depend on the relative liquidity in both markets, and will compensate an investor who invests in the less liquid segment.

On the demand side, the investor base of the two markets is intrinsically different. A wide range of investors populate cash bond markets, though to a large extent bonds end up in buy-and-hold portfolios of funded investors, such as insurance companies and pension funds. Conversely, protection sellers in CDS markets are often more dynamic investors, such as hedge funds and proprietary trading desks, which can easily leverage their exposure due to the unfunded nature of derivatives. Different investor types are also governed by different regulatory frameworks and restrictions, while tax treatment may vary across products that are equivalent in economic terms.

Finally, the off-balance-sheet nature of CDS is an incentive for some types of investors to sell protection in derivatives markets rather than to buy cash bonds outright. Also, on the supply side, the two markets are organized in a different fashion. Protection buyers in CDS markets are often institutions such as banks that want to shed risks in a structural way. On the other hand, bond issuers such as corporations and sovereign states drive bond market supply according to their financing needs.

Hence, on a maturity scale, the cash market for a particular credit name only trades large, liquid, bonds where issuers have decided to sell benchmark bonds into the market. Furthermore, these issues roll down the curve as time elapses, and only a few creditors have regular issuance programmes spread out across the curve. On the other hand, CDS markets ensure liquidity around fixed maturities: the five-year segment attracts by far the most liquidity, while three-, seven- and ten-year CDS are also frequently traded maturities.

SUMMARY: CREDIT DEFAULT SWAPS COMPARED WITH BONDS

As credit default swaps isolate and transfer credit risk, users can buy and sell protection depending on whether they want to hedge (or in some cases speculate) or take on credit risk. Since sellers of protection take on credit risk and earn a premium for this risk, they are equivalent to the buyers of bonds. And since buyers of protection hedge credit risk – paying a premium for getting rid of risk – this is equivalent to shorting a bond. In both cases, the party taking on credit risk loses money if the credit defaults.

The main difference between bond and credit default swap cashflows is timing of principal payments. The bond buyer pays the principal to buy the bond on the trade date, whereas the protection seller pays the principal (or rather, principal less the recovery rate) only when the credit defaults.

CDS bond basis

Basis = Credit swap spread – Cash asset swap spread

The most commonly traded credit default swaps (CDS) generally trade tighter compared with corresponding bond/asset swaps. Credit default swaps are therefore leveraged instruments because the protection seller does not need to put any money down to earn a premium for the risk it takes. Credit default swaps are also referred to as unfunded instruments, because the protection seller – unlike the bond investor – does not need to raise money (or get funding) to buy credit risk.

Figure 3.5 shows the relationship between CDS–bond basis and credit rating. When the CDS is greater than the boxed yield, the basis is positive. When the cash bond yield spread is above the CDS spread, the basis is negative. Figure 3.6 is a quick way to compare a CDS with a bond. The figure shows CDS cashflows compared with bond cashflows.

Bond basis versus bond ratings

Figure 3.5

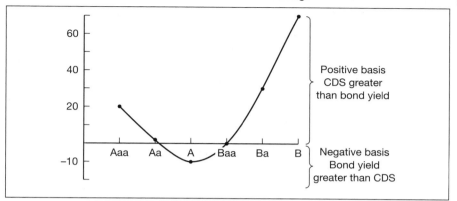

CDS versus bond cashflows

Figure 3.6

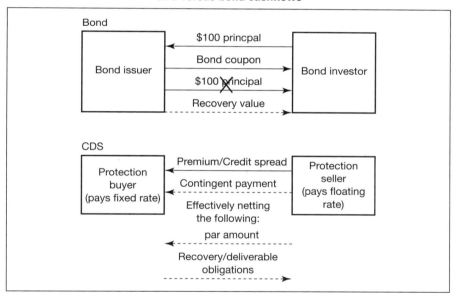

Credit default swap cashflows mean that the protection buyer is exposed to the credit risk of the protection seller. This 'counterparty risk' is the risk that the protection seller cannot or will not pay the par amount, at the time when the protection buyer needs it most. By contrast, the protection seller's only counterparty risk is that the protection buyer will stop making premium payments.

Single-name trading strategies

Single-name credit default swaps can be used as part of a range of relative value trading strategies. Among the simplest are basis trades (Figure 3.7). This strategy is designed to take advantage of the difference (the basis) between credit default swap spreads and cash bond or loan spreads for the same credit.

| Figure 3.7 | Basis trades involving buying a bond and buying protection or vice versa |

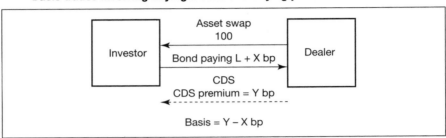

Source: Credit Hedge Ltd

A trader puts on a negative-basis trade when the credit default swap spread is lower than the spread over Libor on a cash asset, allowing the trader to buy the bond, buy protection on the issuer of the bond and earn a positive net spread (this surplus is referred to as positive carry).

The trader either buys a floating-rate asset or a fixed-rate bond that has been asset-swapped into a floating-rate instrument paying a spread over Libor. This trade carries no credit risk and the trader is able to earn a positive spread for taking advantage of the CDS–bond basis.

Because of the bid–offer spread, negative basis trades tend to be worth putting on only when the basis exceeds around 10bp. These opportunities have become increasingly rare as the trade has become well known.

Other single-name trading strategies include convergence trades where a trader believes that the difference between the spreads of two names will decrease.

For example, if Renault spreads are wider than Peugeot spreads, and a trader believes their credit risk is very similar, the trader could sell protection on Renault and buy protection on Peugeot, expressing the view that their spreads will converge and making a gain on the overall trade.

Another strategy is to sell protection on one name whose spreads the trader believes will tighten, and to use the income to buy protection on another name whose spread the trader believes will widen.

For names where there is a liquid market in both senior and subordinated credit default swaps (chiefly financials), traders can use single-name credit default swaps to bet that the reference entity's subordinated debt will outperform its senior debt – or vice versa – without taking an outright view on the creditworthiness of the borrower or the direction of its spreads.

The emergence of a liquid market in seven- and ten-year credit derivatives, starting around 2005, made it possible for traders to express views on spreads at different points on the credit curve (called curve trades) using single-name credit default swaps. These strategies express a view not just on the likelihood of default, but on the timing of any possible default.

A popular curve trade in 2005 and 2006 was a 'curve steepener' (Figure 3.8). A trader who believed that an issuer's long-term credit spreads were likely to widen relative to shorter-term spreads, causing the credit curve to steepen, might sell five-year protection and buy ten-year protection on the name, making money when five-year spreads tighten, ten-year spreads widen or some combination of the two effects. A curve flattener is the opposite bet – that spreads at different maturities will converge.

'Curve steepener' CDS trading strategy   Figure 3.8

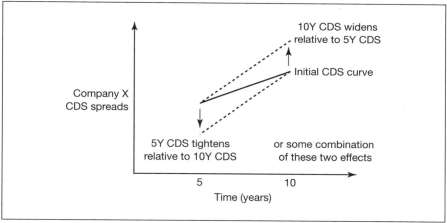

Source: Credit Hedge Ltd

Credit derivatives documentation and regulations

DOCUMENTATION

Flexibility is vital for credit derivatives documentation, which has evolved rapidly. The documentation choices now include original restructuring, modified restructuring and modified-modified restructuring. New Basel rules may facilitate increased trading with no restructuring at all. This chapter sets out the background and some of the issues under discussion and comments on what is needed for the credit derivatives market to thrive in terms of documentation.

Since its foundation in the mid-1990s, the market for credit derivatives has evolved rapidly and grown exponentially. Even as corporate debt default rates have reached historical highs, the growth in the credit default swap market has exceeded all expectations. According to estimates by the International Swaps and Derivatives Association (ISDA)[1], the credit default swaps market grew 44 per cent in the first six months of 2002 and 37 per cent in the second six months. By the end of 2002, the market had grown to $2,150bn; in 2007 it was more than $6,000bn.

The evidence is that this trend continues; participants in the market for credit protection have increased in number and level of activity. As the market for credit default swaps grows in size and importance, few major financial institutions — whether they are natural buyers of protection (usually banks), sellers of protection (typically hedge funds, insurers and reinsurers), or both (dealers) — are without a credit derivatives operation of some kind.

Key features

Basel accords

The original Basel accord was agreed in 1988 by the Basel Committee on Banking Supervision. This accord, referred to as Basel 1, helped to strengthen the soundness and stability of the international banking system by requiring higher capital ratios. Basel 2 revises the framework, aiming to make it more risk-sensitive and representative of modern banks' risk management practices. Its four main components are:

- An explicit measure for operational risk and more risk-sensitive risk weightings against credit risk.
- It reflects improvements in firm's risk management practices. For example, the internal ratings-based approach (IRB) allows firms to rely to a certain extent on their own estimates of credit risk.
- It provides incentives for firms to improve their risk management, with more sensitive weightings as firms adopt more sophisticated approaches to risk managament.

▶

■ The new framework aims to leave the overall level of capital held by banks collectively broadly unchanged.

Basel 2 has been implemented in the EU via the Capital Requirements Directive (CRD). It affects banks and building societies and certain types of investment firms. The framework consists of three 'pillars'. The first pillar sets out the minimum capital requirements required to meet credit, market and operational risk. Under the second, firms and supervisors have to take a view on whether to hold additional capital against risks not covered in the first pillar and take action accordingly. Pillar three aims to improve market discipline by requiring firms to publish details of their risks, capital and risk management.

And this is just the tip of the iceberg. Credit default swaps represent the plain vanilla market in credit derivatives, a product set that extends into baskets and portfolios of such transactions. The appetite to buy into credit markets has created a parallel market in synthesized credit exposure through the synthetic CDO (collateralized debt obligation) market. Ratings agency reports in 2007 even demonstrated that some European banks in particular, though typically considered protection buyers in the default swap market, were net sellers of protection. They are taking on more credit exposure to diversify their holdings than the amount of protection they are buying on their own loan exposures – a significant development.

INFRASTRUCTURE AND ISDA'S ROLE

Against this background of growth, ISDA has taken on several roles in the credit default swap market. One major role in relation to these products has been to establish a secure framework of robust documentation and legal certainty by enforcing such documentation and attendant mechanisms as collateralization and netting. ISDA has done so by working with members from all constituencies of the marketplace, with fellow trade associations, with regulators and with ratings agencies. Only within the context of a secure and supportive legal and regulatory framework can a market the size of that for credit derivatives continue to flourish.

This is far from the only role ISDA has played in discussions around the restructuring issue, however. As a relatively young and fairly complex market, the credit default swap creates a logistical challenge unique even in the realm of derivatives. With the restructuring debate in particular, issues of credit derivatives market practice are entwined with the challenges of documentation and with the regulatory capital requirements that cross the threshold into risk management territory.

Perhaps the most challenging aspect of ISDA's role has been to pull together the strands of the restructuring debate. ISDA has worked with members of the business and trading practice side of the market, with documentation specialists, with risk management specialists and with operations professionals within all constituencies of the marketplace to improve the foundations established by the documentation infrastructure. Along with other trade associations, notably the Risk Management Association (RMA), the London Investment Banking Association, and the International Association of Credit Portfolio Managers, ISDA has worked extensively with regulators on the issue of capital relief for credit hedges.

Credit default swap documentation

Including a restructuring clause in credit default swap documentation is intended to guard against a reference entity's debt losing economic merit after a restructuring of the company's debt schedule. Many participants – notably protection sellers but also certain dealers and banks – have argued there is no need for this clause in the default swap contract. Yet a regulatory requirement for including it as a capital relief mechanism for banks hedging their loans with these products has perpetuated its use in many standard contracts.

The issue of the market requiring that restructuring is considered a standard credit event has therefore become a chicken-or-the-egg argument. The potential relaxation of this requirement has emboldened some participants to drop it from their standard trades. Yet, pending final confirmation on this point means that a large part of the market is adopting a wait-and-see approach before making any all-encompassing decisions on excluding this credit event from their credit default swap contracts.

ISDA documentation for credit default swaps

The ISDA documentation for credit default swaps has evolved more rapidly than that for any other area of derivatives, moving from its original Long-Form Confirmation published in 1998, to the 1999 ISDA Credit Derivatives Definitions, to the extensively revised 2003 Definitions launched in February 2003.

A fast-expanding market is often accompanied by tests of the strength and robustness of the product set and its documentation and the operational infrastructure. Some major tests of the market have been key to defining the 2003 ISDA Credit Derivatives Definitions. The case that began many discussions on the nature of restructuring was Conseco. In September 2000, the restructuring of Conseco's bank loan schedule resulted in some market participants availing themselves of a 'cheapest-to-deliver option', which enabled buyers of protection to deliver lesser-value securities than banks believed they had bought protection on.

Market practice

In January 2001, the ISDA Credit Derivatives Market Practice Committee was formed in an attempt to obtain input from market participants. Members from the three main constituencies of the default swap market – protection sellers, protection buyers and dealers – were formally grouped in London and New York, the two main centres for this market. With an official representative for each constituency in both locations, this working group became known as the Group of Six, or G6.

The task of the G6 was to find a documentation solution by weekly teleconferences that provided business input into the issue of restructuring. Between January and May, this working group operated intensively, in tandem with ISDA. It reported, both to and from the six constituencies, the market's views on an appropriate solution to the cheapest-to-deliver option.

Participating firms in the Credit Derivatives Market Practice Committee moved to close the loophole in the definitional language. They created a supplemental version of the restructuring credit event – modified restructuring – that restricts maturity limitation of deliverable obligations to thrity months after the scheduled termination date.

RESTRUCTURING: THE 2003 DEFINITIONS

This section explains modified restructuring, modified-modified restructuring and old restructuring in a credit default swap (CDS) contract, relative to a contract with only bankruptcy and failure to pay credit events (no restructuring, or no R).

The value of the restructuring credit event in a CDS depends on:

- The contractual maturity restrictions on deliverable obligations.
- The term of the CDS contract.
- The capital structure of the reference entity.
- The likelihood of the restructuring credit event relative to bankruptcy or failure to pay.

Mod R restrictions

The Mod R CDS contract places the most restrictions on the maturity of deliverable obligations, followed by the Mod Mod R variant, with Old R placing least.

For this reason, the value of the restructuring credit event is lowest in Mod R contracts, followed by Mod Mod R and highest in Old R. The value of the cheapest-to-deliver option in CDS with restructuring declines with the term of the contract.

Cheapest-to-deliver option

To settle following a credit event, most CDS contracts allow the protection buyer to deliver a basket of debt that is equal or greater in seniority relative to the contract's reference obligation, which is typically senior unsecured. This feature amounts to a cheapest-to-deliver option: the protection buyer can seek out the lowest-priced debt to settle the contract. If the protection buyer hedged a specific debt issue on its books, delivering lower-priced debt to settle the contract produces a gain.

The pay-off for the cheapest-to-deliver option embedded in a CDS depends on the lowest-priced obligation following a credit event. For example, if a reference entity has long-dated, foreign currency, or otherwise low-priced liabilities following a credit event, the pay-off may be quite large. Alternatively, if all senior unsecured debt is trading at the same price following a credit event the gain is minimal.

Unlike bankruptcy and failure to pay, which usually cause all debt at the same seniority level to trade roughly at the same recovery price, a restructuring often causes deliverable obligations to trade with a term structure. Longer-maturity obligations trade at higher spreads than short-term ones, reflecting the near-term liquidity improvement and continuing long-term uncertainty. The price dispersion of deliverable obligations increases the value of the cheapest-to-deliver option in contracts with restructuring.

The running spread premium in short-maturity CDS contracts is greater than in long ones. Not surprisingly, the more long-maturity or otherwise potentially low-priced liabilities the reference asset has outstanding, the higher the value of restructuring. Finally, the greater the likelihood of the restructuring credit event relative to bankruptcy and failure to pay, the wider is the Mod R, Mod Mod R and old R CDS spread relative to No R.

The question of restructuring

The question of restructuring as a credit event in standard CDO contracts has occupied market participants for several years. Following the publication of the 1999 ISDA credit derivatives definitions, the market-standard set of credit events for corporate reference entities became:

- failure to pay;
- bankruptcy;
- restructuring.

The restructuring supplements provide the CDS market with contract language that limits the ability to deliver debt instruments that are often cheaper than the restructured instrument, while still offering hedges protection from the restructuring credit event. Contracts that specify this limitation as applicable are referred to as 'Mod R', while those that do not are called 'Old R'. CDS that list only failure to pay and bankruptcy are called No R contracts. Failure to pay and bankruptcy are called 'hard' credit events by market participants, while restructuring is deemed a 'soft' credit event.

The 2003 definitions offer four choices relating to restructuring

By the middle of 2001, US dealers had adopted Mod R in the majority of investment-grade corporate CDS contracts. Protection sellers insisted on limiting the value of the cheapest-to deliver option by switching to Mod R.

Four options for restructuring
Key features

- To trade with 'full' or 'old' restructuring, with no modification to the deliverable obligations aspect.
- To trade with modified restructuring, as has been the market practice in North America since the publication of the restructuring supplement in May 2001.
- To trade with Mod Mod R, the new provision, which generally aims to address issues raised in the European market.
- To trade without restructuring.

Modified restructuring

First introduced in May 2001, modified restructuring was widely adopted by the North American market and was one of four choices offered in the 2003 definitions. Under this definition, unlike the original 'old restructuring' definition, the deliverable obligation must be fully transferable with no consent required. Ultimately, the European market chose not to trade with this version because of issues associated with regional regulations on transferability of obligations. The ISDA Credit Derivatives Market Practice (through the G6) and the ISDA Documentation Committee therefore set to work on a third version, commonly referred to as modified-modified restructuring, which was published in the 2003 definitions.

Modified-modified restructuring (Mod Mod R)

Under modified-modified restructuring, the maturity of the restructured bond or loan may be up to sixty months after the restructuring date, but for all other deliverable obligations, the maturity also may be to thirty months. Perhaps more significantly, the deliverable obligation must be 'conditionally transferable', and thus consent may not be unreasonably withheld.

No restructuring (No R)

The fourth choice available is to trade without restructuring. This approach has gained support in several areas, and while not a documentation solution, it demonstrates that the 2003 Credit Derivatives Definitions reflect another stage in the development of a market still in its relative infancy. It stands out among the attempts to shape the infrastructure to fit the requirements of users, because the decision by some market participants to drop restructuring from all trades sidesteps the regulatory requirements of the Basel Committee and, in so doing, forgoes the associated capital benefit. Early in the debate, it became clear that end-user protection sellers wanted to limit their exposure to restructuring risk by using credit default swaps to the extent, in some cases, of deciding to eliminate restructuring from the list of credit events they would sell protection on. An argument in favour of doing so was that many banks wanted to buy protection only against restructuring because it was a requirement under Basel.

Main changes

In addition to the new restructuring clause, changes in the 2003 ISDA definitions include the following.

Test for identifying the successor to a reference entity

In a new approach, the 2003 definitions offer a numerical threshold test. Under the 1999 definitions, the test was whether the new entity had assumed 'all or substantially all' of the assets of the reference entity. However, the test proved to be problematic in circumstances where the quantitative split between the obligation and the assets of the old and new entity were fairly close. Thus, a series of quantitative thresholds are set forth in the 2003 Definitions.

Amendments to credit events, including bankruptcy and repudiation/moratorium

Besides restructuring, the other credit events amended in the 2003 definitions were bankruptcy and repudiation/moratorium. In the context of sovereign CDS, the repudiation/moratorium credit event was amended following discussions among members after the Argentina debt crisis in 2001 and 2002. Under the 2003 definitions, a more specific trigger for the credit event was offered.

Procedures for non-deliverable bonds and loans

A binding notice of physical settlement was introduced. Under the 2003 definitions, the buyer is required to notify the seller of the deliverable obligations it will deliver. The buyer may send the seller notices until the physical settlement date, with the last notice being binding.

Guarantees

The 2003 definitions clarify that the obligations of a reference entity can be its direct obligations. These include an obligation of a 'downstream affiliate', called a 'qualifying affiliate guarantee', or an obligation of a third-party guarantee by the reference entity, called a 'qualifying guarantee'. This last category of third-party guarantees is only included if the parties specify as such in their confirmation.

Novation provision

An article was introduced to address the novation or assignment of credit derivative transactions. A novation agreement and a novation confirmation are also offered to assist parties in documentation and in obtaining the requisite consents to the assignments of such transactions.

Many of ISDA's efforts to document credit derivatives have focused on the deliverable assets in the event of restructuring clause included in a default swap. Looking to the future, ISDA has undertaken to review the trigger events that precipitate a settlement, as well as issues surrounding the bankruptcy trigger in relation to a CDS.

OTHER CONSIDERATIONS

Accounting

Another area of ISDA involvement in the CDS market is that of accounting across jurisdictions. Under IAS 39, the International Accounting Standards Board's standard for fair-value accounting, credit derivatives reporting will come into the balance sheet. This means they will be marked to market, unlike underlying loan books, which are accounted for on an accrual basis.

Under existing accounting standards outside the US, derivatives and other hedges have qualified for hedge accounting treatment, which does not require marking to market (and can therefore be marked-to-model). A concern is that to qualify for hedge accounting treatment, a derivative must exactly match the underlying transaction; this presents a significant issue in respect of a CDS used to hedge loan portfolios.

This standard, which was implemented in 2005, mirrors that of the Financial Accounting Standards Board's (FASB) FAS 133 in the US, which has been in effect for several years.

Taxation

Credit derivatives market participants are also attempting to rationalize a layer of complexity relating to the treatment of these instruments for taxation purposes. The US Internal Revenue Service (IRS) has sought industry guidance on the nature of these instruments as compared with both guarantees and insurance contracts. While credit derivatives are neither of these things, the industry view is that in order to qualify for treatment as financial instruments, they must fit a series of criteria. They must be documented under an ISDA master agreement, to which one party must be a dealer under Rule 475, and reference obligations must not be related to the credit protection buyer or the protection seller.

Regulation

Risk management

ISDA's risk management committee, through its credit risk mitigation working group, has been talking to regulators about clearer rules for capital relief by banks through credit default swaps. It works with other associations, such as the credit risk mitigation subgroup of the Basel Committee. Working with this subgroup, ISDA has often united forces with the London Investment Banking Association (LIBA), The Bond Market Association (TBMA), RMA, and IACPM on issues of capital adequacy.

For the banks' part, the restructuring issue has largely been that of capital requirements. The Basel Committee, through its credit risk mitigation subgroup, requires in the current capital accord that a restructuring clause be used in the default swap contract between a buyer and seller of protection for the bank buyer of protection to qualify for capital relief through that contract. In essence, this means that if the credit default swap contract does not contain a restructuring clause, Basel does not recognize that the loan is fully hedged and will therefore not grant full capital relief as a benefit of the hedge. Inevitably, this has been a source of debate between market participants and with this subgroup of the Basel Committee.

Is it possible to consider the loan fully hedged if the contract by which it is hedged does not contain a restructuring clause? Many market participants believe so, arguing that, in effect, the risk of economic loss as a result of a restructuring is mitigated significantly by the other main credit events under the ISDA documentation. One consideration offered in discussions with the Basel Committee was capital relief on credit default swaps with no restructuring clause as long as the maturity of the swap matched the maturity of the underlying loan. Most banks felt this was a specious argument and that the proffered solution was too easy to arbitrage.

Ultimately, to the delight of many members in the credit derivatives market, ISDA and its fellow associations successfully defended the view that capital relief was warranted in most cases without the need for the derivative to hedge restructuring risk. Early indications have been that the requirement will be dropped, but it now remains to be seen how closely the Basel Committee's third consultation paper (CP3) will be in line with the Committee's thinking on this point.

Summary

In no other area of the derivatives market is the documentation so closely allied with the associated market practice. Neither can exist in a vacuum because of the need for effective documentation in the smooth operation of the trading function and the thorough process of confirmation and, ultimately, settlement. In light of this and the variety of market practices, ISDA attempts to provide as much documentation flexibility as the marketplace requires. The documentation choices now are numerous, including old or original restructuring, modified restructuring and modified-modified restructuring.

BANK REGULATION OF CREDIT DERIVATIVES

The advent of credit derivatives in the international banking forum has yet to be greeted with a definitive regulatory response from the Bank of International Settlements (BIS)[2] for uniform global application.

Rather, regulators regionally, through their publication of guidelines for banks within their respective jurisdictions, have part fuelled and part responded to the rapid growth of the credit derivatives market.

This section outlines the regulatory approach in credit derivatives and discusses certain variations in the treatments of specific issues from jurisdiction to jurisdiction.

BIS

The Bank for International Settlements (www.bis.org) fosters international monetary and financial cooperation and serves as a bank for central banks. BIS fulfils this mandate by acting as:

- a forum to promote discussion and policy analysis among central banks and within the international financial community;
- a centre for economic and monetary research;
- a prime counterpart for central banks in their financial transactions;
- agent or trustee in connection with international financial operations.

Treatment of unfunded credit derivatives in the Banking Book

The reduction in risk from buying protection on an asset via a credit derivative is seen as analogous to that afforded by a bank guarantee on that asset, and in consequence the regulatory approach is consistent with the established approach to the latter as set forth in the Basel Capital Accord.

As the credit exposure of the protection seller to the reference entity in a credit derivative transaction is substantially identical to that of a lender to or bondholder of the same reference entity, the capital that the protection seller is required to hold against the position is just as it would be if a standby letter of credit or guarantee had been written. Accordingly, notional exposure of the protection seller on the Banking Book is registered for the purposes of calculating regulatory capital, dependent upon the risk weighting of the reference entity asset set forth in the 1998 Basle Accord; namely 100 per cent for corporates, 20 per cent for OECD banks and 0 per cent for OECD sovereigns.

Capital relief is afforded the protection buyer provided that it can be demonstrated that the credit risk of the underlying asset has been transferred to the seller. Should the terms of the credit derivative not adequately capture the risk parameters of the underlying instrument – for example through restrictive definitions of credit events or stringent materiality thresholds – then protection cannot be recognized.

Where it is recognized, it has normally been the case in regulatory determinations that the risk weighting of the underlying assets may be replaced by that of the protection seller. For example, protection referenced to a loan to a European corporate bought in credit derivative form from an OECD bank would have the effect of re-weighting the asset from 100 per cent to the risk weighting of the OECD bank, 20 per cent.

While treatment of the bank buying protection in this way recognizes some of the reduction of risk from such a transaction, it is not evident that to require the same amount of capital to be held against a position not at risk until default of two independent credits as against a position at risk to default of one of them only is to recognize adequately the much lower risk profile of the bank in the former scenario. Indeed, in the interests of encouraging prudent and effective risk management techniques by banks, this is an issue highlighted by the Basel Committee on Banking Supervision:

- The committee is aware that the Accord does not fully capture the extent of the risk reduction that can be achieved by credit risk mitigation techniques. Under the Accord's current substitution approach, the risk-weight of the collateral or guarantor is simply substituted for that of the original obligor. For example, a 100% risk-weighted loan guaranteed by a bank attracts the same risk-weight as the bank guarantor. However, in the above example, a bank would only suffer losses if both the loan and its guarantor default.

- On this basis, the size of the capital requirement might more appropriately depend on the correlation between the default probabilities of the original obligor and the guarantor bank. If the default of the guarantor were certain to be accompanied by the default of the borrower, then the current substitution approach would be appropriate. But, if the probabilities of default are essentially unrelated, then a smaller capital charge than currently exists would be justified. In this context, the Committee has considered whether it would be possible to acknowledge the double default effect by applying a simple haircut to the capital charge that currently results from substituting the risk-weight of the hedging instrument for that of the underlying obligor. Such a haircut would need to be set at a prudently low level.

Basel Committee (1999a)

The regulatory treatment of the protection buyer in a credit derivatives transaction also serves to highlight some of the inadequacies of the present risk weighting system, whereby a bank buying protection from a corporate – be it even one of the highest credit rating – is not allowed to reduce capital held against the protected asset.

'Funded' credit derivative structures

'Funded' credit derivatives – i.e. credit-linked note (CLN) structures – are usually distinguished in regulatory treatises from their 'unfunded' brethren, albeit that regulatory treatment of the two is very similar.

For the protection buyer, where an asset is fully or partly hedged by a funded credit derivative, the efficacy of the hedge is again recognized in a reduction of the risk weighting for the buyer. The risk weighting of the hedged asset is replaced with that of the collateral to the credit swap, i.e. where the collateral is cash or government securities that are 0 per cent risk-weighted, there is no capital requirement against the hedged asset.

The exposure of the noteholder – the equivalent of a protection seller in a 'funded' credit derivative transaction – is to the reference credit, to the collateral, and often (and in varying degrees) to the buyer, but regulations have thus far diverged in their approach to this exposure.

The treatment suggested by the Australian Prudential Regulation Authority (ARPA) is conservative in that the risk weighting of the seller's exposure is calculated by summing the risk weights of the protection buyer and the reference credit. BAKred considers that as the amount of the redemption depends both on the financial standing of the debtor of the reference asset and also on that of the buyer, the weighting of the exposure should be at the higher of the risk weightings of the buyer and reference credit.

Guidance from the Financial Services Authority (FSA), the UK regulator, additionally captures situations where the issuer of the CLN is a special purpose vehicle, such that, consistent with the BAKred, the weighting of the exposure is recorded at the higher of the risk weights of the reference obligor and the counterparty holding the funds and, where applicable, the collateral security.

'Basket' structures

For the protection buyer in a first-to-default basket structure, protection is recognized in respect of one of the assets within the basket only. The asset with the lowest risk weighting or smallest dollar amount is usually considered protected and assigned the risk weighting of the protection seller. However, the FSA affords the protection buyer discretion in the choice of asset recognized as protected.

The regulatory approach of the US Federal Reserve and Omni Financial Services to first-to-default baskets is for the protection seller to weight their exposure at the level of the riskiest asset in the basket. That this treatment does not contemplate the increased probability of default from exposure to each of the assets in the basket, implying that the risk of selling protection on a basket of assets with one or more weighted at 100 per cent is equivalent to selling protection on just one of those 100 per cent risk-weighted assets, has caused other regulators to take a more much more conservative approach, summing the individual risk-weighted exposures in the basket such that the resulting capital charge is capped at the maximum payout possible under the swap (i.e. effectively a deduction from capital). The regulators advocating this approach, however, acknowledge its 'shortcoming', particularly in cases where assets in the basket are strongly correlative, in which case the FSA and France's Commission Bancaire advocate bespoke treatment for each case. In the words of APRA:

'The shortcoming of this alternative approach is that it ignores the first-to-default feature of the basket product; by assuming an exposure to each asset in the basket it can be argued that this approach is particularly conservative.'

'In principle then, the appropriate capital treatment is one that incorporates the default correlations between asset values as well as the first-to-default aspect of the credit derivative.'

Asset mismatches

Key to the usefulness of credit derivatives is that a bank's credit exposure arising through ownership of a certain obligation of a certain entity may be completely hedged without making explicit reference to that obligation. For example, a bank with a bilateral loan to a corporate might have difficulties in finding a counterparty willing to sell credit protection referenced to that loan, and instead buy protection referenced to a more well known and liquid bond of the same company.

It is of paramount concern to regulators that, from a credit perspective, the hedged asset be identical to the reference asset in the credit derivative (or, where there is no reference asset, that the hedged asset is eligible for protection under the terms of the credit derivative), i.e. that if a default occurs on the hedged asset, a credit event will be triggered simultaneously under the credit derivative, and recovery rates will be the same.

In consequence, for protection to be recognized and the capital requirement reduced, the two obligations should be issued by the same legal entity, and the reference asset should be *pari passu* or lower in seniority of claim than the hedged asset.

The FSA, BAKred, FRB and APRA also require that there be mutual cross-default clauses between the assets, albeit that while it is necessary that the default of an underlying asset should trigger the credit derivative, it is not clear why the reverse should apply.

Where the hedged asset is exactly the same from a credit perspective as the reference asset, its risk weighting is replaced with that of the protection seller.

On the whole, however, although asset mismatches do not necessarily manifest zero risk reduction, regulators have tended to be conservative in the treatment of their occurrence even to the extent of not allowing any regulatory capital relief on the position thus hedged.

The Commission Bancaire, on the other hand, grasps the problem of non-identical credit hedging in the same currency by limiting the capital reduction effect through taking 10 per cent from the hedge notional, a 'penalty' that can be recognized for capital purposes.

Maturity mismatches

Under certain conditions it can be preferable (principally on the basis of cost efficiency) to hedge an asset of distant maturity for a shorter period.

The problem with this strategy is that the protection buyer retains forward exposure to – and hence a forward capital requirement for – credit risk of the underlying asset.

However, in the example of a ten-year asset hedged through a seven-year credit derivative transaction, there is real economic risk reduction, which ought to be recognized in some risk-weighted asset reduction.

If the hedge has in excess of one year remaining tenure but does not cover the full maturity of the hedged asset, many regulators impose an additional risk weight of 50 per cent of the unhedged weighting of the hedged asset to take account of the forward exposure. For example, the weighting of a 100 per cent risk-weighted asset guaranteed by a 20 per cent risk-weighted counterparty would be 70 per cent.

The assumption here is that forward exposure resulting from maturity mismatching is analogous in risk terms to a committed but undrawn credit facility to a corporate (which is risk-weighted at 50 per cent).

The distinction, however, is that whereas an undrawn commitment may become drawn at any time without notice (whereupon the facility would become 100 per cent risk-weighted to the extent of drawdown), potentially doubling the capital requirement, the fixed maturity of the credit derivative hedge means that a bank knows in advance precisely when the additional capital will be required.

Given that it is generally accepted by regulators that an unfunded commitment to a corporate borrower is weighted at 50 per cent, albeit that it may be drawn down on at any time, it would seem to be an inconsistency that when a ten-year asset is hedged for the next seven, and hence the likelihood of the additional capital requirement in the first seven years is contingent solely on the credit of the OECD bank, the risk weighting should be greater than 50 per cent in the years before the maturity of the hedge.

Indeed, since a hedge to maturity with an OECD bank on a drawn corporate loan is recognized in a re-weighting to 20 per cent (a re-weighting that the Basel Committee has acknowledged may be overly conservative), it is questionable whether in the years prior to the maturity of the hedge the credit position of the bank is such that the risk weighting should be much greater than 20 per cent. Given the economic efficacy of hedging practices such as this, the regulations would seem to be a disincentive to prudent risk management.

In recognition of this, APRA uses a 'straight line' method, which recognises protection on the percentage of the underlying asset that is covered by the hedge. Hence for a ten-year asset protected by a nine-year credit derivative, 90 per cent of the exposure would be risk-weighted according to the protection seller, with the remaining 10 per cent of exposure weighted at the level of the underlying asset. Again, the credit derivative must have a remaining maturity of at least one year to be recognized as a hedge. Pursuit of the ideal economic compromise often leads to the step-up and call structure.

Take, for example, a ten-year loan held by a bank that expects the fee for protection on that asset to be lower in four years' time than it is today. To capture that upside, while prudently protecting against the possibility of severe downside (spreads widen significantly), the bank buys a four-year-into-six step-up callable credit swap whereby the fee for protection increases after four years, at which time the bank has the right but not the obligation to call the swap. Such a structure effectively manifests a total hedge on the loan to maturity for the first four years, eliminating a significant portion of the forward exposure, depending on the level of step-up. Most regulatory treatises do not express a view on the step-up and call, but concern often arises as to the level of step-up.

Post-call protection

Key point

The FSA in the UK, for example, treats the call date as the maturity of the derivative, giving no credit at all for the post-call protection.

Tranched indices

While the market for outstanding synthetic CDOs is vast and quite diverse with respect to structural complexity, it remains fragmented as discussed in Chapter 1. The emergence of standardized, tradable and relatively diverse default swap indices in 2003 provided an opportunity for an on-the-run market for tranches to develop shortly thereafter. Today, tranched index instruments are by far the largest liquidity point in the structured credit market, serve as an entry point in the structured credit market, serve as an entry point for many investors and have been responsible for making the business mainstream.

Key point	**Simple instruments**
	Tranched indices are relatively simple instruments, and are effectively standardized CDOs.

Within the context of synthetic CDOs, tranched indices are relatively simple instruments, and are a simplified standardized CDO. Yet, they deserve special attention given the size of the market and the importance of understanding their subtleties.

This chapter discusses the mechanics of standardized indices of CDS and goes on to elaborate on details of tranched risk in these indices. It is important to understand the nuances of these products before getting into in-depth discussion of correlation and sensitivity risk factors of tranched structures, which is covered in Chapters 6 and 7. The discussion in this chapter applies largely to corporate credit indices and their tranches. Some of the details for emerging market indices may be significantly different.

CREDIT DEFAULT SWAP INDICES

Credit default swap indices are simply portfolios of single-name default swaps, serving both as trading vehicles and as barometers of the market activity. While intuitively very simple, the indices are responsible for the increased liquidity and popularity of tranching of credit risk. Table 5.1 lists the main credit indices.

In buying the protection of an index, an investor protects against default in the underlying portfolio. In return, the buyer makes quarterly payments to the protection seller.

Credit indices: names, regions and number of credits

Table 5.1

Index	Region and type	Number of credits
DJ CDX NA IG	North American investment grade	125 names
DJ CDX NA HVOL	North American investment grade high volume	30 names
DJ CDX NA HY	North American high yield	100 names
DJ CDX NA HY BB	North American high yield	All names rated BB in HY CDX
DJ CDX NA HY B	North American high yield	All names rated B in HY CDX
DJ CDX NA XO	North American crossover	35 names
DJ CDX EM	Emerging markets	14 names
iTraxx Europe	Europe	125 names
iTraxx Europe HiVol	Europe high volume	30 names
iTraxx Europe Crossover	Europe crossover	40 names
iTraxx CJ Japan	Asia Japan	50 names
iTraxx Asia ex-Japan	Asia ex-Japan	50 names

If there is a default, the protection seller pays par in exchange of the reference obligation to the protection seller. Figure 5.1 shows the cashflows in an index.

DJ CDX Investment Grade Index

Figure 5.1

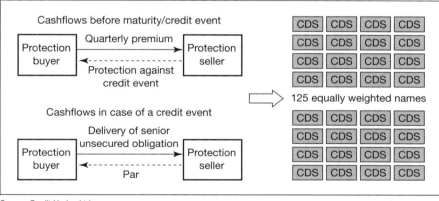

Source: Credit Hedge Ltd

Several investment-grade and high-yield indices trade in the US, covering many maturities, sub-sectors, credit quality, etc. In addition there are similar indices in Europe, pan Asia, and the emerging markets. Pricing levels, descriptions and calculators for these indices are available on a number of bank-sponsored Bloomberg pages (for example MSCD <GO>).

Standardized payment and maturity dates

Deal spread

The indices have a predetermined 'deal spread', which is paid each quarter.

Consequently, if the index is trading away from the deal spread, an upfront payment is required to reflect the difference between the current market spread level and deal spread. Conceptually, it is equal to the present value of the difference between the two, adjusted for default probabilities.

Note also that all the underlying single-name contracts have the same deal spread as the index. Just as a portfolio of bonds with different coupons has better convexity than a corresponding portfolio with the same coupon for each of the bonds (assuming both portfolios have the same average coupon and maturity), the convexity characteristics of the index are different from that of an equal-weighted portfolio of the underlying single-name default swaps.

Payment of accrued premiums

If an investor enters an index transaction between payment dates, the protection seller would make a payment of accrued premium to the protection buyer, to reflect the fact that the protection buyer would pay premium for the full quarter on the next payment date but the protection is in effect only for part of the quarter.

Restructuring definition

The market standards regarding restructuring definitions for indices and underlying credit default swaps are not always the same.

For example, while most of the underlying single credit names for the DJ CDX NA IG index trade with a modified restructuring (Mod-R) definition, the index itself trades on a No-R basis. European indices, however, trade with the same restructuring definition as the underlying, modified-modified restructuring (Mod Mod R). See Chapter 4 for a fuller description of these definitions.

Background to credit default swap indices

A credit derivative index is a basket of single-name credit default swaps with standardized terms. Unlike other multi-name credit default swaps, such as first-to-default baskets, index swaps provide unleveraged exposure to the names in the basket.

The indices act as a global set of benchmarks, allowing investors to buy and sell a cross-section of the credit market much more efficiently than they could if they were buying and selling individual credits. There are credit default swap indices in Europe, North America, Japan, Australia, non-Japan Asia and emerging markets. Unlike in most equity and cash bond indices, constituents are not selected on the basis of their market size, but by specific rules set out for each index. For the main indices, constituents are chosen by liquidity, for example. They are also (for most indices) equally weighted.

Launching new indices

A credit derivative index is launched every six months, usually in March and September, to reflect the names in the credit derivative market that fit the rules for each index at that time. On these 'roll' dates, a new basket of credits is created, with constituents selected by an independent index administrator based on input from dealers. Usually, only a handful of names change from one series to the next.

The current series of the index is known as the 'on-the-run' index and is usually much more liquid than the off-the-run versions. However, some off-the-run indices continue to trade actively after they have ceased to be the current version.

Standardized index trades

Index trades are intended to be highly standardized to ensure liquidity. Not only do all counterparties trade the same list of names for each six-month period, they also trade using a fixed spread for the life of the series. If, as is usually the case, the market spread is different from the coupon, the counterparties exchange money upfront to account for this difference.

Index maturities

Maturities are also standardized, with three-, five-, seven- and ten-year maturities traded for the biggest indices. However, few index trades are held to maturity. To ensure that their positions are as liquid as possible, most counterparties 'roll' into the new version of the index every six months.

Examples

For example, a firm that bought protection on series five of the CDX NA IG index in January 2007, and wanted to keep a position in the on-the-run index, would have unwound this trade at the 20 March 2007 roll date and put on a new trade referencing series six of the index.

Indices are among the most actively traded credit derivatives because they provide a way to buy or sell diversified credit risk quickly and with low dealing costs. The main indices trade with bid–offer spreads of one-half of a basis point. See the prices at the end of this chapter.

Indices and their trading dynamics

These patterns of trading give credit indices their own trading dynamics. Although there is little fundamental reason why the spread of the index should not be the same as the average spread of its constituents (its 'theoretical value'), in practice indices often trade wider or tighter than their theoretical value.

Theoretical price versus market price

When the market price of the index is higher than its theoretical value, it is said to trade with a positive basis to theoretical. When the index price is lower than the average of the single names, the basis is said to be negative.

Single name versus indices basis

One reason for the existence of a basis is that indices, because of their ease of execution, tend to react more quickly to changes in market sentiment than single names. And while the basis should present an opportunity for traders to put on arbitrage trades to narrow the gap, the execution cost of trading single names against the index makes this an expensive and difficult strategy (although it is one that some participants implement).

In fact, the index basis acts as a barometer for credit markets. A positive basis typically occurs when most participants want to buy protection on the market as a macro hedge, reflecting a bearish sentiment. (One of the times that the index had its largest positive basis was around the time that Italian food group Parmalat defaulted in December 2003, reflecting nervous market sentiment.)

A negative basis typically occurs when most participants want to go long the market, pushing index spreads below their theoretical value due to high demand for credit risk, reflecting a bullish sentiment.

Early indices

Although the first tradable credit derivative index was JPMorgan's Hydi, which referenced high-yield names, most credit index trading to date has been in the investment grade indices, especially North America's CDX NA IG and iTraxx Europe.

New indices

The low spreads and low volatility of investment-grade credit since 2003 have encouraged the creation of a number of indices (typically subsets of the main index) which consist of riskier investment-grade names and those whose spreads have a tendency to move around more than the market as a whole. In both North America and Europe, HiVol inidices (comprising high-volatility credits) and Xover (pronounced 'crossover') indices (including some high-yield names) are now actively traded.

DETERMINING THE UPFRONT PAYMENT

As mentioned earlier, if an index is trading away from the deal spread, an upfront payment is required to reflect the difference between the current market spread level and the deal spread. Theoretically, the present value of the two-premium stream should match when the default probabilities and timing of cashflows are taken into consideration.

The first step for calculating the upfront premium is to estimate default probabilities from the credit curve. Using these probabilities, the present value of the current spread is calculated, by multiplying the spread with the probability of survival at the time of payment and then discounting back using risk-free zero rates. Now, the present value should equal the present value of upfront and running premiums (the deal spread), based on the same default probabilities. So if the deal spread is higher than the current par spread, the protection seller makes a payment to the protection buyer.

A convenient way to do this conversion is to use the CDSW function on Bloomberg. Simply input the 'deal spread' and value the contract using the current par spread. The 'market value' represents the equivalent upfront payment. In addition to the upfront calculations, this function can be used to calculate mark-to-market, DV01 and cashflows. The DV01 is especially helpful in delta hedging of portfolio credit exposures using indices.

IMPACT OF DEFAULTS ON INDEX CASHFLOWS

When an underlying name defaults, it is separated from the index and settled separately. For example, in the CJ CDX NA IG index, which has 125 names, if one of the underlying names defaults, the remaining index would have 124 names and the same deal spread. The 1/125th of the notional would be separated and the protection seller would pay par to the protection buyer in exchange for a deliverable obligation (Figure 5.2).

After a default, the premium payments for the index would be (124/125) times the deal spread, irrespective of which of the 125 names defaulted (this methodology applies to CDX series 3, and may not hold for previous indices).

This is due to the same deal spread for all underlying names in the index portfolio, as mentioned earlier. It is important to note that an equal-weighted portfolio of underlying names could now have a different spread; given that each of the underlying names has its own spread level and depending on which of the 125 names defaults, the average spread for the remaining 124 names could be different from 124/125 of the original spread.

Figure 5.2

Impact of default on index

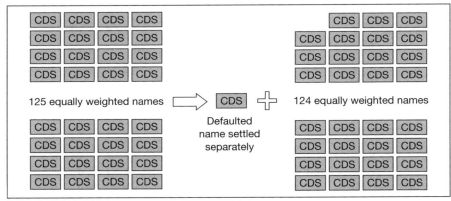

Source: Credit Hedge Ltd

TRANCHES OF STANDARD DEFAULT SWAP INDICES

Co-existence of synthetic CDOs and liquid benchmarks indices resulted in the logical next step of applying the tranching techniques to the indices, which led to standardized synthetic CDOs. This section discusses the basic structure of these instruments, followed by a more detailed analysis of their characteristics.

The basic mechanics

Borrowing the CDO technology, the credit risk of an index can be tranched into a number of slices, each with a different level of subordination. The most junior tranche covers initial defaults, and once losses exceed the notional of the tranches, they are passed on to the next senior tranche in the capital structure.

For example, the most liquid standardized CDX index tranches are:

0–3 per cent;

3–7 per cent;

7–10 per cent;

10–15 per cent;

15–30 per cent.

See Figure 5.3.

The first tranche, also referred to as the 'equity' tranche, takes the first 3 per cent of the losses of the portfolio. When the portfolio has accumulated large enough losses to exceed 3 per cent of the notional, the next tranche,

3–7 per cent, will incur losses from any potential further defaults, and so on. The standardized tranches for the high-yield index, CDX NA HY, are:

0–10 per cent;

10–15 per cent;

15–25 per cent;

25–35 per cent;

35–100 per cent.

Tranched CDX IG

Figure 5.3

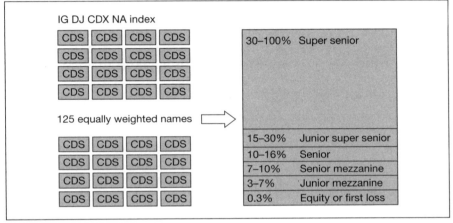

Source: Credit Hedge Ltd

How are the standardized tranches determined?

The attachment and detachment points of standardized tranches are partly driven by the synthetic CDO market and expected ratings of tranches.

It is important to note above that the IG equity tranche takes 3 per cent of overall portfolio losses, not defaults. Assuming a 40 per cent recovery, 5 per cent of the portfolio would have to default to wipe out the entire equity tranche.

CHARACTERISTICS OF BENCHMARK TRANCHES

Attachment and detachment points

The attachment point determines the subordination of a tranche. For example, a 3–7 per cent tranche's attachment point of 3 per cent implies that the tranche will incur losses only after the first 3 per cent of the notional has been lost due to defaults over the term of the index. The detachment point determines the point beyond which the tranche has lost its complete notional. In other words, the 3–7 per cent tranche is completely wiped out if the portfolio losses exceed 7 per cent of the index. The difference between the attachment and detachment points is referred to as the 'thickness' of the tranche.

Market quoting convention

Tranches that are expected to incur significant default losses, i.e. the equity tranche and some other junior tranches, are typically quoted with a sizeable upfront payment and some running premium, while more senior tranches are typically quoted on a running premium basis.

For investment grade (CDX IG), the equity tranche is currently priced on an upfront plus 500bp running, while other tranches are priced on a running premium basis. (In early 2008, it was 47.7 per cent; it varied between 30 per cent and 61 per cent upfront over two weeks in July/August 2007, due to an increase in credit volatility around US subprime debt and the housing market. See Table 5.2 at the end of this chapter for some example prices.) However, in case of high yield (CDX NA HY) the first two tranches were priced in early 2008 on an upfront basis with 0bp running, while the more senior tranches were priced only on a running premium basis.

Typically, when a tranche is expected to face material losses, an upfront payment helps reduce the volatility of returns and sensitivity of the tranche to spread changes. The reason being that in case of high defaults the running premium would drop significantly along with the outstanding notional, implying lower expected premiums. Conversely, the protection seller collects higher premiums in a low default case. For more detail on this, see Chapter 9.

Tranche 'delta'

The delta of a tranche reflects its sensitivity to changes in spreads of the underlying index portfolio. It is typically measured as a ratio of PV01 of the tranche to PV01 of the index.

Key point | **PV01**
PV01 is the change in the marker-to-market for a single basis point move in each of the underlying credits in the portfolio.

Typically, dealer quotes assume that the counterparty will enter into a delta-neutral amount (i.e., delta times tranche notional) of the index simultaneously with a tranche transaction.

Broadly speaking, junior tranches have higher deltas than senior tranches, if both are quoted on a running premium basis. However, the presence of upfront payments for junior tranches (equity tranche for investment grade CDX and the first two tranches for higher yield CDX) lowers tranche delta. See Chapter 10 for more on this topic.

Rolling over indices

As time passes, the maturity term of tranches and the underlying index decreases, making them significantly shorter than the benchmark terms. So, tranches on the new on-the-run indices are introduced, as the indices roll over.

Standardized maturity dates

Just like the underlying indices, the cashflow dates of index tranches are also standardized – the 20th of March, June, September and December every year.

Payment of accrued premiums

If an investor enters an index tranche transaction in between the payment dates, the protection seller would make a payment of accrued premium to the protection buyer, to reflect the fact that the protection buyer would pay premium for the full quarter on the next payment date but the protection is in effect only for part of the quarter.

Restructuring definitions

The restructuring definition of market standards for index tranches matches the underlying index convention (no-restructuring for US indices).

Hybrid settlement in case of default

When one of the names of the index defaults, the loss is transferred to the relevant tranche (say, the equity tranche assuming that this is the first default in the portfolio). Determining the realized recovery on the defaulted name is very important, as it not only affects the cashflows of affected tranches but also determines the erosion of subordination for other tranches.

To determine the recovery rates more accurately, the market has adopted a 'hybrid settlement' for index tranches. The goal of hybrid settlement is to balance the protection seller's desire for a high valuation with the protection buyer's interest in keeping recoveries low. Hybrid settlement has two stages: partial physical settlement followed by a cash settlement valuation. The first phase consists of obligations being delivered up to the amount of the defaulted name's delta in each tranche. The second phase involves an auction process, which determines the amount by which each tranche is written down.

INVESTMENT STRATEGIES WITH CREDIT DERIVATIVE INDICES

Credit derivative indices: a simple application

Credit derivative indices are used for many purposes. One of the most common applications is to provide a macro hedge. Buying protection on the credit derivative index allows users to hedge themselves against a general downturn in the credit market. Sometimes, they express a positive view on a particular credit, sector or tranche, but buy protection on the index as an overall hedge.

Another important use for the index is for asset managers and CDO managers that need to put allocated funds to work quickly, before they have had a chance to select or find specific assets that they believe will outperform the market.

Because of their low execution costs, credit indices are also the product of choice for hedge funds, which often want to place short-term bets on the direction of the market. As a result, indices are often used in momentum trades, where traders believe they can ride the general direction of the market for a short period.

Hedge funds and other relative value traders also use index swaps in curve-steepening and curve-flattening trades. Some hedge funds and proprietary trading desks also trade the index versus all its component single-name credit default swaps to arbitrage the basis to theoretical.

Trading example: premium payments

Let us suppose that on 1 December 2007, a market maker quotes 98 basis points for selling protection on the five-year DJ CDX IG (series 9) index. An investor buys protection on $125m notional of the index.

The running spread on the index is 90bp. Therefore the investor will be making 21 quarterly premium payments of $281,250 (one quarter of 90bp of $125 million; note that the CDX/iTraxx indices follow an Actual/360 convention) starting on 20 December 2007, with the last payment on 20 December 2012.

In addition to quarterly payments, the investor will make an upfront payment to account for two factors:

- The contract is settled on 98bp and the investor is paying only 90bp running; therefore, the investor must make an upfront payment equivalent to the 8bp running premium.

- The investor will be making a whole quarterly payment on 20 December 2007, but will enjoy the protection provided by the product for only 20 days of the quarter; thus, the accrual amount needs to be deducted from the upfront payment. Following the ACT/360 day count convention, the investor deducts $221,874 for the period 21 September 2007 to 1 December 2007.

The net upfront payment is calculated as $217,776 (calculation is based on a flat credit curve and a 40 per cent recovery).

Trading example: credit event

Suppose an investor bought protection on $125m notional of five-year DJ CDX IG Index on 1 December 2007, and one of the names in the index defaults on 15 January 2008. Since the investor bought protection on $125m notional on the index, it includes $1m notional on the defaulted name.

Assuming a physical settlement, the investor will get $1m from the seller of protection and deliver $1m face value of deliverable reference obligation for the defaulted credit. The index contract will be reduced to $124m and the defaulted credit will be removed from the reference portfolio. Since the next premium payment (on 20 March 2008) will be only $27,800 (a quarter of 90bp, assuming the offer side is 90bp, of $124m), the investor will have to make an accrual premium payment of $625 to cover the protection on $1m of the defaulted credit for the period from 21 December 2005 to January 2006.

As CDX/iTraxx indexes gained popularity, they began to be used in various ways. Because of their liquidity and transparency, they react quickly to new market information, especially during sell-offs. But more important, they are an efficient tool to gain access quickly to specific credit asset classes and sectors. Although many single-name CDSs are liquid, it is more efficient to use the indexes when trying to gain or reduce exposure to the market quickly. This property is important for investors trying to rebalance, diversify, or hedge their portfolios, particularly during volatile periods.

Applications include the following:

- A quick way to take long or short market positions. Investors can use credit derivative indexes to express credit macro views.

- Portfolio diversification and rebalancing. Indices allow investors to access asset classes that are harder to obtain in cash or single-name form. The property is especially important for portfolio managers who want to diversify or rebalance their portfolios.

■ Asset ramp-up. Many of the structured finance collateralized debt obligations (CDOs) include synthetic buckets. Using credit derivatives indices, CDO managers can quickly fill a core position in those lines.

■ Hedging. Credit derivatives indices are an efficient toll to take short positions in the market and are commonly used to hedge market-wide spread risk inherent in credit portfolios. An index hedge can be fine-tuned using additional selected positions in single-name CDS.

■ Relative value trading. A rich family of CDX/iTraxx credit derivatives indexes (see prices for iTraxx and CDX in Table 5.1) provides relative value players with a variety of potential strategies. Liquidity in the indexes accommodates efficient execution of relative value trades. Examples of relative value trades are the following:

— Index versus index trades. The CDX /iTraxx family provides a variety of relative value trades.

— Index versus intrinsic trades. Although harder to execute, indices sometimes trade at a substantial spread compared with the intrinsic. Index versus intrinsics relative value trades are suitable for indices with a lower number of credits in the portfolio or for indices where the reference CDS are less liquid.

■ Trades around the index roll. Around the index roll date, technicals can play a significant part. Under normal conditions, investors are more likely to roll their short positions than long positions. Rolling the short positions allows staying in the on-the-run product and providing a more liquid hedge. These trends lead to potential relative value opportunities around the roll time.

■ Curve trades. Increased liquidity across the credit curve allows for various index curve trades.

Key point	**Accurate indices**

The subprime credit crunch has been reflected very accurately throughout by the CDX/iTraxx indices. The widening in credit spreads has been noticeable and a good barometer of the crisis. Table 5.2 shows such prices.

A snapshot of iTraxx and CDX index prices

Table 5.2

Europe investment grade (iTraxx 8) at 8 February 2008

5-year	Bid	Offer	Mid change
Full index	95.0	95.5	3.8
0–3%	34.3%	35.3%	–0.2%
3–6%	410.3	416.3	22.5
6–9%	258.3	263.3	11.3
9–12%	187.0	192.0	10.0
12–22%	82.5	86.5	–0.4

North America investment grade (CDX NA IG 9) at 8 February 2008

5-year	Bid	Offer	Mid change
Full index	129.8	130.9	6.5
0–3%	56.8%	57.5%	1.6%
3–7%	567.0	573.0	27.5
7–10%	310.5	315.5	28.0
10–15%	163.3	169.7	14.0
15–30%	83.0	86.0	12.5
30–100%	39.8	41.8	3.8

All 0–3% tranches are quoted as percentage upfront plus 500bp running premium

Tranche prices and base correlation (Europe) at 7 February 2008

Index	Bid (bp)	Offer (bp)	Correlation	Change
iTraxx 8 (5-year)				
Full index	91.2	91.7		
0–3%	34.5%	35.6%	42.05%	1.7
3–6%	388.8	393.0	53.79%	1.5
6–9%	246.5	252.5	59.16%	0.9
9–12%	176.5	182.5	64.29%	0.5
12–22%	82.9	87.0	76.37%	0.8
iTraxx 8 (7-year)				
Full index	–	–		
0–3%	40.7%	41.8%	41.44%	1.7
3–6%	470.9	476.8	51.47%	1.4
6–9%	298.8	306.0	57.26%	1.4
9–12%	220.2	226.8	59.90%	0.6
12–22%	94.7	99.6	76.25%	1.2
iTraxx 8 (10-year)				
Full index	–	–		
0–3%	45.7%	46.8%	41.80%	2.0
3–6%	577.9	588.6	49.21%	1.8
6–9%	350.3	358.1	54.05%	1.6
9–12%	240.3	247.0	58.44%	0.9
12–22%	107.8	113.7	74.07%	0.9

Tranche prices and base correlation (US) at 7 February 2008				
Index	Bid (bp)	Offer (bp)	Correlation	Change
CDX NA IG 9 (5-year)				
Full index	123.4	124.2		
0–3%	55.1%	56.0%	38.81%	2.3
3–7%	538.9	546.1	59.56%	2.7
7–10%	277.4	292.6	67.24%	2.7
10–15%	148.4	156.6	79.96%	1.6
15–30%	69.5	74.5	98.54%	1.1
CDX NA IG 9 (7-year)				
Full index	–	–		
0–3%	61.0%	61.4%	37.62%	1.4
3–7%	618.3	625.5	55.60%	1.9
7–10%	359.1	373.1	61.67%	1.5
10–15%	200.7	205.9	71.58%	2.3
15–30%	79.7	84.8	96.66%	3.1
CDX NA IG 9 (10-year)				
Full index	–	–		
0–3%	65.1%	65.5%	37.86%	2.1
3–7%	724.7	731.9	51.11%	2.5
7–10%	436.6	449.1	55.57%	2.4
10–15%	221.4	225.9	66.40%	1.8
15–30%	92.5	99.2	91.12%	1.7

INVESTORS

Credit derivatives and index-linked products used to be primarily in the domain of leveraged accounts, such as credit hedge funds and proprietary desks in investment banks. But real-money investors such as hedge funds have also started participating in credit derivatives markets and using CDX/iTraxx indices for a variety of reasons, especially as the index can be structured in the form of credit-linked notes.

Although credit derivatives indexes are gaining in popularity among real-money investors, mark-to-market accounting rules and regulations are one of the main roadblocks to wider acceptance. This is because a significant portion of credit positions held by banks and insurance companies are in hold-to-maturity books that are not market-to-market. But regulations governing credit derivatives, for the most part, do not allow them to be held in such books.

What is correlation?

Before addressing correlation, it is worth saying why correlation is of interest to credit investors. Portfolio structured credit products are generally based on portfolios of assets whose performance is interrelated. For example, default rates are economically cyclical and entire sectors can suffer from downturns, resulting in more defaults than expected. These baskets of correlated assets behave differently from identical baskets of independent assets. For example, retailers such as Tesco and Wal-Mart are correlated assests, but one is in the UK, the other in the US. Markets have long since recognized these differences and prices have reflected the different risks. Correlation[1] is the missing link between today's standard derivatives pricing models and the prices observed in credit markets, and vice versa.

WHAT DO WE MEAN BY CORRELATION?

In financial markets, correlation is best understood by describing the price changes (or returns) of two assets. Consider the classic Capital Asset Pricing Model (CAPM), which implicitly uses the idea of correlation between return of a given asset and the overall market in the definition of Beta.

$$\text{Beta} = \text{Cov}(R_i, R_m) / \sigma^2 (R_m)$$
$$= \rho(R_i, R_m) \times \sigma (R_i)/ \sigma(R_m)$$

Where R_i and R_m are the the return on asset i and the market, respectively Cov is covariance, ρ correlation, and σ is standard deviation.

This is the type of correlation many investors and asset allocators are most accustomed to, and it has long been discussed in the financial literature.

Another example of this same type of correlation is in the world of equity index options where we can examine the correlation between securities, rather than the correlation between a security and the market. Consider the market for options on the Dow Jones Industrial Average and all of the components. Traded option markets tell us that the weighted implied volatility for the portfolio was roughly 21 per cent on 23 March 2005 while the observed implied volatility for options on the actual index was about 11 per cent. The difference is explained by the correlation among the components.

Table 6.1 summarizes the implied index volatility as calculated under several correlation assumptions, as well as that observed from the options market. If the credits are 100 per cent correlated, there are no diversification benefits and the volatility of the portfolio is simply the weighted average of the components, which is 21.3 per cent. If the components are independent of one another, there are significant diversification benefits, with implied index volatility of 4.3 per cent. The reality is somewhere in between, and on this particular day, the correlation implied by market pricing was approximately 24.5 per cent.

Portfolio volatility affected by correlation Table 6.1

Correlation	Index volatility
0.0%	4.3%
50.0%	15.3%
100.0%	21.3%
24.5%(index option implied)	11.0%

Source: Credit Hedge Ltd, Bloomberg

To simplify the analysis above, one common correlation variable has been used for each pair of components and the number varied. In reality, the assumption of a single correlation between these assets is probably inadequate and the market pricing is likely to reflect the varying levels of correlation among the assets of the portfolio. While historical correlations among the returns of the index components are observable (because there are equity markets for all the components), these are backward-looking estimates, such as realized volatility.

CORRELATION IN STRUCTURED CREDIT MARKETS

Correlation in the structured credit markets has a very different meaning from that in most financial markets. (This section focuses on the correlation measure used in standard copula implementations rather than rating agency approaches. For a discussion on rating agency approaches, please see Chapters 8 and 9.)

First, the correlation quoted in structured credit markets[2] is generally implied from the market price of a tranche, under certain assumptions using a given model. Therefore it is usually an output, rather than an input, and it is generally forward-looking rather than historical.

This might not have been the case in the early days of the market or in some of today's bespoke structures, but standardization in both models and contracts has occurred almost organically, allowing market participants to quote correlations to communicate price, given all the other market variables. Interpreting an implied[3] correlation generated by one of today's standard 'copula' models requires market data or assumptions regarding all of the variables listed in the section on valuation in structured credit markets later in this chapter.

Default correlation not spread correlation

Second and probably the most important, the correlation actually being measured is not the correlation of the change in prices (or spreads) but rather it is more closely related to the correlation of the timing of default events within the portfolio.

In contrast to equity derivatives models, structured credit models generate values based on default probabilities derived from today's market prices of the underlying instruments rather than the expected value based on the future market prices of the underlying instruments. This is a fundamental difference in the way credit derivatives are valued as compared with derivatives based on other asset classes.

The current generation of structured credit models rely on the distribution of aggregate default losses for the portfolio to derive tranche price. Aggregate losses for the portfolio are generated by combining the likelihood of default for each credit with a measure of how correlated the default events are. The expected timing of default events for the individual credits is directly related to today's spreads for the portfolio components (but do not reflect the potential movements in spreads in the future).

Aggregate correlation – if you can call it that

Third, the quoted correlation is a single number that represents the relationship between all the pairs of names in a given portfolio. Correlation is generally a concept that measures the relationship between any two assets. In structured credit markets, the same number is used to represent the relationship between every pair in the portfolio (as in Table 6.1).

Key point

Tranche correlation

When we say the price of the tranche has an implied correlation of 30 per cent, we are essentially saying that the correlation for each distinct credit pair is implied by the market price to be 30 per cent. While the definition does not allow us to vary correlation for each pair, it does provide a measure of the aggregate correlation in the portfolio.

As with the equity index example of Table 6.1, there are likely to be levels of correlations for the various pairs of names, but deriving correlations for all pairs can be an exercise in futility. Unlike the example, the historical correlation for two given credits cannot be observed (if a name had a correlated default to observe, would it be in the portfolio?), so approximations of the pair-wise correlations add the risk of significant estimation errors. Spread correlations can be observed, assuming spread markets are liquid, but these are imperfect proxies for default correlations (which are discussed below). Additionally, the sheer number of estimates required makes the process an unmanageable exercise fairly quickly. Consider a typical 100 name portfolio, which would require 4,950 distinct correlation estimates.

100 x 100 = 10,000

Using only half of this matrix, because the other half is a reflection, gives 5,000 combination/correlations factors and removing 50 pair collations, that are for example duplicates, leaves 4,950 correlation factors.

For all but the most junior tranche, the aggregate correlation of a portfolio is a more important driver of pricing the correlation between any two credits. For the most subordinate tranche, the correlation between a single pair of credits can be an important driver as well, given their exposure to idiosyncratic risk.

For example, if the widest trading names in the basket announced a merger for which the financing plan indicates leverage (and by implication, higher levels of default risk) for the joint entity, this would be doubly bad for the most junior tranches, while having only a marginal effect on the most senior tranche because of the idiosyncratic nature of the risk. Default propensity increases only for the two names and not for the broader universe, and correlation jumps between only those two entities, but their correlation to the rest of the portfolio is likely to have dropped. Consider how muted the benefit would be to the same tranches if two of the most high-quality credits announced a credit-enhancing merger. Situations like this help, in part, to explain the difference in implied correlation for actively traded tranches of the same portfolio.

OBSERVING DEFAULT CORRELATION

Implied correlation in structured credit is similar to implied volatility in the equity options market. It provides a way to communicate price, given all the other inputs, which are generally observable.

Under this framework, observing implied correlation for different tranches is like observing different implied volatilities in options markets: it measures the supply and demand dynamics in the market and, if persistent, can point to weakness in the assumptions or the model that is being used.

There is one critical difference, however, between implied volatility and implied correlation. If we want to test implied volatility against realized volatility in markets, we can do so. We can observe the returns in markets during the periods and compare realized return volatility against the implied option prices. This type of comparison is not possible in structured credit markets, largely because defaults are generally low probability events and hence infrequent, particularly in investment-grade markets. What we really want to observe is the correlation between two events, each of which is itself fairly unlikely.

<table>
<tr><td>**Key point**</td><td>**Observable peril**

Users in today's market have turned to observable data to get a sense of default correlation by proxy for a variable that is difficult to observe. This can be an exercise fraught with peril.</td></tr>
</table>

To illustrate the point, consider two measures of correlation for the components of the Dow Jones Industrial Average from January 1995 to the end of March 2005. The first metric, 'price correlation', is the average correlation of the daily percentage returns for each pair of index components. This measure is consistent with the correlation that is most frequently encountered in the financial markets.

The second metric, on the other hand, is designed to be similar in concept to the time to default correlation used in today's structured credit models. It is defined as the average of the 'timing correlations' for the components, where 'timing correlation' is defined as the correlation of 'extreme return' days in a given month for each pair of index components. 'Extreme return' is a daily return greater than ±5 per cent. The idea for this metric is to capture the correlation of extreme daily moves only, assuming a month is a sufficient period to capture any lag among the components.

For the full period in question, it was found that the average return correlation for the DJIA was roughly 16 per cent, while the timing correlation was roughly 34 per cent, or more than double the price correlation. Similar (albeit flipped) results are found when spread markets are examined: the realized spread (price) correlation for the components of CDX IG 3 was 56 per cent for the year ending 29 March 2005 while the implied (timing) correlation in the 0–3 per cent tranche on that date was 19 per cent. The implication is that day-to-day equity prices are only slightly correlated, while extreme events are much more correlated. For credit spreads, the opposite is true: daily price changes are highly correlated, but default events are less so. The point here is that when talking about the correlation of extreme events such as default, care needs to be taken in extrapolating from correlations that capture both large and small changes in valuation, such as the correlations of the prices of equities, assets or spreads.

Hidden meaning of default correlation in credit markets

After such a discussion of exactly what 'correlation' is in the structured credit market, it is worthwhile highlighting what correlation does to the implied behaviour of structured credit portfolios. Below is a view on portfolio optimization space, in which the focus is on portfolio size and the influence of correlation on credit portfolio performance.

Figure 6.1 shows the volatility of expected losses of similar investment-grade portfolios with different numbers of independent credits. As the portfolio size increases from fifty names to 1,000 (think of 1,000 as the investable universe), the uncertainty of expected losses of the portfolio declines to some minimum level (0.4 per cent over five years for the largest portfolio).

If we then perform the same analysis for the same portfolio and superimpose 20 per cent default correlation on the portfolio, Figure 6.1 shows that the absolute level of uncertainty declines much less than in the independent case. This points to the first effect of correlation on the portfolio (this may sound obvious). Alternatively, the diversification effect of adding names to the portfolio is much less important for correlated names.

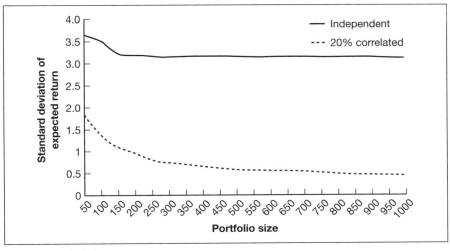

Correlation affects the relationship between volatility and portfolio size (expected losses = 3.0%)

Figure 6.1

Source: Credit Hedge Ltd

The real insight comes from examining these results against real experiences. The coefficients of variation (standard deviation divided by mean) of the simulation results are summarized in Table 6.2 alongside the same for Moody's five-year cumulative default statistics for 1970–1999. The most valid comparisons are the 1,000 name portfolios against the Moody's result, because the fifty-name portfolios have much more idiosyncratic risk. Most notable is that the volatility of expected losses for large portfolios is much greater for correlated portfolios and this is broadly consistent with actual default experiences observed from Moody's.

Table 6.2

Table 6.2   Volatility in the models and in the real world

	50 credits 0% correlation	1000 credits 0% correlation	50 credits 20% correlation	1000 credits 20% correlation	Moody's A	Moody's Baa	Moody's A & Baa
Coefficient of variance	0.6x	0.1x	1.1x	1.0x	1.5x	0.7x	0.9x

This is the hidden effect of correlation: to make aggregate default experiences inside the models more similar to what is actually experienced, given the cyclical (correlated) and volatile nature of credit risk.

VALUATION IN STRUCTURED CREDIT MARKETS

Valuation for the structured credit market has developed in several ways. The most recent introduction, in 2004, is in the synthetic space and has been largely based on a derivative pricing framework not dissimilar to that used to price single-name credit derivatives. As with single-name credit derivatives, pricing tranches or nth-to-default baskets is a function of the:

■ single-name par spread levels;
■ the spread at which the contract is struck;
■ the risk-free interest rate and the recovery assumption.

But we need also to add the following variables for tranches:

■ attachments;
■ detachment points (either in losses or in number of defaults);
■ the correlation of default events.

As with single-name models, spreads are converted into risk-neutral default probabilities, which is effectively the same as generating a loss distribution for the single-name credit. Think of single-name default probability as being represented by a simple Bernoulli probability distribution, where default for a given single name is distributed in the following way:

■ 1 is default probability p;
■ 0 if no default with probability $1-p$.

Therefore, losses are distributed as follows, using a fixed recovery assumption:

- (1 – recovery) × notional amount if defaulted with probability p;
- 0 if no default with probability $1 - p$.

The key to valuing tranches of a given portfolio is the ability to generate a distribution for the number of defaults in the entire portfolio over a given time. This, in turn, gives the ability to calculate the probability that losses in the portfolio exceed given thresholds (like the attachment and detachment points of tranches).

Once these probabilities of various levels of default for the portfolio are known, we can generate expected losses, cashflows and value tranches accordingly.

GETTING TO A PORTFOLIO LOSS DISTRIBUTION

To explore why copular models for structured credit products were developed, consider a simplified example. Assuming the default probability for each credit in a given portfolio (say, with 100 names) is the same and all the credits are independent of one another, generating the distribution of portfolio losses from the single-name default probabilities is a simple matter. From statistics theory, if the single-name loss distributions look like Bernoulli trials, then the sum of 100 Bernoulli variables with the same probability of default has a binomial distribution.

Then, add the complication that the probability of default varies by credit and the problem becomes more complex. There is no longer a clean, closed-form solution, but the problem can still be solved using simulation (or numerical approximations). The simulation process is straightforward. Simulate 100 independent random numbers, check whether the random number for each credit generates a default for that credit and add up the individual losses caused by each default to generate a loss for the entire portfolio. Then, repeat the process many times to generate a distribution for the portfolio losses like those graphically illustrated in Figure 6.2.

Figure 6.2 shows the aggregate loss distribution for a portfolio in which all the credits are independent and have the same default probability (5.5 per cent) and a portfolio in which all the credits are again independent and have different default probabilities (although with an average default probability of 5.5 per cent). Both were generated using a simulation with 10,000 trials. The portfolios underlying these assets are similar to investment-grade CDX index products in that the average spread is 66bp and, in the second case, the distribution of spreads is similar to the CDX portfolios. What should immediately jump out is the similarity of the distribution and also that distribution of losses in both cases is very concentrated, with more than half of the scenarios inside the 4–6 per cent range.

| Figure 6.2 | **Correlation creates portfolio loss distribution with fatter tails** |

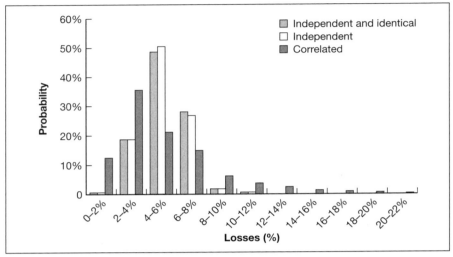

Source: Credit Hedge Ltd

The third set of data in Figure 6.2 reflects the idea that the individual credits are not independent but are positively correlated. There are a few things worth noting here. First, the resulting portfolio loss distribution is much less concentrated, with no single bucket accounting for more than 36 per cent of the simulations. Additionally, the distribution has a much fatter tail. To illustrate the point, consider the likelihood of aggregate portfolio losses exceeding 10 per cent, which is less that 0.1 per cent for both scenarios in which defaults are independent. This compares with roughly 8 per cent for the correlated scenario. The probabilities from the independent simulations would imply that the spread on tranches with attachment points above 10 per cent is nearly zero, so positive correlation is a way to explain the pricing observed in the marketplace. It is also consistent with the idea that credit risk is driven by cyclical changes in the underlying economy.

COPULA FUNCTIONS

To generate the results in Figure 6.2, a simulation-based approach was used, which reflected positive correlation among default events. To do this needs a way to generate correlation random numbers from which to generate the default scenarios. This is where copula functions come into play.

While copula functions can be derived from statistical distributions, the most common implementation (in structured credit markets) involves combining many normal distributions into a correlated multivariate normal distribution (also referred to as the multivariate Gaussian copula). These correlated normal variables are then mapped into default times based on the spreads (and implied default probabilities) for the underlying credits. These correlated single-name default times can be mapped into losses for a contract with a given maturity, which can, in turn, be aggregated into portfolio losses for the same maturity. In a simulation context, this process is repeated many times to generate the portfolio loss distribution in Figure 6.2.

Copula benefits **Key point**

Copula functions are mathematical functions that allow us, in a simulation context, to transform independent random numbers into correlated random numbers.

Why use the normal distribution? As with most other derivative models, the computation efficiency and theoretical attractiveness of the normal distribution were probably important drivers in selecting this as the basis for most structured credit pricing models. There are obviously options to this, with the Student-T copula function being the most notable.

CORRELATION AS A RELATIVE VALUE METRIC (BASE CORRELATION)

The language of implied correlation has evolved to provide a useful relative value metric in the form of the often-quoted base correlation. In the early days of correlation trading, the term used was 'implied correlation'. It referred to what we now call 'compound correlation', that is the correlation implied by the price of a tranche, given all other market inputs. The problem with compound correlation is that it fails to give meaningful results in some of the mezzanine parts of the capital structure. Table 6.3 summarizes the implied compound and base correlation for one of the first liquid-traded index products, Dow Jones TRAC-X Series 2. Note that the implied correlation for the 3–7 per cent tranche is different from the other deviations.

Implied correlation and base correlation **Table 6.3**

Index	Bid	Ask	Compound correlation	Base correlation
Index	68	69		
0–3%*	43%	47%	21%	21%
3–7%	395	435	3%	25%
7–10%	138	158	17%	28%
10–15%	56	66	21%	34%

* Point upfront plus 500 bp running
Source: Credit Hedge Ltd

Figure 6.3 shows the spreads implied by compound correlation levels with a range of 10–90 per cent. There are two solutions for the 3–7 per cent with a spread (mid) of 415bp. This complicates the use of compound correlation as a relative value measure. Additionally, the idea of using compound correlation as a relative value metric is even more complicated by the fact that rising correlation is good for some tranches and bad for others, as the differing slopes of the lines in Figure 6.3 illustrate.

Figure 6.3

Correlation sensitivity varies with seniority

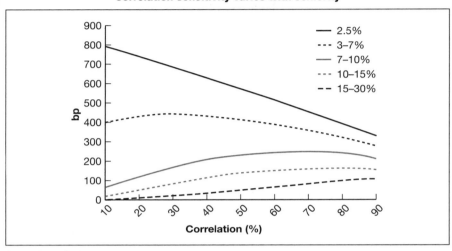

Source: Morgan Stanley

Base correlation, which uses the implied correlations from a series of first-loss tranches with detachment points equal to the detachment points of the actual tranches, does not suffer from either of the two issues above. It does not have tranches for which there are several solutions because all the correlations are implied from the first-loss tranches. An example of one implementation of a base correlation approach is shown in Table 6.4. Base correlation provides a good relative value benchmark because it is fairly

Table 6.4

Tranche equivalence – long/short combination for replicating portfolio

Benchmark tranche	First loss tranche	Tranche position	First loss implied correlation	First loss delta	Implied benchmark tranche delta
	0–3%	Short	21.2%	12.2x	
3–7%	0–7%	Long	27.5%	10.1x	8.5x
7–10%	0–7%	Short	27.5%	10.1x	
	0–10%	Long	31.6%	8.3x	3.9x
10–15%	0–10%	Short	31.6%	8.3x	1.9x

Source: Credit Hedge Ltd

uniform in its meaning (i.e. rising base correlation means tighter spreads on the tranche, all else being equal), and it provides a unique price for a given base correlation.

Additionally, base correlation provides price sensitivities that are more in line with what is observed in the marketplace when compared to compound correlation, which can imply unreasonable price-sensitivity values for very high or very low implied correlation values.

BASE CORRELATION

Base correlation is central to pricing for all bespoke tranche trades, which make up the bulk of any correlation trading book. The role of base correlations requires an explanation of single tranche pricing methodology.

Currently there are several highly liquid credit indices, the most significant being Itraxx Europe and CDX Investment Grade, each containing 125 predominantly European or US names. Standard tranches (on standard attachment and detachment points) on each index there are also liquidly traded.

Base correlation methodology is used to price tranches using inputs of the index constituent spreads and the *pair-wise default correlation within tranche* (known as *compound correlation*). This correlation parameter can only be determined by taking market prices for index tranches and backing out the correlation using the Gaussian copula model (this is similar to using Black–Scholes to get the implied volatility from option prices).

These correlations can then be used to build a base correlation curve for each index. A bespoke single tranche is a tranche on a portfolio of names that does not match Itraxx or CDX exactly and has non-standard attachment and detachment points. To price this, depending on the closeness of the names to CDX or Itraxx, correlations are taken from the index base correlation curve (interpolated between known points from market prices) along with the spreads in the portfolio and the Gaussian copula model is used.

Each index that has liquidly traded tranches has an associated base correlation curve. This moves with tranche, index and single-name prices. As the base correlation curve moves, any bespoke tranches that are priced from the curve will also be strongly affected.

Base correlation movements affect equity and mezzanine tranche prices in different ways. Increase in base correlation leads to a reduction of risk in the equity tranche and corresponding reduction in price.

For mezzanine and more senior tranches, this is reversed, with the risk and price increasing for lower correlation. The effect of correlation can be illustrated by taking extremes: for a perfectly correlated portfolio, the first default would wipe out all tranches. This would mean that senior tranches would have no credit enhancement over the equity tranche and risk would move out of the equity tranche and be redistributed equally across the tranches.

If there was zero correlation then each default in the portfolio would occur independently. Here, the risk is shifted towards the equity tranche and away from the more senior tranches.

PRACTICAL USE OF CORRELATION

Fixed-income professionals are focusing intently on 'correlation' as a factor that drives the value of their portfolios. Recent waves of bond defaults in certain sectors have prompted heightened attention on correlation. Correlation arguably has become most important in the areas of credit derivatives, such as collateralized debt obligations (CDOs) and baskets of credit default swaps (CDS). In those sectors, some market participants recently have long been trading correlation.

This section provides a more detailed look at the use of a simple 'copula' approach for modelling correlation of credit risk. It then illustrates how certain structured credit products can be priced using the copula technique.

Why we care about correlation

Correlation is important in the credit markets. It affects the likelihood of extreme outcomes in a credit portfolio. Therefore, it plays a central role in pricing structured credit products, such as tranches of CDOs, traded CDS indices and first-to-default baskets. Intuitively, when correlation among credits in a portfolio is high, credits are likely to default together (but survive together, too). In other words, defaults in the portfolio would cluster.

Correlation between two variables generally is expressed by a 'correlation coefficient', sometimes denoted by the Greek letter rho (ρ). A correlation coefficient ranges between −1 and +1. When a correlation coefficient is +1, it reflects 'perfect positive correlation' and the two variables always move in the same direction. On the other hand, if the correlation coefficient is −1, the variables always move in opposite directions – 'perfect negative correlation'.

Diversification presumes that movements in the values of individual assets offset each other. More formally, a diversification strategy relies on the assumption that movements in asset values are not perfectly correlated. In fact, diversification can achieve the greatest reduction in risk when assets

Key point | **Correlation and diversification**

Correlation is closely related to the idea of diversification. 'Diversification' describes a strategy of reducing risk in a portfolio by combining many different assets together.

display negative correlation. For example, suppose a portfolio consists of two assets of equal value. If returns on the two assets are perfectly negatively correlated, a decline in the value of one asset would be exactly offset by an increase in the value of the other.

In the real world, there is usually some degree of positive correlation among the credit risk of individual assets in a portfolio. The actual degree of correlation strongly influences the distribution of outcomes that the portfolio may experience. Slicing the portfolio into several 'tranches' of credit priority magnifies the importance of correlation because the degree of correlation affects the value of different tranches differently.

Consider the most junior and most senior tranches of a CDO. All else being equal, if the credit risk among the underlying assets is strongly correlated, there is a higher likelihood of either very few or very many of the assets defaulting. Conversely, if correlation is weak, the likelihood of extreme outcomes is low, and the likelihood of an intermediate number of defaults is higher. Consider a hypothetical portfolio of ten assets of equal size, where each asset has a 20 per cent probability of default. If the risk among the assets is uncorrelated (*i.e.*, $\rho=0$), the most likely outcome would be two defaults, and the chance of more than five assets defaulting would be extremely small. However, if the risk among the assets is correlated to a significant degree, the odds of either no defaults or more than five defaults increase substantially. Figure 6.4 illustrates this with the results of a simulation.

Frequency of portfolio default and tranche losses (simulation results)*   **Figure 6.4**

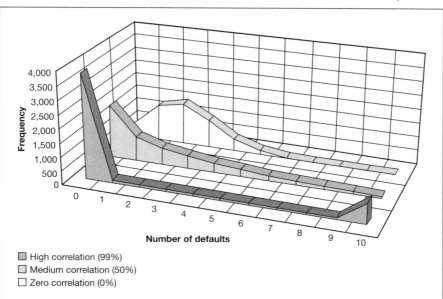

High correlation (99%)
Medium correlation (50%)
Zero correlation (0%)

* Based on simulations with 5,000 iterations assuming a 20% probability of default

Figure 6.4 shows the frequencies of defaults in three hypothetical portfolios of ten assets with zero ($\rho=0$ per cent), medium ($\rho=50$ per cent), and high ($\rho=99$ per cent) levels of correlation, based on the results of a Monte Carlo simulation.

The simulation results show that the distribution of defaults can vary greatly depending on the level of correlation. In the graph, the default frequency for the zero-correlation case looks somewhat like a bell-shaped curve. In contrast, the medium- and high-correlation cases exhibit downward sloping and U-shaped curves, respectively.

The high-correlation portfolio has the highest frequency for zero defaults, while the low-correlation portfolio usually has a modest number of defaults. Also notable are the differences in the frequencies of large numbers of defaults. The right end of the graph shows that the high-correlation portfolio has a much higher frequency of all assets defaulting compared with the zero- and medium-correlation portfolios.

Returning to the hypothetical CDO backed by ten assets, assume that the equity tranche (i.e., the most subordinated tranche) represents 10 per cent of the deal. Assume also that each asset pays nothing if it defaults. Thus, the equity tranche would be wiped out if any of the ten assets defaulted. On the other hand, if none of the assets defaulted, the equity tranche would receive its cashflow. Given such a structure, the value of the equity tranche would be highest in the case of the high-correlation portfolio. The reason is that the high-correlation portfolio has the greatest likelihood of experiencing zero defaults. Moreover, after one default, it makes no difference to the equity tranche whether there are additional defaults because the first default wipes out the tranche.

Now consider the CDO's senior tranche. Suppose that the senior tranche accounts for 60 per cent of the deal and, therefore, does not incur losses until there are more than four defaults. The situation for the senior tranche is exactly opposite to that of the equity tranche.

When the portfolio's correlation is zero, there is only a slight possibility that many defaults occur and cause losses for the senior tranche. On the other hand, a high correlation means an increased possibility of a large number of defaults, where all junior tranches are exhausted and losses reach the senior tranche. Accordingly, an increase in correlation decreases the value of the senior tranche. Hence, correlation affects equity and senior tranches in opposite directions.

In the past, correlation in structured credit products, such as CDO tranches or first-to-default baskets, was analysed and priced mostly at individual banks and dealers. The introduction of tranche trading on the CDX US indices and iTraxx Europe changed that. Tranche trading in the indices put correlation in the spotlight and drove development of common valuation methods.

ANALYSING A PORTFOLIO OF CREDIT RISK

Market participants usually use Monte Carlo simulations to analyse the effect of correlation in portfolios of credit risk. When one needs to take correlation into account (i.e. variables are not independent), Monte Carlo simulations allow greater flexibility than non-simulation techniques.

This section describes the use of 'default time' as a tool for modelling the credit risk on individual credits and then illustrates the use of a copula approach for analysing correlated risk on a portfolio of credits through a simulation. After simulating correlated defaults, we can value an individual tranche of a portfolio tranche and a 'first-to-default' basket of credit risk. Discussion of more advanced versions of copula models is beyond the scope of this book.

MODELLING CORRELATED DEFAULTS

Modelling default time of individual credits

One popular way to model correlated default risks is to focus on correlation between 'default times' (i.e. when assets or companies default). An asset's 'default curve' plots the asset's default probability over time.

A default curve permits calculation of the likelihood that the asset will survive (i.e. not default) for a specified period. For example, if an asset has a constant default probability of 5 per cent a year, it means that the likelihood that the asset will survive for one year is 95 per cent. The survival probability goes down over a longer time horizon: over five years, the asset's survival probability is 77.38 per cent (=0.95^5).

Accordingly, the asset's default probability over five years is 22.62 per cent (100 per cent − 77.38 per cent). Within the context of a simulation, the process is reversed. The goal is to determine whether the asset defaults over a certain time, starting with the survival probability and arriving at an asset's default time. To generate a simulated default time, a uniform random variable is used with the range 0 to 1 and the asset's survival curve. The random variable is treated as the survival probability and the corresponding default time is found on the asset's survival curve. For example, a simulated random value of 0.5 means that the survival probability to a specific time point is 50 per cent.

The simulated default time is found using the equation:

95 per cent$^\tau = u$

Where:
95 per cent = the annual survival probability
τ = the default time, expressed in years
u = simulated uniform random variable

Replacing *ui* with 0.5 gives τ = 13.513 years. In general, when there are many assets, 'default correlation' refers to the tendency of assets to default together over a particular time. Credit risk simulations often capture correlation by linking the default times of different assets (Figure 6.5).

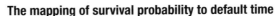

| Figure 6.5 | **The mapping of survival probability to default time** |

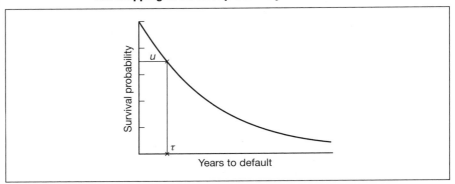

What is a copula?

The most commonly used method for modelling and simulating correlated default risk is the 'copula approach'. The word 'copula' comes from the Latin word for 'connecting' or 'linking'. In technical terms, a copula function is a multivariate, or joint, distribution that links a set of univariate, or marginal, distributions. While the marginal distributions describe the default risk of each individual asset, the copula describes relations among individual default risks through a multivariate distribution. So, the copula can separately specify the characteristics of individual default risks and the relationship among them. Although it is possible to use a multivariate distribution to directly model individual default risks together, it is usually much easier to use the copula approach when more than two variables need to be modelled.

A popular model for simulating correlated credit risks is the 'one-factor Gaussian copula'.

The term 'one factor' refers to using one extra variable to which the performance of each individual asset is linked. The extra variable can be viewed as expressing the condition of the overall economy.

The term 'Gaussian' refers to the underlying assumption that the correlations among the underlying assets can be expressed with 'normal' distributions, even if the individual credit risks themselves are not normally distributed.

Another key assumption is that correlation among the underlying assets remains stable over time. For now, it remains unclear whether this assumption fairly reflects reality. However, dropping the assumption arguably complicates the modelling process without necessarily improving predictive power.

SIMULATING CORRELATED DEFAULTS WITH A COPULA

A Monte Carlo simulation using a copula model involves a few simple steps. Suppose that we have credit exposure to a portfolio of three assets. To use a one-factor Gaussian copula to simulate the portfolio, we would need the following ingredients:

- For each of the three assets, an assumption about its risk of default over time (i.e. the asset's default curve and its corresponding survival curve).

- For each of the three assets, an assumption about the level of recovery that would be associated with a default.

- An assumption about the correlation between the credit risk of each asset and the overall economy. Intuitively, correlation describes the degree to which different assets default around the same time. In the simplest case, we would assume a uniform correlation structure, where all the assets have the same correlation of credit risk to the overall economy. In that case, we have one ρ for all calculations.

The term 'univariate' refers to a distribution that involves just one variable. Multivariate refers to a distribution that involves two or more variables. A multivariate, or joint, distribution describes the behaviour of two or more variables. We can visualize the multivariate distribution of two variables with a three-dimensional graph. For example, Figure 6.6 shows a hypothetical joint distribution of height and weight for a group of people.

Hypothetical joint distribution of height and weight   Figure 6.6

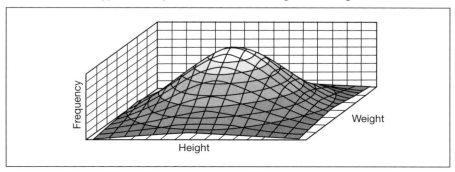

Each iteration of the copula-based simulation involves four steps:

- To generate a normally distributed random variable for each of the three assets, plus a fourth one for the overall economy. Let the random variable for the three assets be $\varepsilon 1$, $\varepsilon 2$, and $\varepsilon 3$, respectively. Let the random variable for the overall economy be y.

■ The second step is to use the εi variables, together with the correlation coefficient, to produce a group of three *correlated* normally distributed random variables: $x1$, $x2$, and $x3$. Assuming a uniform and stable correlation structure, we can use the following formula to produce the xi variables:

$$xi = \rho y + 1 - \rho \varepsilon i$$

■ Next, produce corresponding set of variables in the range of 0 to 1. Each of the xi variables is normally distributed and we can use the cumulative distribution function of the standard normal distribution to convert it into a corresponding value in the 0–1 range. We denote those values as $u1$, $u2$, and $u3$.

The use of the normal distribution in this step is why the process is called a 'Gaussian copula'. (The right-hand graph in Figure 6.7 illustrates this step.)

■ The final step of the process is to convert the ui values into default times for each of the assets. The easiest way to do this is to use the survival curves. The survival curves allow us to map each ui variable to a corresponding default time (τi). The default time for a particular asset tells whether (and when) the asset defaulted in that iteration of the simulation. (The left-hand graphic in Figure 6.7 illustrates how to map each ui to the corresponding τi.)

| Figure 6.7 | The mapping of simulated correlated random variables to default time |

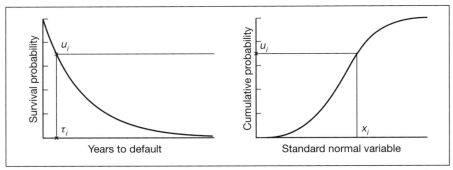

Valuing tranched transactions

Once we have simulation results, how do we value a tranche trade?

A Monte Carlo simulation generates a large number of randomly generated scenarios of correlated defaults. Based on the simulation results, we can calculate expected losses and, hence, breakeven spreads of tranches.

Let's consider a portfolio of CDS consisting of five reference entities. We assume that each reference entity has a notional amount of $100, an annual default probability of 5 per cent, and a fixed recovery rate of 45 per cent. Assume 1 per cent a year for the discount rate. Also assume that the time horizon is five years. A simulation path might look like that in Table 6.5.

Sample simulated path of default times Table 6.5

	Default time	Default before maturity (5 years)
Credit 1	2.5 years	Yes
Credit 2	4.5 years	Yes
Credit 3	8.0 years	No
Credit 4	10.0 years	No
Credit 5	11.0 years	No

In this simulation path, default times of two reference entities are less than five years, indicating that the two defaults occurred during the term of the portfolio. Given the recovery rate of 45 per cent, the loss amount is $55 for each of the two defaulting credits. The next section illustrates how to value two simple structured credit products: loss tranches and nth-to-default baskets.

Valuing a loss tranche

Percentage loss tranches are constructed so that one tranche absorbs losses until the total loss reaches the size of the tranche. After the first-loss tranche is exhausted, the next junior tranche starts to absorb losses until it is exhausted. In other words, a loss tranche has an 'attachment point' and a 'detachment point', characterizing the seniority and size of the tranche. For example, a tranche with an attachment point of 0 per cent and a detachment point of 20 per cent bears exposure to the first $100 of losses in a portfolio of $500.

For example, Table 6.6 shows the same simulated path discussed above. In the column for the 0–20 per cent tranche, the tranche suffers a loss in the third year (2.5 years) of $55, as the first default occurs. Furthermore, the same tranche suffers another $45 in the fifth year (4.5 years) as the second default occurs in the portfolio. The tranche size is $100, so the second default wipes out the 0–20 per cent tranche ($55+$45=$100) and losses reach the next tranche (the 20–40 per cent tranche). Accordingly, this particular path results in a $100 loss (with a present value of $96.66) to the 0–20 per cent tranche and a $10 loss (PV of $9.56) to the 20–40 per cent tranche.

Table 6.6

Losses to % tranches – the sample path

Year/Tranche	0%–20%	20%–40%	40%–60%	60%–80%	80%–100%
1	0	0	0	0	0
2	0	0	0	0	0
3	$55	0	0	0	0
4		0	0	0	0
5	$45	10	0	0	0
Total loss	$100	10	0	0	0
Loss PV	$96.662	$9.560	0	0	0

Once tranche losses for one path are calculated, we can calculate the breakeven spread based on the present value of the tranche losses so that the present values of losses equal the present value of premium paid by the protection buyer. Table 6.7 shows actual simulation results with 10,000 iterations and correlation of 0.5. In Table 6.7, the average present value of tranche losses is $41.88 and the breakeven spread is 1,129 bp.

Table 6.7

Combined simuation results for the 0–20% tranche

Simulation path	Portfolio defaults	PV of tranche loss	Breakeven spread
1	0	0	
2	0	0	
3	1	$53,642	
⋮	⋮	⋮	
10,000		0	
Average	1.112	$41.876	1129 bp

Calculating a breakeven spread

To calculate a breakeven spread, we need to get the tranche loss and the average notional amount for the tranche. We calculate the average notional amount to take into account that the tranche's notional amount is reduced when defaults occur.

For example, if just one default occurs at 2.5 years for the 0–20 per cent tranche in the above example, the tranche's notional is reduced by $55 to $45. After that point, the protection buyer pays an annual premium to the seller based on the reduced notional amount of $45, not $100. In this particular case, the notional amount is $100 for year 1; $100 for year 2; $72.5 for year 3; $45 for year 4; and $45 for year 5. (Note that the third year starts with a notional amount of $100 but ends with $45.)

Hence, the present value of the average notional is about $71, at a discount rate of 1 per cent a year. We aggregate all the simulation paths and calculate average present values of the average notional amounts and the tranche losses. Finally, we divide the average present value of annual losses by the average notional amount, also in present value terms, to arrive at a breakeven spread for the tranche.

In a first-to-default (FTD) basket, the buyer of protection receives the par amount minus the recovery if one or more reference entities default before maturity. On the other hand, the protection seller receives periodic premium payments (spread) until one or more defaults occur. Likewise, the buyer of a second-to-default protection receives a payment if two or more defaults occur, while the protection seller continues to receive spreads until two or more reference entities default, and so on.

Unlike in loss tranches, each default knocks out one tranche at a time, sequentially moving from junior to senior ones.

Table 6.8 shows the same sample path as before. The first default occurs in the third year (2.5 years) and the second default occurs in the fifth (4.5 years) year. Accordingly, the first-to-default and the second-to-default protections cease to exist after the third year and the fifth year, respectively.

The nth-to-default basket – a simulated path of default losses **Table 6.8**

Year	Credit 1	Credit 2	Credit 3	Credit 4	Credit 5	
1	0	0	0	0	0	
2	0	0	0	0	0	
3	$55	0	0	0	0	⇐1st-to-default is knocked out
4		0	0	0	0	
5		$55	0	0	0	⇐2nd-to-default is knocked out

As shown in Table 6.9, this particular path dictates very large losses for the first-to-default tranche ($53.64) and the second-to-default tranche ($52.58). However, because two out of the five credits defaulting within five years is a highly unlikely event, such a scenario is associated with a small probability. As before, we collect all simulated paths and calculate the average present value of losses to the first-to-default tranche to arrive at the breakeven spread for that tranche.

On a 10,000-path simulation with correlation of 0.5, the first-to-default tranche is expected to suffer an average loss of $28.49 in present value and the breakeven spread is 849bp (Table 6.10). In a similar manner, breakeven spreads for more senior tranches can be calculated.

Table 6.9

Losses for the *n*th-to-default

Year	FTD	2nd to default	3rd to default	4th to default	5th to default
1	0	0	0	0	0
2	0	0	0	0	0
3	£55	0	0	0	0
4		0	0	0	0
5		$55	0	0	0
Total loss	$55	$55	0	0	0
Loss PV	$53.642	$52.580	0	0	0

Table 6.10

Combined simulation results for the 1st-to-default basket ($\rho = 0.5$)

Simulation path	Portfolio defaults	PV of tranche loss	Breakeven spread
1	0	0	
2	0	0	
3	1	$53.669	
⋮	⋮	⋮	
10,000		0	
Average	0.112	$28.486	849 bp

WHAT IS CORRELATION MISSING?

Key point

In structured credit markets, it has never been the case that all the tranches of a given index/portfolio traded to the same correlation.

There are several likely explanations for this (aside from liquidity), but most relate to assumptions in today's standard models. The use of a single correlation number fails to capture that there are stronger relationships between specific companies and even entire sectors. These subtleties are more important for the subordinate parts of capital structures and can move prices in ways that force the single implied correlation metric to move away from the correlation in other parts of the capital structure.

Copula models are risk-neutral and therefore assume investors are indifferent when faced with a choice between risky assets that can be hedged and assets that are free of risk. While single-name CDS are clearly a traded commodity, pricing in this market is far from continuous and investors in subordinate portions of capital structures have levered exposure to the risk that default swap prices in the underlying portfolio jump. Lower correlation for more subordinate portions of the capital structure can reflect the increasingly levered exposure to (and subsequent risk premium charged for) jumps in single-name prices or exposure to idiosyncratic risk.

Another factor in the relative pricing of tranches is the willingness of rating agencies to assign a rating to a particular tranche. The most severe dislocations in the pricing (and largest implied correlation skew) in the market for liquid tranches occur at points between what are typically unrated portions of the capital structure and what are typically the most subordinate rated portions of the capital structure. In this case, the difference of correlation skew simply represents the supply and demand dynamics for instruments with various risk levels. The rating may add an institutionalized component, exacerbating these supply/demand dynamics and increasing the skew in correlation.

Finally, most standard models use the normal distribution (or the Student-T) to generate correlation defaults. It is likely that the assumed distribution is not the best approximation of the real world.

A SUMMARY OF CDO PRICING

Copula functions are a relatively new tool in finance, where they are used to construct multivariate distributions and to investigate dependence structure between random variables. This section discusses the drawbacks of using copula functions to value multi-tranche synthetic collateralized debt obligations.

Typically, synthetic CDOs are constructed to meet client risk preferences and are sold in tranches.

Risk-adverse investors will seek tranches higher in the capital structure for lower risk and consequently lower expected returns. Conversely, investors seeking a higher return with associated risk will source lower equity tranches.

The iTraxx credit card swap index in Europe and the Dow Jones CDX index in the US have provided greater transparency and liquidity in the synthetic CDO market.

When a bank quotes a price on standardized tranches or on a bespoke structured tranche, by extension, it runs risk on the remaining capital structure. It is, therefore, vital to measure the correlation between the constituent components to manage risk in a disparate portfolio of credit derivatives.

The standard market model for valuing default swaps on multi-constituent credit baskets is the Gaussian copula model, which uses one parameter to describe the correlations between the individual names' credit default times. This standard market approach also assumes these correlations are constant for the life of the basket swap. It is also assumed that the recovery rates and swap spreads are constant. This simple, standard approach allows dealers to quote in terms of implied correlation rather than a swap spread.

CORRELATION TRADING RULES OF THUMB

Since 2001, CDO investors have been painfully aware of correlation risk in their structures. As a result, investors are now focused on understanding the correlation of credits in portfolios backing synthetic cash structures, although debate was sparked in the subprime and credit crunch about what this actually means. As correlation relationships can be puzzling, this chapter gives some rules of thumb to correlation, which has been covered in previous chapters. Note that:

■ The street has a standard technique to price baskets, given correlation assumptions.

■ A market exists for first-to-default baskets and credit indices CDX and iTraxx, and implied correlation can be seen in these transactions.

Key features

Rules of thumb

■ In subordinate tranches, risk and spread decrease as correlation rises.
■ In senior tranches, spread increases as correlation rises.
■ Investors in subordinate tranches are long correlation (spreads tighten when correlation rises).
■ Investors in senior tranches are short correlation (spreads widen when correlation rises).

The subordinate v. senior divide

In graduating from small baskets to large baskets, two things happen. First, the range of possible (implied) correlation values narrow because large baskets are less sensitive to the idiosyncratic behaviour of a small number of companies. Second, the tranche sizes that trade are typically much thinner than in small baskets, which makes their interrelationship very interesting from a correlation perspective. Typically you can have about five tranches all within the bottom 30 per cent of the capital structure. By comparison, in a five-name, first-to-default basket, one can think of the implicit tranche size as being 0–20 per cent.

COPULA DRAWBACKS

The standard Gaussian copula model has drawbacks. It is argued that one should use stochastic models with negative correlation between recovery rates and default probabilities. The model assumes that default rates implied from

CDS spreads are constant and equal. Another drawback is the assumed flat correlation structure across reference names, which misrepresents the complex default relationship between entities and sectors. One of the strongest arguments against the model is the computation resource required to produce stable values, particularly when using Monte Carlo simulations.

Despite the drawbacks, the Gaussian copula model has the advantage of simplicity and tractability. The introduction of the one-factor approach has reduced the computation burden. Also, extensions to the model, allowing clustered correlation for inter- and intrasector modelling and random recovery rates that allow for correlation between recovery rates and default probabilities, give more accurate results.

7

First-to-default (FTD) baskets

While the lion's share of attention and liquidity in the tranched credit markets is focused on cash CDOs (see Chapter 8), synthetic CDOs (see Chapter 9), and the tranched indices (see Chapter 5), first-to-default baskets or, more generally, nth-to-default baskets are the simplest tranched credit instrument. First-to-default baskets look similar to a credit default swap, but the uncertainty associated with whether a credit in the basket will trigger a credit event makes the risk and return profile intuitively more similar to CDO tranches. There are important differences as well, which this chapter will address.

BASKET DEFAULT SWAP MECHANICS

An nth-to-default basket product is one in which the investor gains either long or short exposure to a relatively small basket of credits. The typical size of the basket ranges from four to ten credits. The investor is either selling or buying protection on the nth credit to default in the basket, as with a plain credit default swap, except that the reference credit is a basket instead of a single name. Five-name baskets are most common and protection is typically bought or sold on either a first-to-default (FTD) or second-through-to-fifth default basis.

Suppose an investor sells FTD protection on a five-name basket of reference credits. The investor will receive a periodic payment (the 'premium') in exchange for taking on the credit risk of the basket. If no credit events occur during the term of the basket default swap, the swap expires. If a credit event occurs during the term of the basket, the swap is terminated and the 'buyer' of protection delivers the reference credit that experiences the credit event to the 'seller' of protection in exchange for a par payment (equal to the notional amount of the swap). This process is analogous to a single-name credit.

The settlement in case of default can be done either through a cash settlement or physically, with a security that qualifies for delivery under the terms of the underlying default swap on the credit. A credit event is defined as it is in the single-name market, with investors having the option of choosing the restructuring definition. When a credit event occurs, the seller of protection in the basket is effectively losing par minus the recovery value of the defaulted asset. For detailed definitions of credit events and deliverable obligations, refer to Chapter 2. Figure 7.1 shows an FTD swap with an underlying basket of five names.

First-to-default swap

Figure 7.1

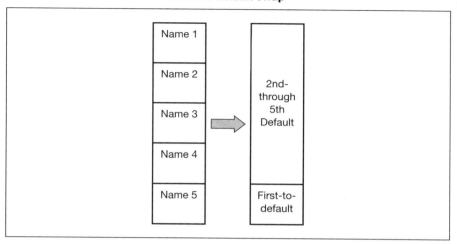

Selling FTD protection: looks like a default swap, feels like CDO equity

Although basket default swaps resemble single-name credit default swaps optically, their risk/return and valuation profiles are much more like CDO tranches. FTD baskets are much more similar to CDO equity, albeit with less leverage in that the investor receives a premium in exchange for taking on first-loss risk. Even if fully funded, the default swap basket can be thought of as a leveraged investment in a basket of credits, with the non-recourse leverage being provided by the counterparty. The seller of protection in an FTD, however, is only exposed to the first credit event, and the principal loss is directly related to the recovery value of the defaulted asset. This aspect is unlike CDO equity, where the CDO structure is still active after the first loss and continues to be active until it matures, is called or amortizes.

Basket default swaps are correlation products

As in CDO tranches, correlation can have a dramatic effect on the pricing of basket default swaps. As an example, consider a first-to-default on a basket of five credits, with each default swap trading at a premium of 50bp. In the case of no correlation, a first-to-default swap would carry a premium of approximately 250bp, the sum of the individual swap premiums. In the case of 100 per cent correlation, the first-to-default would have a premium of 50bp, the maximum of the individual default swap premiums. Figure 7.2 shows an example. A graph of the premiums on the various swaps as a function of correlation is shown in Figure 7.3.

Figure 7.2	Two examples of an FTD. Basket 1 has high default correlation and Basket 2 has low default correlation

HSBC 20bp	HSBC 20bp
HSBC 20bp	Audi 40bp
HSBC 20bp	IBM 30bp
HSBC 20bp	Carfour 20bp
HSBC 20bp	Lufthansa 100bp

- First default results in payment $(1 - R)$ on whole notional. (R is the recovery amount)
- Pricing depends on level of *default correlation* – tendency of two names to default at the same time
- Basket 1 – high default correlation – price 20 bps
- Basket 2 – low default correlation – price between 100bp (highest single default spread) and 210bp (sum of all default spreads) depending on level of correlation.
- Risks: single-name spread risk, jump to default, correlation
- Spread risk – delta hedge with single-name CDS

Figure 7.3	Basket default swap premium depends on correlation

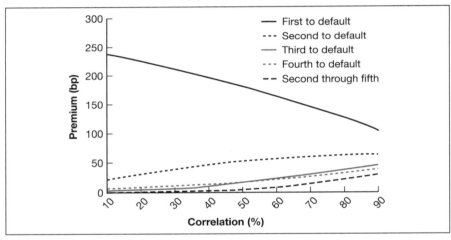

INVESTOR MOTIVATION

Why would an investor either buy or sell protection on a basket of credits? Say an investor has a positive view on a basket of five credits and that each credit pays a premium of 50bp in the five-year default swap market, as in the previous example. By entering into five individual default swaps, the investor could gain $2m exposure to each credit and effectively receive 50bp of premium per annum on $10m notional exposure for five years if no credit event occurs. If one or more credit events occur, there will be a principal loss on each default swap (equal to par minus the recovery value of the default asset).

Or, an investor could express a positive view on the same basket of credits by selling first-to-default protection on the basket with a notional amount of

$10m. From Figure 7.3, assuming a correlation of 30 per cent, the premium earned would be about 214bp (86 per cent of the portfolio spread); therefore, implementing this view via an FTD basket results in a higher-yielding investment for a given notional exposure. To get an equivalent yield from a single name, an investor would have to write protection on more than four times the notional. Therefore, an FTD is a much more levered way of expressing a positive view on credits, which is obviously a double-edged sword.

Buying protection on a basket of credits is effectively a way of shorting a basket of credits with a lower premium outlay than buying protection individually on each underlying credit. However, the swap gets terminated when the first credit event occurs, so the upside for the protection buyer is equal to par minus the recovery value of the defaulted credit only. This makes the basket a better hedge for default risk than spread risk.

Buying protection is also a way of hedging long exposure to credits, particularly for investors who want to reduce concentration risk but not necessarily have an outright negative view on credits. For example, rather than buying protection individually on a portfolio of names, buying protection on the basket will be cheaper and more useful if the investor has a genuine positive view on the credits but would like to reduce concentration risk. The buyer of protection is effectively short correlation.

Table 7.1 summarizes the motives for basket trading.

Investor motivation for basket trading   Table 7.1

Basket	Protection seller	Protection buyer
FTD	Receive higher yield for notional by taking more levered exposure to basket	Avoid idiosyncratic risk on a basket
	Expressed credit views in levered form	Buy cheaper protection versus individual swaps on all underlying names, but retain tail risk
	Position for rising correlation (for example as a result of mergers)	Express views of taking correlation between individual names or industry
Second through to fifth	Express position views on a basket, while avoiding idiosyncratic risk, but taking tail risk	Buy cheaper protection against the tail risk or buying protection of underlying names
	Receive possibly higher yield than ome of the low-yielding names in the underlying basket	Manage risk for extreme scenarios
	Position for failing correlation (for example expressing views that expected mergers won't materialize)	Position for rising correlation (for example as a result of mergers)

MERGERS AND FTD BASKETS

The seller of protection on an FTD basket is long correlation, i.e. rising correlation among the names in the basket would result in a positive mark-to-market. This is also evident in Figure 7.3. This aspect of an FTD basket makes it an effective instrument for positioning for mergers and acquisitions (M&A) activity among a set of names (assuming no 'replacement language', which will be explained shortly).

For example, if an investor expects M&A activity in a sector, he/she can write protection on an FTD basket, including names that are likely to be involved. If there is a merger, the correlation between the merged names will effectively go to 100 per cent, resulting in an overall rise in basket correlation, benefiting the FTD protection seller. From another perspective, the FTD protection writer has to worry about only four credits after the merger as opposed to five credits previously (assuming that the basket initially includes five credits).

Replacement language in FTD baskets

What happens if two of the names in a basket merge? It is important to understand the mechanics behind merger treatment in baskets because there are two forms that trade in the market (see Figure 7.4). In the simplest form (i.e. without replacement language), a five-name, first-to-default basket where two reference entities merge effectively becomes a four-name basket once the merger closes.

Figure 7.4   **Replacement language matters: the effect of a hypothetical merger between credits 1 and 2. Assume $10m notional of first-to-default exposure**

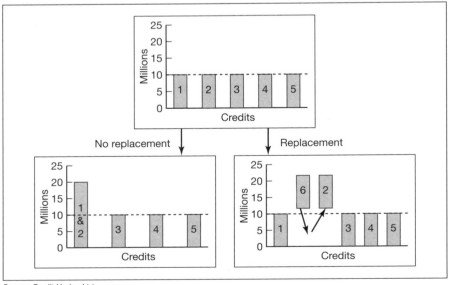

Source: Credit Hedge Ltd

However, the 'contractual' notional amount of the merger entity in the basket doubles to reflect that it was once two reference entities. Yet, this change in exposure size of merger entity does not matter to the seller or buyer of first-to-default protection. A credit event in any of the four names (including the merged entity) would still trigger the contract. A credit event experienced by the merged entity, however, has a larger notional impact. Therefore, it would simultaneously trigger both a first-to-default and a second-to-default contract.

Replacement language: operationally puzzling

The effect of a lack of replacement language seems intuitive, given either the correlation or leveraged reduction analogies described earlier. The seller of first-to-default protection sees a reduction of risk when there is a merger, so the seller of second-to-default protection must see an increase in risk, for which he or she must be compensated. Market clearing levels should be taken into consideration, if the market is efficient about this. In fact, I would argue that the merger option is one factor that keeps implied correlation in small baskets higher than in large baskets.

First-to-default baskets trade with 'replacement' language in the marketplace, as well (see Table 7.1). Here, when a merger occurs, instead of dropping an entity from the basket, the buyer and seller of protection must agree on a replacement credit, and often this replacement credit is one that trades at a similar spread level. Clearly, there is significant correlation risk in this exercise, and the buyer and seller of protection have opposite correlation views. Furthermore, the operational aspects of going through this process for each basket that experiences a merger can be tedious. In my experience, there are more baskets that trade without replacement language, which seems more intuitive. Generally, both buyers and sellers of first-to-default protection should avoid replacement language.

The merger effect: what is it worth?

To gain a better understanding of the value of the merger option, consider the pricing effect across credits with a variety of spreads and correlations. Generally, the merger effect becomes more valuable for riskier (e.g. higher spread) credits as well as for baskets where implied correlation (before the merger announcement) is low. For example, the expected spread move in a basket with an average premium of 50bp, at a correlation of 40 per cent (which is typical for diversified industrial first-to-default baskets), would be 32bp (see Table 7.2). At 150bp of average premium, it would be worth 80bp. This assumes no movement in spread of the merged entity or other credits in the basket.

| Table 7.2 | What is the effect of a merger worth? | | | |

Average spread of credits in basket (bp)

Correlation	20	50	100	150
20%	18	41	78	111
40%	15	32	57	80
60%	11	22	39	53
80%	6	13	22	29

Source: Credit Hedge Ltd

To the extent that the mergers drive the merged entity's spread wider, the effect of the merger would be more muted than indicated in Table 7.2. As an example, for a basket with average spread of 50bp trading at 60 per cent correlation, the gain of the merger of two entities (roughly 22bp of the first-to-default premium) would be fully offset by a 33bp (66 per cent) widening in spread for the merged entity.

SECOND-THROUGH-FIFTH DEFAULT BASKETS

A second-through-fifth default basket (assuming five credits) is similar to a senior CDO tranche, and any credit event after the first default triggers the contract. Unlike FTD baskets, the swap remains in effect until maturity or until all the covered credits default. The risk/return profile is similar to that of a CDO senior tranche in that a protection seller is protected from idio-syncratic risk, but exposed to severe loss where several credits default (also known as 'tail risk'). However, a significant difference is that the return profile of the protection seller in a second-through-fifth default basket is independent of the severity of the first loss.

Second-through-fifth default baskets: investor motivation

Why would an investor sell or buy protection on a second-through-fifth default basis?

As with senior versus equity in a CDO, selling protection in a second-through-fifth default basket is potentially a safer or less volatile way to gain long exposure to a basket of credits. In exchange for a smaller premium, the protection seller has direct exposure to any defaults after the first credit event, but is protected from the first credit event. An investor with a positive view on the underlying credits can sell protection in this swap and potentially earn more premium than selling protection on some of the individual names. In contrast to first-to-default baskets, the seller of protection is short correlation (i.e. an increase in correlation among the underlying names would be bad).

Why would an investor buy protection on a second-through-fifth default basket?

In general, it can be a significantly cheaper way of hedging existing long credit exposure when the investor is willing to take the risk of some losses on the first credit event, but wants to hedge against more severe default scenarios.

FUNDED BASKETS

Most basket default swaps are structured and executed in 'unfunded' form and are not assigned credit rating. However, it is possible to combine an FTD basket with a deposit to create a funded product. In that case the protection writer would buy a note with spread over Libor coming from an FTD position. In case of default in the underlying portfolio, the note holder would incur a loss of principal on the note, reflecting the payment of par minus recovery on the FTD basket.

Example: ex-HiVol first-to-default basket

Among the more common types of first-to-default basket transactions in the marketplace are those involving high-quality credits from relatively unrelated industry groups. In such baskets, first-to-default protection sellers receive significantly higher premiums than the average for the basket because the low correlation among the credits effectively raises the probability that at least one credit will experience a credit event.

Table 7.3 shows the FTD basket excluding high-volatility credits (Ex-HiVol) as an example, with five investment grade credits and individual default swap premiums averaging 37bp. Investors confident that none of the credits will experience a credit event over a five-year term can implement the view by selling first-to-default protection on the basket. In exchange for taking on the risk that any one of the credits experiences a credit event, the investor receives a premium of 153bp. This premium is 4.1 times the average of the five names and 84 per cent of the total, assuming correlation of 38 per cent.

Ex-HiVol benchmark first-to-default basket　　　Table 7.3

Names	CDS level (bp)	Bid/Offer (bp)	Bid/Offer % total	Implied correlation of bid/offer (%)
DOW	22	153/164	84/90	38/25
SRAC	90			
DUK	25			
GECC	21			
VZ	25			
Total	183			

The quoted price can assume that the FTD protection seller/buyer would also buy/sell a delta-neutral amount of protection on the underlying credits. However, if the investor is not interested in entering into a delta-neutral transaction, the bid/ask would be wider, reflecting the transaction cost that the dealer has to incur for hedging delta.

Clearly, the correlation assumption is an important input in valuation of FTD baskets. Chapter 7 spent time developing ideas that are central for an understanding of correlation. As mentioned earlier, sensitivities of baskets to spread changes, correlation changes, time decay, etc. are intuitively similar to those of CDO tranches (see Chapters 8 and 9).

8

Cash CDOs

The emergence of a market for collaterized debt obligations (CDO) is a significant development for credit risk. The cash CDO[1] market has now been in existence for more than 18 years, with considerably substantial issuance volumes since the mid-1990s, and is established as a mature asset class having withstood the peaks and troughs of a full credit cycle. CDOs have emerged as a major segment of the overall asset-backed securities market as well.

While the CDO market started as an efficient mechanism for managing credit risk on bank balance sheets and for obtaining regulatory capital relief, CDOs have evolved into complex instruments to achieve leveraged returns for investors with a wide range of credit risk appetites. Today's CDOs encompass a vast array of underlying assets ranging from unsecured debt instruments such as high-grade, high-yield and emerging market bonds, secured debt instruments such as middle-market and leveraged loans, and subordinate instruments such as trust-preferred securities to all forms of structured finance obligations, including ABS, CMBS and RMBS, hedge fund obligations and, finally, CDO tranches themselves.

Key features

CDO – a definition

CDOs are asset-backed securities used to tranche the credit risk and return characteristics of a diversified pool of assets into notes with different risk/return profiles. They are usually structured by setting up a special purpose vehicle (SPV), which is a bankruptcy-remote entity. The sole purpose of an SPV is to hold a pool of assets. To finance the purchase of the asset pool, the SPV issues various classes/tranches of debt securities.

CDOs provide usually non-recourse term financing for the collateral portfolio.

The elements that define a CDO are:

- portfolio;
- purpose;
- structure.

---

[1] While CDO is an all-encompassing term, it is common to use the terms collateralized bond obligation (CBO), collateralized loan obligation (CLO) and collateralized fund obligation (CFO), depending upon the predominant assets in the collateral portfolio – bonds, loans and hedge funds, respectively. CDO refers to the special purpose vehicle (SPV) that holds assets and issues obligations. CDO also refers specifically to the obligations the SPV issues, leading to the seemingly circular phrase 'the CDO issues CDOs'. Finally, CDO is an umbrella term encompassing the various subclasses, including the CDO species listed later.

CDO TERMINOLOGY

Unfortunately, CDOs bring with them a bewildering array of terminology, such as: arbitrage CBO; cashflow CDO; CBO of ABS; synthetic arbitrage CLO; balance sheet CLO; EMCBO; synthetic CDO; investment-grade CBO; market value CDO; repacks; re-REMICs; and CBO of real estate.

CDO variety　　　　　　　　　　　　　　　　　　　　　　**Key point**

These names, for different types of CDOs, reflect the variety of features and forms a CDO can take and still be called a CDO. A CDO can hold bonds, loans, emerging market debt, ABS, RMBS and CMBS. It can also gain exposure to these assets synthetically.

The CDO can issue floating- or fixed-rate obligations tranched in a variety of ways with respect to seniority and payment. Its obligations can be revolving, have delay-draw features and be guaranteed by a third party. CDOs are done for one of two purposes and use either of two credit structures or a combination of the two.

The CDO names above do not fully describe any CDO's structure and are not mutually exclusive. The easiest way to both classify and understand CDOs is by taking a component or 'à la carte' approach. A CDO can be described by the choices made with respect to its:

- underlying assets;
- tranche structure;
- purpose;
- credit structure.

Looking at CDOs in this way will also allow innovations to be placed in the context of a conceptual framework.

ASSETS, TRANCHES, PURPOSES AND CREDIT STRUCTURES

Assets

Its assets, more than anything else, define a CDO. The general definition is that a CDO is a securitization of corporate obligations. By order of volume, CDOs have securitized (or re-securitized) commercial loans; corporate bonds; ABS, RMBS and CMBS; and emerging market debt. Even tranches of CDOs have been re-securitized into CDOs of CDOs. Table 8.1 gives an idea of the relative values of the types of debt.

Table 8.1

Cash CDO outstandings (January 2007)

Cash CDO outstandings, January 2007		
	$bn	%
Structured finance	492	50
Corporate	412	42
Trups	26	3
Other	56	6
Total	986	100

Source: Creditflux Data+

However, CDOs do not always own these assets outright. Sometimes, a CDO achieves exposure to these assets synthetically by entering into a credit default swap. In a credit default swap, the CDO receives a periodic payment from a counterparty that seeks protection against the default of a referenced asset. In return for this payment, the CDO must pay the protection buyer default losses on the referenced asset if the obligor of the referenced asset defaults.

The definitions of 'default' and 'default losses' can be negotiated to suit the requirements of the CDO and the protection buyer, but typically follow standard ISDA definitions.

The protection-buying counterparty in a credit default swap is usually exposed to the referenced credit by, for example, having made a loan to the name. Any credit loss the counterparty sustains from its dealings with the referenced credit is offset by a payment from the CDO. Because the CDO assumes credit exposure to the referenced asset without buying it, the protection buyer gets rid of credit risk without selling the asset.

A CDO may have a few synthetic exposures or be comprised entirely of synthetic exposures (see Chapter 9).

Tranches

Tranches are sized to minimize funding costs within the constraints of investor requirements. In most CDOs, the top-most tranche provides the majority of the vehicle's financing. Other debt tranches are sized around 5 per cent to 15 per cent. Equity is generally around 2 per cent to 15 per cent of the CDO's capital structure, depending on the credit quality and diversity of the assets. Seniority can also be created synthetically outside the CDO structure by the terms of a credit default swap so the protection buyer retains a first-loss position.

The CDO's payment under the credit default swap may occur only if losses on referenced assets exceed some set amount. This first-loss carve-out might be expressed on a per-name basis (losses up to so much on a name) or on an overall portfolio basis (losses up to a certain level across the entire portfolio). In the language of insurance, the protection-buying counterparty in the credit default swap essentially has to meet a deductible before being able to make a claim under the credit default swap.

Subordinated CDO debt tranches protect more senior debt tranches against credit losses and receive a higher coupon for taking on greater credit risk. Coupon payments on subordinated tranches may be deferrable if the CDO does not have sufficient cashflow or if it is in violation of certain tests.

Sometimes a CDO senior debt tranche is structured with a 'delayed draw' feature. This is useful if the CDO's assets are to be purchased over time, as draws against the facility can be taken as they are needed. A revolving tranche can allow the CDO to adjust its leverage. Often a double structure of tranches is used where the same seniority tranche is comprised of separate fixed- and floating-rate sub-tranches. Finally, debt tranches are sometimes guaranteed by third parties, such as bond insurers.

Purposes

CDOs are classified as either balance sheet or arbitrage CDOs, depending on the motivation behind the securitization and the source of the CDO's assets. Balance sheet CDOs are initiated by holders of securitizable assets, such as commercial banks, which want to sell assets or transfer the risk of assets. The motivation may be to shrink the balance sheet, reduce required regulatory capital, or reduce required economic capital.

The most straightforward way to achieve all three goals is the cash sale of assets to the CDO. But for a variety of reasons, the risk of the assets may be better transferred to the CDO synthetically, as described above. This second method can reduce required capital, but cannot shrink the balance sheet. Nevertheless, synthetic CDOs done to adjust required capital are referred to as balance sheet transactions.

Arbitrage CDOs, in contrast, are generated by asset managers and equity tranche investors.

Leveraged return   **Key point**

Equity tranche investors hope to achieve a leveraged return between the after-default yield on assets and the financing cost due for debt tranches. This potential spread, or funding gap, is the 'arbitrage' of the arbitrage CDO. The asset manager gains a management fee from monitoring and trading the CDO's assets.

An arbitrage CDO's assets are purchased from a variety of sources in the open market, over a period that may stretch for months from a warehousing period before the CDO closes to a ramp-up period after the CDO closes. The asset manager often invests in a portion of the CDO's equity tranche or subordinates a significant portion of its fee to debt and equity tranches. There is generally more trading in an arbitrage CDO than in a balance sheet CDO, where trading of the portfolio is not allowed or limited to replacement of amortized assets.

By number, 74 per cent of CDOs are arbitrage transactions, but because balance sheet transactions are typically larger, the division is an almost perfect even split by volume.

The distinction commonly drawn between balance sheet and arbitrage CDOs ignores the fact that the asset seller in a balance sheet CDO also enjoys potential 'arbitrage' profits from retention of the equity tranche. After the close of the transaction, there is nothing very different between the economic position of an equity investor in a CDO that buys assets in the open market and the equity investor in a CDO that buys assets the equity investor originated.

Origination CDOs can be considered as a third CDO purpose and method of obtaining CDO assets.

Perhaps the most practical distinction between balance sheet, arbitrage and origination CDOs is how likely the proposed CDOs are to be accomplished. The key to the successful closing of a CDO is the placement of the CDO's equity. A balance sheet CDO often has the advantage of a pre-packaged investor for most or all of the equity tranche. Thus, a typical balance sheet CDO is more likely to close than the typical arbitrage CDO where the asset manager only commits to a portion of the equity tranche.

Credit structures

A CDO can have either a market value or a cashflow credit structure, depending upon the way the CDO protects debt tranches from credit losses. In a market value structure, the CDO's assets are marked-to-market periodically. The mark-to-market value is then haircut, or reduced, to take into account future market value fluctuations.

If the haircut value of assets falls below debt tranche par, CDO assets must be sold and debt tranches repaid until haircut asset value once again exceeds debt tranche par.

In contrast, there is no market value test in a cashflow CDO. Subordination is sized so that after-default interest and principal cashflow from the CDO's asset portfolio are expected to cover debt tranche requirements.

This expectation is based on assessment of default probability, default correlation and loss in the event of default. A common cashflow structuring technique is to divert cashflow from subordinated tranches to senior tranches if the quality of CDO assets diminishes by some objective measure.

But while the manager of a troubled cashflow CDO can sell CDO assets, and the senior CDO obligation holders can sell CDO assets after a CDO default, there is generally never a requirement to sell CDO assets. Nine out of ten CDOs, both by number and volume, use the cashflow credit structure.

THE À LA CARTE CDO MENU

Figure 8.1 shows the four CDO attributes. A wide variety of CDOs can be constructed by picking one attribute from each menu column.

The à la carte CDO menu

Figure 8.1

Assets	Liabilities	Purpose	Credit structure
High yield corporate bonds	Different number of tranches possible	**Balance sheet transaction:** A seller desires to shed assets to shrink its balance sheet and adjust economic and regulatory capital. Existing assets are transferred to the CDO and the seller often takes back the CDO's most subordinate tranche	**Market value:** The haircut value of CDO assets is periodically compared with CDO tranche par. If haircut assets are less than tranche par, CDO assets must be sold and tranches repaid
Commercial and industrial loans	Sequential, fast/slow, or contemporaneous paydown of principal		
Emerging market corporate and sovereign debt			
ABS, CMBS, RMBS and other CDOs	Coupon can be fixed rate or floating rate		**Cashflow:** CDO subordinate tranches are sized so that senior tranches can survive asset default losses. If portfolio quality deteriorates, asset cashflow may be redirected from subordinate tranches to senior tranches
Investment-grade debt	Variety of portfolio tests to divert cashflow from subordinate to senior	**Arbitrage transaction:** A money manager wants to expand assets under management and equity investors desire non-recourse leverage. Assets may be purchased over warehousing and ramp-up periods	
Distressed securities			
Equity	Delay-draw tranches possible		
Assets can be purchased or exposure can be gained synthetically	Revolving tranche possible		
	Guarantee by a third party possible		
		Origination transaction: (not a recognized term) Underlying CDO assets are issued for a CDO	

Source: Credit Hedge Ltd

Types of collateral portfolios

The portfolio underlying a CDO is referred to as the 'collateral portfolio'. Collateral portfolios tend to consist of assets of the same type. However, multi-class CDOs have been issued. The most common types of assets underlying CDOs are investment-grade bonds, high-yield bonds and leveraged loans. In recent years, the range of asset types used as CDO collateral has broadened to include:

■ emerging market debt;

■ project finance debt;

■ mortgage-backed securities;

■ REIT debt;

■ DIP financings;

■ mezzanine debt;

■ asset-backed securities;

■ stripped securities (interest only and principal only);

■ distressed debt;

■ hedge funds.

The range of CDOs offered allows investors access to asset classes that might not otherwise be available for their portfolios.

Motivation

Companies have many reasons for creating or sponsoring CDOs. For example, some CDOs are created by investment advisory firms (i.e. money market firms). Such a firm earns fees based on the amount of assets that it manages. By creating a CDO, the firm can increase its income by increasing its assets under management. This kind of CDO is usually called 'arbitrage CDO' because of the (hopefully) positive spread between the yield that the CDO earns on its portfolio and the yield that it must pay on its own securities. In many cases, the profit goes mostly to the holder of the equity class, with some portion going to the manager as a performance-based fee.

Other CDOs are created by banks as a way to remove assets from their balance sheets. A bank can remove assets from a balance sheet by creating a CDO and transferring assets to the CDO's portfolio. Such a CDO is a 'balance sheet CDO'. Removing assets from its balance sheet can be advantageous for a bank when it reduces regulatory capital requirement.

Motivations for the owners of the assets and SPV

There are different motivations for the participants within a CDO. For the SPV, the CDO is income-motivated: the SPV gets fees for placing, structuring and managing the CDO. These fees can be quite substantial, reaching up to 10 per cent of the notional amount. SPVs can also make a profit on the difference between the generated income from the tranches and the default swap premiums and coupons of the risk-free asset. This type of CDO is termed an 'arbitrage CDO'.

The SPV can also initiate a CDO to achieve regulatory capital relief by removing an asset from its balance sheet. For example, an SPV might already own assets, and create a tranched CDO, thus transferring the credit risk to the investors of the tranches. This type of CDO is termed a 'balance sheet CDO' and can extend a client's credit line and raise funding.

The motivation for the owners of the assets is in laying off credit risk via a default swap without having to inform the original debtor, thus maintaining a good creditor–debtor relationship. Synthetic structures are also more convenient from an administrative point of view, because no physical transfer of the original asset takes place. Finally, synthetic structures are flexible, allowing customized credit risk transfer of an individual credit. The motivation for the investors in the tranches is primarily yield enhancement. The tranches often pay a higher return than assets with the same risk in the cash markets. However, the investor is advised to keep an eye on the high fees in CDOs. Another motivation for the investor is that a CDO allows them to access payoff profiles that would be difficult, if not impossible, to create with cash products.

Diversification

A CDO sponsor tries to create value by assembling a well-diversified portfolio of assets to back its CDO. In principle, diversification within a CDO's portfolio can make it stronger than merely the sum of its parts. Diversification, tranche behaviour and correlation are themes throughout this book.

The idea of diversification is central to estimating the riskiness of a CDO's different classes. Professionals grapple with diversification through the statistical concept of 'correlation'. They gauge the riskiness of a CDO's different classes by running computer simulations where they make assumptions about correlation. The rating agencies often use the same approach when they analyse CDOs for the purpose of rating them. For example, when a CDO's underlying portfolio consists of corporate bonds, Standard & Poor's assumes a constant correlation of 0.3 for companies within a given industry and zero correlation among companies of different industries. Similarly, when a CDO's underlying portfolio consists of asset-backed securities, S&P assumes constant correlations of 0.3 within an asset-backed security (ABS) sector and 0.1 between ABS sectors.

Assumptions about correlation have a strong effect on the predicted credit quality of a CDO. A few years ago, many outstanding CDOs performed worse than the rating agencies and other market participants had predicted. Some professionals now feel that wrong assumptions about correlation around 2004 were the cause of the inaccurate predictions. Following a wave of poor CDO performance around 2004, each of the rating agencies modified its CDO rating approach to place greater emphasis on correlation.

Correlation can produce opposite effects on different tranches in a CDO. Senior tranches tend to benefit from low correlation of credit risk among the assets in the underlying portfolio. Conversely, junior tranches tend to benefit from high correlation.

Think of it like this: strong diversification (i.e. low correlation) dampens the overall performance volatility of a CDO's underlying portfolio. That is, strong diversification makes extreme outcomes less likely. The CDO's senior tranche can suffer only if extreme outcome of very high losses occurs. Conversely, the CDO's equity tranche may survive only if the extreme outcome of very low losses occurs. Thus, the senior tranche favours low correlation but the equity tranche favours high correlation.

HOW DO CASH CDOs WORK IN PRACTICE?

While CDO issuance using credit derivatives technology has become very popular (see Chapter 9 for a primer on synthetic CDOs), the issuance of CDOs in their original form as cash instruments remain substantial. This section focuses on cash CDOs and provides an overview of their types, structure, motivation and performance metrics.

Key point | **Special vehicles**

CDOs are standalone, special purpose vehicles (SPVs) that invest in a diversified pool of assets. The investments are funded through the issuance of many classes of securities, the repayment of which is a function of the performance of the pool of assets that serves as collateral.

These classes of securities are sold to investors who assume the risks of the pool of assets in different order of seniority, with each class representing a priority of cashflows generated by the underlying collateral. When the SPV purchases the pool of assets outright, as opposed to acquiring risk exposure using credit derivatives, the CDOs are called cash CDOs.

Figure 8.2 shows the workings of a cash CDO. In this simplified illustration, the SPV issues three classes of securities, all at par: senior notes, junior notes and preferred shares.

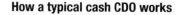
How a typical cash CDO works

Figure 8.2

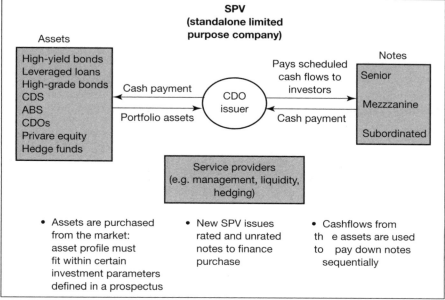

Source: Credit Hedge Ltd

The senior and junior notes are the debt tranches and the preferred shares constitute the equity tranche of the transaction. The proceeds are used to purchase a diversified pool of assets. Cashflows from the assets are used to pay the manager and trustees of the transaction and make principal and interest payments to the note holders in the order of seniority – senior notes first, followed by the junior notes. Preferred shares are the residual of the transaction and receive a current coupon out of the residual interest proceeds generated by the collateral. The coupon may be deferred or eliminated depending upon available cashflow.

As assets in the portfolio default, residual cashflows and consequently, the payments of the proffered share holders decrease. If defaults reach a certain level, the principal amount invested by the proffered shares may be written down, followed by the principal of the junior notes and so on. The coupons of the senior notes are set to be lower than the coupons on the junior notes, reflecting the lower risk assumed by the senior note holders. The proffered shares represent a leverage investment in the underlying collateral pool of assets. Being in a first-loss position, they have the highest risk exposure and consequently the highest return potential. They also face higher volatility of return than the underlying collateral pool.

In some cash CDOs, the collateral pool of assets may predominantly have fixed-rate coupons, while the liabilities may be predominantly floating-rate. This mismatch introduces interest-rate risk into the transaction, which is usually addressed through an interest-rate hedge (fixed–floating-rate swap or an interest rate cap/swap) at deal inception. The notional amount of the hedge is a function of expected amortization of the floating-rate liability traunches. If the realized amortization differs from the expected amortization at deal inception, the hedge may introduce a degree of risk into the transaction.

Monoline reinsurance

In some transactions, the SPV enters into an insurance contract with a monoline bond insurance company to buy external credit enhancement. The bond insurer guarantees the payment of principal and interest on one or more classes of the debt tranches. The notes so insured are said to have been 'wrapped'. Usually, the ratings of the notes reflect the financial strength rating of the bond insurer.

CDO collateral manager

The assets are purchased and managed by a collateral manager in accordance with guidelines, which are designed to provide investors with an exposure to a diversified pool of assets. Typically, trading within the portfolio ceases 3–5 years after the CDO issuance. Around that time, the debt tranches start to amortize. Structural mechanisms are put in place to protect the integrity of the capital structure and to maintain the balance between the interests of the debt and equity traunches.

CDO trustee

Each transaction also involves a trustee who acts as the custodian responsible for the safe custody of the assets and for ensuring compliance with trading guidelines and other structural features. Frequently, the trustee is also the calculation agent for the transaction, responsible for computing the payments due to parties in the transaction according to deal documentation. Periodically, the trustee provides reports to investors regarding the status of the CDO's assets and liabilities as well as compliance with regard to structural mechanisms specified in the CDO documentation at deal inception. The reports are critical for monitoring transactions.

CDO debt tranches

Finally, debt tranches are typically callable at the option of the preferred share-holders after a stated non-call period, usually 2–5 years. The call option embedded in senior CDO notes is generally a Bermuda-style option, in that the call is exercisable on discrete exercise dates after the non-call period.

Structurally, the embedded callability is intended to provide a way for equity investors to unwind the CDO transaction once it has de-levered to the point that, looking forward, returns are no longer deemed attractive.

In addition, the call enables equity investors to realize capital appreciation in the underlying collateral pool. In some cases, callability involves make-whole premiums, which require payments greater than the par amount of outstanding liabilities of the CDO.

Figures 8.3 and 8.4 show the workings of a cash CDO. In the illustration, the SPV issues three classes of securities, all at 1(Par)-recovery.

CDOs are tranched investment vehicles. Typical CDO debt structure   **Figure 8.3**

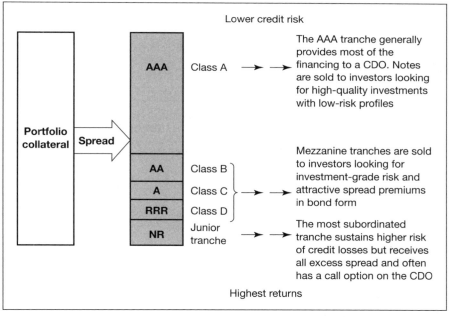

| Figure 8.4 | The CDO 'waterfall' |

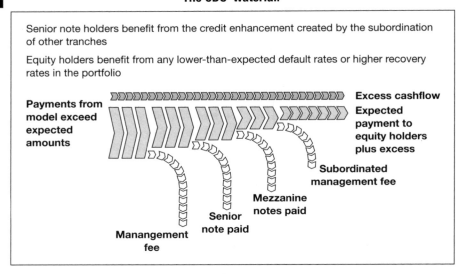

Senior note holders benefit from the credit enhancement created by the subordination of other tranches

Equity holders benefit from any lower-than-expected default rates or higher recovery rates in the portfolio

Payments from model exceed expected amounts

Excess cashflow

Expected payment to equity holders plus excess

Subordinated management fee

Mezzanine notes paid

Senior note paid

Manangement fee

Capital structure example

A typical CDO may have an underlying portfolio of roughly one hundred corporate bonds with an average of single-B-plus (Moody's, B1; S&P, B+). If the total size of the portfolio is $300m, the CDO might issue six classes of securities as in Table 8.2.

| Table 8.2 | Example of basic CDO capital structure |

Class	Amount ($m)	Pct. of Deal	Subordination (%)	Ratings (Moody's/S&P)
Class A	243.0	81.0	19.0	Aaa/AAA
Class B	13.5	4.5	14.5	Aa2/AA
Class C	10.5	3.5	11.0	A2/A
Class D	9.0	3.0	8.0	Baa2/BBB
Class E	9.0	3.0	5.0	Ba2/BB
Equity	15.0	5.0	0.0	not rated

In buying and selling assets for the portfolio, the manager would be required to maintain an average portfolio rating of single-B-plus or higher. If the average rating of the portfolio slipped lower, the terms of the deal might curtail the manager's discretion in managing the portfolio. In addition, the rating agencies might downgrade the securities.

Naturally, investors demand higher yields on classes exposed to greater credit risk. In the example of Table 8.2, the class A securities would command the lowest yield because they carry the highest rating. Conversely, the equity class would command the highest yield because of its station at the bottom of the deal's capital structure.

CASH CDOs: A TAXONOMY

CDO investors are faced with an overabundance of terminology to describe different types of structures. This section explains some terms.

Depending upon the motivation behind the transaction, cash CDOs can be categorized into two types – balance sheet and arbitrage transactions.

Balance sheet transactions

Balance sheet transactions are intended to obtain regulatory and/or economic capital relief for financial institutions holding bonds and/or loans, and achieve a higher return on assets through redeployment of capital. The financial institutions often retain the equity tranche of the CDO. Usually, the assets securitized through balance sheet CDOs are already on the balance sheets of the financial institutions; therefore, balance sheet CDOs require very short ramp-up periods. In addition, during the life of the transaction they experience only limited trading in the underlying collateral pool of assets.

Arbitrage transactions

Arbitrage transactions are motivated by the aspirations of equity tranche investors and collateral managers. The former seek to achieve leverage return on the spread between post-default yield of the collateral pool of assets and the cost of financing the assets through the issue of the debt tranches. This spread, also known as the funding gap, is the arbitrage that the equity investors are seeking to capture. The collateral managers seek to expand assets under management to realize fees for the management (acquisition, trading and monitoring) of the collateral pool of assets.

Depending upon the mechanics of structural protection to the debt tranches, cash CDOs are categorized into cashflow and market value structures. Cashflow structures are based on the ability of the collateral to generate sufficient cashflow to pay the coupon and principal of the debt tranches. If the credit quality of the collateral falls below specified levels, cashflows are diverted from subordinated tranches to the senior tranches to pay their coupons. If certain triggers are breached, cashflows are diverted to repay the principal of the senior tranches in an accelerated fashion until the metrics of the collaterization revert to the levels above the triggers.

Market value structures

Market value structures, in contrast, depend upon the ability of a fund manager to maintain the market value of the collateral to pay the CDO debt tranches. In a market value transaction, assets in the CDO collateral pool are valued (marked-to-market) periodically, incorporating cushions to account for future variability in the market value of the assets. If the value of the assets falls below the sum of the par amounts of the debt tranches, some assets are sold and a par of the debt tranches is repaid until the market value of the assets exceeds the par value of the remaining debt tranches.

Though it was not always the case, the vast majority of cash CDOs now tend to be arbitrage transactions.

CDO lifecycle and performance tests

It is useful to view a CDO as having a lifecycle that consists of several phases (Figure 8.5). The first phase is the ramp-up, when the manager uses the proceeds from issuing the CDO to purchase the initial portfolio. The CDO's governing documents generally specify parameters for the initial portfolio but not the exact composition. For example, the terms of the CDO might require that the initial portfolio have a minimum average rating, or a minimum degree of diversification. During the ramp-up phase, the manager must select assets so that the portfolio satisfies all the parameters.

Figure 8.5

Stages in the life of a CDO

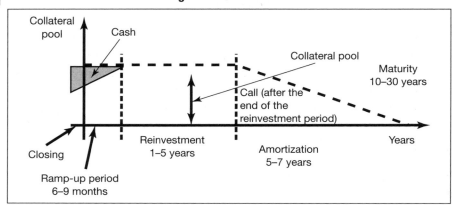

The second phase is the revolving period, during which the manager manages the portfolio and reinvests cashflow from the portfolio. The reinvestment allows a CDO to remain outstanding – without amortization of the CDO's own bonds – even though the assets in the underlying portfolio reach their maturity dates.

The third period is the amortization phase, in which the manager stops reinvesting cashflow from the portfolio. Instead, the manager must repay the CDO's debt securities.

A manager generally is required to follow certain rules in managing the portfolio. The rules protect investors by limiting the manager's discretion. For example, one rule might require the manager to maintain the average yield or spread on the managed assets above a certain level. Another rule might require the manager to maintain the average maturity of the assets within a certain range.

Many CDOs include performance tests that can trigger the early start of the amortization phase if the deal performs poorly. For example, many deals include an 'over-collateralization' test based on the ratio of portfolio balance to the balance of the CDO's debt securities. Likewise, many CDOs also include an interest coverage test, based on the ratio of interest cashflow on the portfolio to the interest the CDO must pay on its own securities. If either ratio falls below a specified threshold, the deal would enter early amortization. The tests are designed to protect investors by triggering amortization if a deal's performance deteriorates. However, CDO managers sometimes manipulate the tests to avoid early amortization. In such cases, rating agencies are likely to downgrade the CDO's securities.

STRUCTURAL FEATURES AND PERFORMANCE TESTS IN CASH CDOs

This section focuses on arbitrage cashflow CDOs to describe typical structural features and performance tests that determine the priority of payments designed to maintain the integrity of the CDO capital structure. The priority of payments is also referred to as the cashflow waterfall (Figure 8.6).

Senior notes in a cashflow CDO transaction have a priority claim on all cashflows generated on the underlying collateral pool and are protected by:

■ subordination;

■ over-collateralization; and

■ coverage tests

that serve to accelerate the redemption of the senior notes if the tests are violated. Other structural features and limitations are imposed to ensure that the collateral pool is well diversified and remains consistent with the intended credit quality at deal inception.

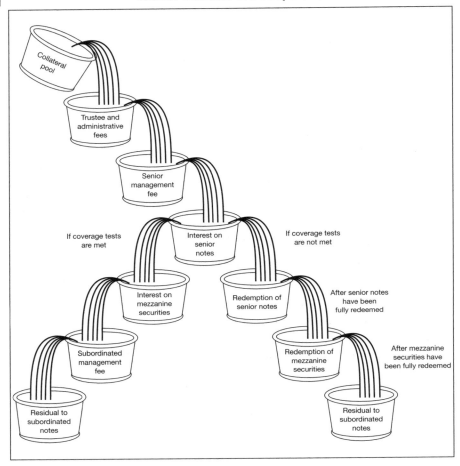

Figure 8.6

Interest 'waterfall' of a sample CDO

Subordination

The priority of claims of the senior notes means that the claims of junior notes and the equity tranches are subordinate, in that order. The size of the junior and equity tranches therefore describes the amount of subordination available to the senior note holders.

Key point

Subordination

The amount of subordination is a function of the credit quality of the underlying pool of assets, their expected losses given defaults and desired rating. The lower the credit quality of the underlying pool of assets, the higher the level of subordination required for the senior notes to obtain a desired rating.

Over-collateralization (O/C) and coverage tests

The mechanisms most used to ensure the priority of payments are collateral coverage tests. Over-collaterization (O/C) is the excess of the par amount of the collateral available to secure a class of CDO notes. If $100 of par assets is available to service $80 of senior notes, the ratio 100/80 = 125% suggests that the senior notes are over-collateralized by 25 per cent.

Coverage tests

In the senior tranche par coverage test, the adjusted par value of defaulted assests reflects the expected recoveries for defaulted assets whose final valuation is yet to be determined. So:

Senior tranche par coverage test = (PVofPA + APVDA)/PASN

Where PVofPA is the par value of performing assets; APVDA is the adjusted par value of defaulted assets; and PASN is the par amount of the senior notes.

The junior tranche par coverage test (JTPCT) is:

Junior tranche par coverage test = (PVofPA + APVDA)/(PASN+PAJN)

Where PAJN is the par amount of the junior notes.

Along the same lines, there are two interest coverage tests. For the senior tranche interest coverage test, if IPA is the interest expected to be collected on the performance assets for the current period and IS is the interest due on the senior notes for the period:

Senior tranche interest coverage test = IPA/IS

If ISJN is the interest due on the senior and junior notes for the current period:

Junior tranche interest coverage test = IPA/ISJN

Trigger levels

Trigger levels for these tests are set in the deal documentation. In general, junior notes will have par coverage triggers set at lower levels than the senior notes. At deal inception, the actual deal for these tests will be well above the trigger levels. A breach of the coverage tests below the trigger level results in additional trading restrictions and/or potential diversification of cashflows as identified in the deal indenture's property of payments (see Figures 8.6 and 8.7).

If the par coverage test for the senior tranche is breached, the senior notes will be redeemed until the test comes back into compliance. Likewise, if interest coverage tests are breached, all interest payments will be redirected to the senior bonds until the trigger is cured. In general, interest coverage tests are less onerous than par coverage tests. Still, the presence of these tests contributes to maintenance of higher levels of current coupon income than would otherwise be the case.

Figure 8.7 **Principal 'waterfall' of a sample CDO**

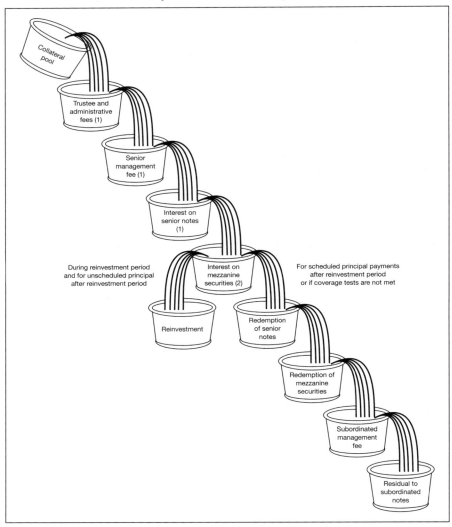

The level at which the O/C test triggers is an important consideration in a cash CDO, given its effect on the cashflow waterfall. For each set of notes, triggers should be set at levels high enough to ensure that the class can withstand a certain level of defaults in the underlying pool of assets. The higher the trigger level, the more likely that a given level of default will cause the O/C trigger to be breached. From the perspective of investors of subordinate tranches, O/C triggers set too high increase the likelihood that cashflows are diverted away from them. Ideally, transactions should be structured such that O/C tests for the junior notes are triggered before the senior notes.

Another structural provision frequently seen in CDOs is the payment-in-kind provision ('PIKing'). Some CDOs provide for the deferment of interest to subordinate debt tranches upon the breach of certain coverage tests. PIKing results in the deferred interest being added to the principal of those tranches, where it earns interest at the same rate as the original principal.

Supplemental O/C test

During the 2001–02 downturn in the credit cycle, several CDO notes experienced downgrades that were attributed to structural weaknesses. The argument made was that the trigger levels of par coverage tests were set at levels so low that a violation would occur only after significant deterioration. Such criticism was addressed by the introduction of the supplemental O/C test that becomes binding before the par coverage tests are breached by setting its trigger level higher than the par coverage test triggers. A violation of supplemental O/C tests results in reinvestment of excess cashflow rather than redemption of the senior notes. Some part of collateral management fees and payments to the equity tranche are not paid until the test is cured. This mechanism enables a collateral manager to build up over-collateralization over time and offsets downward pressure on rating without paying down the least costly portion of a CDO's capital structure.

Excess CCC haircut

Another issue that became prominent in 2001–02 was the level of assets rated at CCC in CDO portfolios because of severe downgrades in the corporate sector. These securities were still performing but were highly likely to experience potential par losses in the near term as their downgraded ratings suggested. Nevertheless, for the purpose of the computation of par coverage tests, they were being given full par credit.

Barbelling | **Key point**

In some cases, collateral managers were resorting to 'barbelling' of the credit portfolio – buying deeply discounted CCC bonds whose risk potential was not reflected in the coverage tests.

The excess CCC haircut was a proviso introduced to address this issue. In short, securities rated in CCC in excess of some predetermined levels would be treated at their market value instead of at par value.

If coverage tests are not met

It is worth noting that if coverage tests are not met, and not corrected with principal proceeds, the remaining interest proceeds will be used to redeem the most senior notes to bring the structure back into compliance with the coverage tests. Interest on the mezzanine securities may be deferred and compounded if cash is not available to pay current interest due.

Collateral quality tests

Unlike the coverage tests, the purpose of quality tests in CDOs is not to redirect cashflows in the waterfall but to ensure that the composition of the portfolio does not change drastically over time. When the quality tests are breached, trading within the portfolio becomes restricted.

Some of the frequently used collateral quality parameters are: minimum diversity score; maximum weighted average factor (WARF); issuer concentration limits; maturity weighted life (WAL) limits; and weighted average spread (WAS).

Diversity score

Diversity score is a statistical development by Moody's to reflect the degree of diversification within the collateral pool. Assets in the collateral pool are mapped into a hypothetical portfolio of N uncorrelated, homogenous assets with identical default probabilities and equal par values. The number N in the hypothetical portfolio is the 'diversity score'. The higher the diversity score, the more diversified the reference portfolio. The formula for calculating the diversity score incorporates obligor and industry concentrations in the reference portfolio as well as default correlations across industries.

Trading guidelines restricting the diversity score of a CDO's portfolio to a minimum lever are frequently used to prevent the portfolio from becoming overly concentrated in a single issuer or sector. A manager may not execute a trade that will result in a breach of the minimum diversity score restriction. In the same vein, individual issuer, sector, country and currency concentration limits are used to ensure that the collateral pool of assets remains diversified during the life of the CDO.

Weighted average rating factor (WARF)

WARF is the numerical metric used by Moody's and Fitch to express the credit quality of a collateral pool of assets. It is interpreted as the expected ten-year cumulative default probability for a rating level. For example, for a B3 rating, 3,490 implies a cumulative default probability of 34.90% over ten years. WARF is derived by computing the weighted average of a numerical value assigned to each rating category to reflect the expected defaults for that rating category. Table 8.3 shows the values that Moody's equates to each rating level; these values are averaged across the collateral pool, weighted by the par balance of the respective asset in the WARF statistic. The higher the WARF statistic, the more likely the portfolio is to experience defaults. As with the diversity score, trading guidelines restrict a collateral manager from adding or removing assets from the portfolio if such an action would violate the maximum WARF test.

Moody's rating factors

Table 8.3

Rating	Factor
Aaa/AAA	1
Aa1/AA+	10
Aa2/AA	20
Aa3/AA–	40
A1/A+	70
A2/A	120
A3/A–	180
Baa1/BBB+	260
Baa2/BBB	360
Baa3/BBB–	610
Ba1/BB+	940
Ba2/BB	1350
Ba3/BB–	1766
B1/B+	2220
B2/B	2720
B3/B–	3490
Caa1	4770
Caa2	6500
Caa3	8070
Ca–C	10000

Source: © Moody's Investor Services, Inc. and/or its affiliates. Reprinted with permission. All Rights Reserved

WAL and WAM

Maximum weighted average life (WAL) and weighted average maturity (WAM) tests are intended to deter collateral managers from taking duration bets inconsistent with the dimensions of the CDO liabilities. Other collateral quality tests include limitations on discount purchases – purchases of par assets with steeply discounted market value, payment-in-kind or deferred interest securities, and, in the case of CLOs, the purchase of securities rated CCC/Caa.

UNDERSTANDING CDO EQUITY RETURNS

If the coverage tests are not met, and they are not corrected with principal proceeds, the remaining interest proceeds will be used to redeem the most senior notes, so that the structure can be brought back into compliance with the coverage tests. Interest on the mezzanine securities may be deferred and compounded if cash is not available to pay current interest due.

The debt tranches used to fund CDO assets are collateralized by the assets, and if the assets do not perform to expectations, the claims of the holders of the debt tranches are limited to the CDO assets. It is useful to make comparisons with of the repo market, which is another way to finance assets. In the repo market, the lender is not only collateralized by the pledge of the assets being financed but also has recourse to borrow if the collateral is insufficient. With CDOs, the recourse is limited to the assets in the collateral pool of the CDO. Further, repo financing is relatively short term compared to the non-recourse financing achieved by equity tranche investors in cash CDOs.

Effectively, equity investors seek to obtain leveraged return as the positive difference between post-default yield on the CDO's assets and the cost of financing.

Remember that the pricing of credit-risky assets compensates investors for expected credit losses and incorporates risk and liquidity premiums.

The spread over the risk-free rate in an asset's yield of a non-callable, fixed-rate instrument is a measure of the reward for the credit risk and liquidity risk. As such, CDO equity investors are betting that the difference between the expected credit losses in the portfolio will be favourable and thus seek to capture risk and liquidity premiums in the assets in the collateral portfolio.

In contrast to competing asset classes such as hedge funds, the cashflow return profile for CDO equity investors begins from deal inception. It is front-end loaded and does not depend on the discretion of the collateral manager but on a predetermined set of rules. At deal inception, all structural protections and compliance mechanisms are in place. Therefore, for the first few years of the transaction, there may be residual cashflow available to equity tranche investors, which explains the front-loaded nature of CDO equity investments. For investors with exposures to first loss, the likelihood of residual cashflows being available decreases over time as assets default.

UNDERSTANDING CDO DEBT RETURNS

The risks to an investor with exposure to a portfolio of credit-risky assets may be thought of as having four dimensions:

- default probability;
- default severity or loss given default;
- default correlation;
- default timing.

In a CDO these risks are distributed to tranches using the waterfall mechanism, with the debt tranches receiving the benefit of structural protection in the form of subordination, over-collateralization and coverage tests.

Compared with an investor holding assets in a collateral pool directly, an investor in a debt tranche of a CDO that holds the identical collateral pool of assets will experience narrower default distributions because of the structural protection embedded in a CDO.

The effects of diversification on the risks to investors are well known. Not only does a CDO offer the benefits of such diversification by requiring the collateral pool of assets to be diversified through the collateral quality tests but, in addition, the structural protections ensure that each additional default in the collateral pool will have a small effect on the return of the debt tranche.

The application of the CDO technology enables investors to gain exposure to asset classes they might not otherwise have access to.

For example, investors mandated to limit investments to investment-grade securities have very limited opportunities to invest in emerging-market securities, few of which are rated investment grade. However, CDOs make it possible for such investors to get exposure through investment-grade tranches of CDOs with a collateral pool of emerging market securities. The same is true of other asset classes, such as leveraged and middle-market loans.

DETAILS OF A CASH CDOs STRUCTURE

Nomura CRE CDO 2007-2, Ltd notes as follows:

Key features

- $471,131,250 Class A-1 at 'AAA'
- $75,000,000 Class A-R at 'AAA'
- $60,681,250 Class A-2 at 'AAA'
- $70,537,500 Class B at 'AA'
- $26,600,000 Class C at 'AA–'
- $27,075,000 Class D at 'A+'
- $20,425,000 Class E at 'A'
- $21,612,500 Class F at 'A–'
- $24,937,500 Class G at 'BBB+'
- $20,187,500 Class H at 'BBB'
- $25,175,000 Class J at 'BBB–'
- $22,800,000 Class K at 'BB+'
- $8,787,500 Class L at 'BB'
- $5,700,000 Class M at 'BB–'
- $8,075,000 Class N at 'B+'
- $12,825,000 Class O at 'B–'.

Deal summary

Nomura CRE CDO 2007–2 (Nomura 2007–2) is a revolving commercial real estate (CRE) cashflow CDO that closed on 27 March 2007. It was incorporated to issue $950m of floating-rate notes and preferred shares. At 24 December 2007 and based on Fitch categorizations, the CDO was substantially invested as follows: commercial mortgage whole loans and A-notes (81.3%); B-notes (9.4%); commercial real estate mezzanine loans (1.1%); CMBS (5.0%); and CMBS rake bonds (0.8%). The CDO was permitted to invest up to 5.0% in CDOs.

The portfolio is selected and monitored by Nomura Credit & Capital, Inc. (NCCI). Nomura 2007–2 has a six-year reinvestment period during which, if all reinvestment criteria are satisfied, principal proceeds may be used to invest in substitute collateral. The reinvestment period ends in March 2013.

Asset manager

NCCI is wholly owned by Nomura America Mortgage Finance (NAMF), a newly formed subsidiary of Nomura Holding America, Inc. (NHA). NAMF was formed in October 2006 to expand NHA's commercial mortgage origination and acquisition operations and establish an asset management platform.

Within NCCI is the Commercial Real Estate Finance (CREF) group, which was established in 2001. CREF is responsible for the majority of collateral management functions, including origination, underwriting and CDO administration for its commercial real estate CDO platform.

Nomura CRE CDO 2007–2 is the first CDO managed by the CREF group, which is responsible for originating and allocating collateral appropriate to the CDO. The CDO serves as a financing vehicle for the CREF group and is held off balance sheet.

NCCI has engaged Centerline Servicing as the primary and special servicer for the CDO. Additionally, Centerline purchased a substantial amount of the below-investment-grade notes and approximately 65% of the equity. Centerline and NCCI work together to manage borrower requests and work out distressed assets.

For more details, see Fitch's CDO asset manager review (www.fitch ratings.com).

Performance summary

Nomura CRE CDO 2007–2 became effective on 24 December 2007. Since it closed in March 2007, the as-is poolwide expected loss (PEL) has increased to 24.500% from 21.125%. The CDO has below-average reinvestment flexibility with 5.750% of cushion based on its PEL covenant of 30.250%.

The portfolio's increased PEL is primarily attributed to an increase in the concentration of higher leveraged assets, including junior debt positions. Generally, these asset types carry higher-than-average expected losses.

The portfolio's weighted average spread (WAS) has decreased to 2.22% from 2.31% since close. The weighted average coupon (WAC) has increased to 6.14% from 5.76% over the same period. Additionally, the over-collateralization (O/C) and interest coverage (IC) ratios of all classes have remained above their covenants, as of the 31 December 2007 trustee report.

Collateral summary

As of the effective date, the pool consists of 94.9% commercial real estate loans, 5.0% CMBS, 0.8% CMBS rake bonds, and 2.4% uninvested proceeds. At close, the CDO was 83.4% ramped, and the asset manager has since invested the majority of its available capital. Based on the fully ramped balance, exposure to whole loans and A notes increased to 81.3% from 79.7% at close. The CDO is also more concentrated in subordinate loan positions. Exposure to B notes increased to 9.4% from 2.3%, and mezzanine debt increased to 1.1% from 0.5% at close. Investment in CMBS rake bonds remained the same at 0.8% of the portfolio. The CDO now invests in two CMBS positions from the same obligor, representing 5.0% of the portfolio. The weighted-average Fitch-derived rating for the two rated securities is 'BBB/BBB−'.

Since Fitch's last review in 2007, seven assets representing six obligors ($195.1m) have been added to the pool, including five commercial real estate loans, and two CMBS. In general, the loans added to the portfolio carry higher expected losses compared with those that were paid off, based on Fitch's modelling of the transaction. The weighted average expected loss of loans added to the portfolio is 33.8%, while the expected loss of the repaid loan is 16.4%. As noted above, the added assets include highly leveraged assets. The weighted average Fitch loan-to-value (LTV) for the added assets is 134% and weighted average Fitch debt service coverage ratio (DSCR) is 0.82 times (×). The credit quality of the loans remaining in the pool since close remained relatively flat.

The portfolio is invested in traditional property types. The CDO does not contain any exposure to land, condominium conversion, or construction loan assets. Office properties remain the largest concentration at 37.6%, increasing from 23.6% at close. Property type concentrations are based on Fitch categorizations, which may differ from the trustee report. As of the

December 2007 trustee report, the CDO is within all its property type covenants. The CDO is also within all of its geographic covenants, with the highest concentration in California at 41.8%.

The pool has below-average loan diversity relative to other CRE CDOs. Fitch's Loan Diversity Index (LDI) increased to 596 from 556 at close, reflecting slightly less pool diversity. The LDI covenant is 625. The two largest loans represent 23.9% of the portfolio, and the five largest loans represent 43.3% of the portfolio.

Rating definitions

The ratings of the class A, B, and C notes address the likelihood that investors will receive full and timely payments of interest, as per the governing documents, as well as the aggregate outstanding amount of principal by the stated maturity date. The ratings of the class D through O notes address the likelihood that investors will receive ultimate interest and capitalized interest payments, as per the governing documents, as well as the aggregate outstanding amount of principal by the stated maturity date.

Upgrades during the reinvestment period are unlikely given that the pool could still migrate to the PEL covenant. The Fitch PEL is a measure of the hypothetical loss inherent in the pool at the 'AA' stress environment before taking into account the structural features of the CDO liabilities. Fitch PEL encompasses all loan, property and poolwide characteristics modelled by Fitch.

Synthetic CDOs

Since their appearance in 1997, synthetic collateral debt obligations[1] have become very popular and have been the most fertile area for growth and innovation in structured credit markets. They have contributed to – as well as benefited from – explosive growth in the use of credit default swaps (CDS). From their initial application as a means of risk transfer from bank balance sheets to manage regulatory capital requirements, they now encompass every facet of credit risk covering a wide range of assets from corporate bonds and loans to structured finance obligations and CDO tranches themselves.

Given that the bulk of CDO issuance takes place in private transactions, the amount of public data is limited.

WHAT ARE SYNTHETIC CDOs?

Synthetic CDOs are the result of an innovative combination of two technologies – the securitization techniques applied to transfer credit risk by cash CDOs and credit derivatives, which enable the isolation of credit risk from other components of risk. Effectively, synthetic CDOs are CDOs using CDs. Within that broad description, there is a wide variation in the underlying credit-risky assets, whether or not they are managed, and the extent of associated funded issuance and the motivation behind the risk transfer, each of which defines a type of synthetic CDO.

To build an understanding of how synthetic CDOs work, it is worth revisiting the mechanics of a credit default swap (Figure 9.1). Recall from Chapters 1 and 2 that a CDS is akin to an insurance policy that protects the buyer of protection against the loss of principal in an underlying asset when a credit event occurs. The protection buyer pays a premium, typically each quarter, to the protection seller until a credit event occurs or the contract matures, whichever is earlier. The underlying asset is defined by a reference obligation, which informs the scope of the protection. When a credit event occurs, depending upon the settlement mechanism specified in the CDS contract, the buyer of protection delivers a reference obligation of the seller to the seller and receives par in return (physical delivery) or receives the difference between the par amount of the reference obligation and its recovery from the seller (cash settlement). Standard credit events include bankruptcy, failure to pay and restructuring of the debt.

How a typical CDS works

Figure 9.1

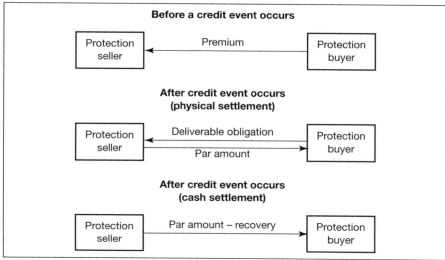

Before a credit event occurs

Protection seller ← Premium — Protection buyer

**After credit event occurs
(physical settlement)**

Protection seller ← Deliverable obligation / Par amount → Protection buyer

**After credit event occurs
(cash settlement)**

Protection seller — Par amount – recovery → Protection buyer

Source: Credit Hedge Ltd

The special purpose vehicle (SPV) sells protection on the collateral pool of assets to the sponsoring financial institution or other market participants and receives a premium for the risk being assumed. The credit risk so acquired is distributed to investors of different tranches who receive a por-tion of the premium depending on the amount of credit risk assumed by each tranche. When a credit event occurs with respect to any asset in the collateral pool, the SPV pays the protection buyer an amount linked to the loss incurred on the asset. The loss is then passed on to investors in reverse order of seniority (i.e. the most junior tranche bears the first loss). Often, some of these tranches are funded, analogous to credit-linked notes, with the difference being that the risk and return are linked to a portfolio of assets as opposed to a single asset. The proceeds of the funded note issuance are invested in low-risk 'eligible collateral'. (Eligible collateral mainly con-sists of investments in cash or government bonds or guaranteed investment contracts issued by highly rated insurance companies.) There is more on funded and unfunded CDOs later in this chapter.

Thus, in any synthetic CDO, investors act as the sellers of protection on a pool of underlying assets, the sponsoring financial institution or the market participants are the buyers of protection and the SPV is the international vehicle that effectively distributes the cashflows involved. As such, syn-thetic CDOs are the derivative counterparts of cash CDOs.

Figures 9.2 and 9.3 show how a typical CDO works. The SPV sells pro-tection on the collateral pool of assets to the sponsoring financial institution or other market participants and receives a premium for the risk assumed.

Figure 9.2

How a typical CDO works

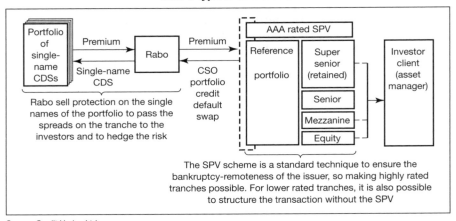

The SPV scheme is a standard technique to ensure the bankruptcy-remoteness of the issuer, so making highly rated tranches possible. For lower rated tranches, it is also possible to structure the transaction without the SPV

Source: Credit Hedge Ltd

Figure 9.3

Example of a typical CDO

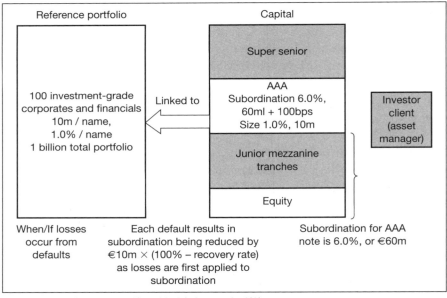

Notes rated single AAA are protected from eight defaults, assuming 30% recovery rate

Loss rate analysis for a tranche rated AAA: (assuming 30% recovery rate)

Table 9.1

No. of defaults	Loss amount (million)	Loss %	Outstanding subordination notional (million)	Outstanding subordination (%)	Outstanding tranche notional (million)	Outstanding tranche (%)
0	0	0.0	60	6.0	10	100
1	7	0.7	53	5.3	10	100
2	14	1.40	46	4.6	10	100
3	21	2.10	39	3.9	10	100
4	28	2.80	32	3.2	10	100
5	35	3.50	25	2.5	10	100
6	42	4.20	18	1.8	10	100
7	49	4.90	11	1.1	10	100
8	56	5.60	4	0.4	10	100
9	63	6.30	0	0	7	70
10	70	7.00	0	0	0	0

Source: ISDA

Table 9.1 shows a simple loss analysis for a tranche rated AAA, assuming a 30 per cent recovery rate. One can see the erosion of the subordination 'cushion' or the outstanding subordination, if the numbers of defaults increase.

Figure 9.4 identifies the main reasons for investing in synthetic CDOs.

Investor reasons for using a synthetic CDO

Figure 9.4

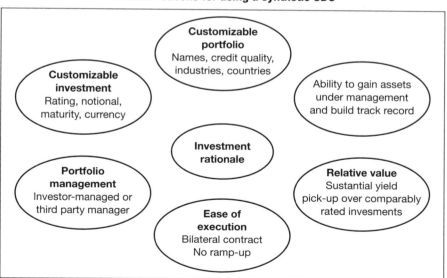

Table 9.2 demonstrates the main areas in synthetic CDOs and the types of investors prone to invest in them. Looking at the financial logic, it's worth going back to the early days of the market (1997–1999), when nearly all synthetic CDOs were motivated by balance sheet considerations.

Table 9.2	Synthetic CDOs and investors		

Client	Typical tranche	Investment logic
Banks, insurance	Mezzanine	Yield pick-up for investment grade rating
Real money accounts	Mezzanine, equity	Yield pick-up, management fees, assets under management
Leveraged trading accounts	Equity, mezzanine	Relative value arbitrage, correlation trading
Re-insurers	(Mezzanine) Super-senior	Insurance-type tail risk for low premium

However, arbitrage deals have been growing rapidly and now account for the majority of the market activity. Also, in the early days of the market, deals included a complete set of tranches (equity, mezzanine, senior) whose notional amounts summed to the notional amount of the reference portfolio. Now, most synthetic CDO activity consists of single-tranche CDOs, where only one tranche of the CDO's capital structure is sold.

Synthetic CDO tranches can be either funded or unfunded. If a tranche is funded, the CDO investor pays the notional amount of the tranche at the beginning of the deal and any defaults cause a writedown of principal.

Throughout the deal, the investor receives Libor plus a spread that reflects the riskiness of the tranche. The investor's funds are put into a collateral account and invested in low-risk securities (government or debt rated AAA). Unfunded tranches are similar to swaps. No money changes hands at the beginning of the deal.

The investor receives a spread and pays when defaults in the reference portfolio affect the investor's tranche (after any subordinate tranches have been eaten away by previous defaults).

Because unfunded tranches rely on the investor's future ability and willingness to pay into the CDO, they create counterparty credit risk that must be managed.

How do CDOs make economic sense when they merely rearrange the payment priority of other credit-risk-sensitive instruments such as credit default swaps, bonds and loans? First, regulatory on credit risk can at times exceed the economic capital the market requires to bear the risk. Banks cite reducing regulatory capital as a motive for their participation in credit derivatives markets, more so in the early days of the market than today.

Second, CDOs help investors overcome market imperfections associated with the illiquidity of bonds and loans. Few corporate bonds trade more than twice a day. Loans trade even less frequently. Illiquidity makes it costly for credit investors to assemble a portfolio that meets their diversification and risk-return targets.

Managing portfolio credit risk is a dominant motive for commercial banks' participation in credit derivative markets.

The economic value of a CDO is apparent in the fact that the CDO's spread income from the reference portfolio can compensate investors in the CDO tranches and also cover transaction costs.

The rapid adoption of CDO technology by credit investors suggests that the cost of creating a CDO is less than the cost a credit investor would incur to assemble a portfolio of bonds and/or loans to meet the investor's diversification and risk-return targets.

Table 9.3 compares some relative values that an investor will consider when using synthetic CDOs. The high cost of investing directly in a portfolio of bonds or loans is presumably driven by the high bid–ask spreads an investor would pay, reflecting the illiquidity of such markets.

Relative value investor rationale

Table 9.3

Rating	Static single-tranche CSO	Cash CDO	Corporate bond
AAA	120	60	15
AA	175	110	25
A	250	195	40
BBB	400	325	75
B	800	800	300

Source: Credit Hedge Ltd

EXAMPLE OF A FULLY UNFUNDED SYNTHETIC CDO

A fully unfunded deal can be on a balance sheet or source its reference assets externally. Because it is unfunded, the liabilities of the deal structure are comprised purely of credit default swaps, meaning it can also be structured with or without an SPV. This example shows a hypothetical deal structure with the following terms:

■ originator: banking institution.

■ reference portfolio: €900m notional, 80–100 corporate names sourced in the market.

- CDS tranching: super-senior CDS €815m notional:
  - 'Class A' CDS €35m notional.
  - 'Class B' CDS €15m notional.
  - 'Class C' CDS €20 million notional.
  - 'Class D' or equity CDS €15 million notional.

Key point

No SPV

The main feature of this structure is that it can be arranged by the originating institution directly: there is no need to set up an SPV. In fact, this is also an on-balance-sheet deal. The rating of the tranches is based on the loss allocation, with credit events among the references being set up so that the junior note suffers losses first. This follows traditional structured finance technology.

However, unlike traditional structures, interest payments on the liability side are not subject to a waterfall, but are guaranteed to investors. This increases the attraction of the deal for investors. Thus, on occurrence of a credit event, interest payments are still received by an investor. It is the notional amount, on which interest is calculated, that is reduced, thereby reducing the interest received. Losses of notional value above the Class D threshold eat into the Class C swap notional amount.

This is a version of an arbitrage deal, with the originating bank taking the role of a funded manager. It displays the following features.

The bank selects the initial portfolio of credits in the market, which are referenced via CDs. The bank sells protection on these assets; the premium received exceeds the premium paid out on the liability side, creating an arbitrage gain for the bank. The reduced premium payable on the liability side reflects the tranches' arrangement of the liabilities.

The reference assets are sourced by the bank on its own balance sheet, before the CDO itself is closed in the market.

The bank has the freedom to manage the portfolio dynamically during the life of the deal, taking a view on credits in line with its fundamental analysis of the market. Trading profits are trapped in a 'reserve account', which is also available to cover trading losses and losses suffered from credit events.

As part of the rating requirements for the deal, the originating bank will follow certain eligibility constraints on which exposure it can take on. Restrictions may include:

- Reference entities being rated investment grade by the rating agencies.
- No single reference credit may exceed a total exposure of more than €10m.

- The reference entity being incorporated in a specific list of countries.
- Specific geographical and industrial concentration.
- A trading turn over limit of 20 per cent of notional value per anum.
- A Moody's diversity score of at least 45 on closing and no lower than 42 during the life of the deal.

In addition to the 'guaranteed' nature of interest payments of investors (subject to leave of credit events), the main advantage of this structure is that it may be brought to the market.

There is no requirement for the originator to set up an SPV, and no need to issue and settle notes. The originator can therefore take advantage of market conditions and respond to investor demands for return enhancement and diversification fairly quickly.

EXAMPLE OF AN AAA REFERENCE PORTFOLIO CDO

This illustration is of a hypothetical managed collateral synthetic obligation (CSO) that generates value from low-risk reference assets. During an economic downturn with widening spreads, higher yields on AAA-rated securities enable synthetic CDOs to be structured with the backing of a pool of AAA-rated collateral. Thus, a very low-risk CDO vehicle can be created, providing investors with favourable risk/reward profiles. In this structure, investors are exposed to ratings downgrade risk rather than default risk, because it is extremely unlikely that an AAA-rated entity will experience default during the life of the deal.

This transaction features:

- A reference portfolio comprised solely of AAA credits. This can be a mixture of conventional bullet bonds, ABS and MBS securities and CDSs.
- A liability note has tranches so that the junior note is rated BBB, but its effective risk is lower than this rating suggests – a favourable risk/reward profile to create for an investor.
- A return on a note that is rated BBB (and hence paying BBB note interest spread over Libor) but which is, in effect, rated AAA given the nature of the collateral backing.
- All notes paying a fixed spread over Libor.

The proceeds of the notes issues are held in a reserve account that is authorized to invest in 'eligible investments'. These are typically a cash account (or guaranteed investment contract (GIC) account), Treasury bills and Treasury securities or other AAA-rated sovereign bonds. This reserve account is used to pay for any losses incurred by the reference portfolio; surplus reserves benefit the originating bank.

Risk/reward profile

The risk/reward profile of the issued notes is made possible because the reference assets are all rated AAA. Investors in the deal are being exposed to the spread risk rather than default risk (because an asset rated AAA can be downgraded). Nevertheless, BBB note holders are able to earn an attractive return at what is, for practical purposes, a risk exposure considerably lower than risk rated BBB.

CASE STUDIES OF MANAGED SYNTHETIC CDOs OR CSOs

The most common manifestation of synthetic securitization is the managed synthetic CDO, known as a CSO. Typically, in Europe these have been originated by fund managers, with the first examples being issued in 2001.

Although they are effectively investment vehicles, the discipline required to manage what is termed a 'structured credit product' is not necessarily identical to that required for a corporate bond fund. Investment banks' arrangers are apt to suggest that a track record in credit derivatives trading is an essential pre-requisite to being a successful CSO manager.

There is an element of reputational risk at stake if a CDO suffers a downgrade; e.g. in 2007 Moody's downgraded elements of 83 CDO deals, across 174 tranches, as underlying pools of subprime assets experienced defaults and fell in value during the subprime credit crunch. So, managing a CDO presents a high-profile record of a fund manager's performance. Managing your way out of a crisis such as the subprime crisis is as important as managing well in normal conditions.

In Europe, fund managers that have originated managed synthetic deals include Robecco, Cheyne Capital Management, BAREP Asset Management and Axa Investment Managers.

Certain deals can be considered as milestones in the development of synthetic CDOs.

BISTRO – the first synthetic securitization

The Broad Index Secured Trust Offering (BISTRO) from JPMorgan is a deal that exemplifies innovative structures and a creative combination of securitization technology and credit derivatives. It shows how a portfolio manager can use vehicles of this kind to exploit credit trading expertise as well as provide attractive returns to investors.

Managed synthetic CDOs also present fund managers with a vehicle to build on their credit derivatives experience because the market in synthetic credit, in Europe at least, is frequently more liquid than the cash market for the same reference names.

BISTRO is viewed as the first synthetic securitization. It is a JPMorgan vehicle brought to market in December 1997. The transaction was designed to remove the credit risk on a portfolio of corporate credits held on JPMorgan's books, with no effect on funding or balance sheet. The overall portfolio was $9.7b, with $700m notes being issued in two tranches by the BISTRO SPV.

The proceeds of the notes issued were used as collateral for the CDS entered between JPMorgan and the vehicle. This is a five-year swap written on the whole portfolio, with JPMorgan as the protection buyer. BISTRO, the protection seller, pays for the coupons on the issued notes from funds received from the collateral pool and the premiums of the CDS. Payments on occurrence of credit events are paid out from the collateral pool.

Under this structure, JPMorgan has transferred the credit risk on $700m of its portfolio to investors, and retained the risk on a first-loss piece and the residual piece. The first-loss piece is not a note issue, but a $32m reserve cash account, held for the five-year life of the deal. First losses are funded out of this cash reserve which is held by JP Morgan. This is shown in Figure 9.5.

JPMorgan trade

Figure 9.5

The asset pool is static for the life of the deal. The attraction of the deal for investors included a higher return on the notes compared with bonds of the same credit ratings and a bullet maturity structure, compared with the amortizing arrangement of other asset-backed security (ABS) classes. The bullet maturity means there is no pre-payment of the principal, as is the case with ABS classes.

The BISTRO deal featured:

- the credit exposure of a pool of assets being transferred without moving the assets themselves from the balance sheet;
- a resultant reduction of the credit exposure for the originator;
- no funding element for the originator – i.e. a securitization deal that separates the liquidity feature from the risk transfer;
- the application of structured finance rating technology; and
- unfunded liabilities that were still tranched, as in traditional cashflow securitization, so that these liabilities could be rated.

Investors in the deal, who are in fact taking on the credit risk of the assets on the originator's balance sheet, were attracted to the deal because:

- The deal provides exposure to particular credits and a certain credit risk/return profile, but without a requirement for this exposure to be funded.

- The deal economies are aimed at a precise transfer of specifically packaged segments of risk, with the investor realizing greater value.

- The equity holder gains from a leveraged exposure, which means the cost of this exposure is lowered.

The originating bank retained a comparative advantage on the funding while the investor gained the required exposure to the credit risk. The investor effectively provided the comparative advantage because it is not subject to regulatory capital requirements. In short, the deal benefits both bank and investor. The investor – in this instance, typically a fund manager or insurance company – is an expert in the market, so can price the risk very efficiently. It also benefits from the cheap(er) funding that the bank is able to source.

SINGLE-TRANCHE CDOs (STCDOs)

In a typical STCDO transaction, there are three decision steps for potential investors:

- Select a portfolio of credits to which they want exposure.

- Choose a subordination level (attachment point) and a tranche size corresponding to their risk/return preference or yield target.

- Dynamically manage their position and substitute credits in the collateral portfolio throughout the life of a STCDO.

Selection of reference portfolio

The first step in structuring an STCDO transaction is the investors' selection of the credits in the underlying reference portfolio according to their preferences. For example, investors can choose a portfolio of credits different from their current positions, and by selling the protection on those names they achieve more diversification of their overall credit exposure. They can also sell protection on the subset of names in their current portfolios in case they want to overweight certain credit sectors. Alternatively, investors can designate the whole or a part of their portfolios as the reference pool, and by buying protection they hedge themselves against spread widening of individual defaults.

A common option is that investors choose as a reference portfolio the CDX/iTraxx default index, which is based on a diversified set of liquid names in the credit default market. The main reason for that choice is the liquidity and diversification of the index. The standard tranches on the CDX/iTraxx indices also trade as liquid instruments in the broker/dealer market.

Single-tranche CDO investment strategies

A single-tranche CDO uses credit defaults swaps in its portfolio of assets and issues only one tranche tailored for a single investor instead of issuing the entire capital structure to a variety of investors. The single tranche is in the form of a credit default swap. It may also be offered in note format by creating a credit-linked note referenced to the tranche swap (Figure 9.6).

Single-tranche CDO cash flows

Figure 9.6

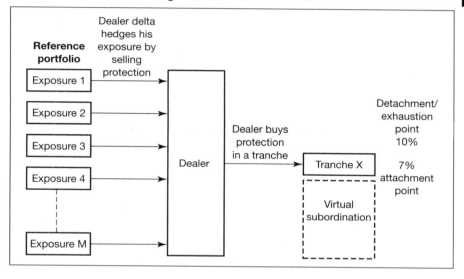

Bespoke single tranches are almost always settled in cash. When there is a default in the portfolio, the calculation agent (usually the protection buyer) calculates the recovery rate for the credit and determines the loss as a percentage of the portfolio. However, the protection seller only needs to make a payment once losses exceed the 'attachment point'. Once losses increase to reach the detachment point, the protection seller's investment is wiped out and the protection buyer no longer enjoys any protection on the portfolio.

For example, an insurance company might invest in a €20m 5–6 per cent tranche of a portfolio of ninety equal-weighted investment-grade credits with a dealer as the buyer of protection. The dealer pays a premium of 50bp a year to the insurance company, and the first few defaults in the portfolio do not affect the investment. After the tenth default (based on 50 per cent recovery rates for the various defaults), losses in the portfolio will hit the 5 per cent tranche attachment point.

If, for example, the eleventh default brings losses in the portfolio to 5.4 per cent, the insurance company's investment will be written down to €12m and the 50bp protection payments will made on the reduced €12m notional.

Most single tranches are rated – though, unlike cashflow CDOs, the rating is usually given by only one rating agency – and the deal in this example could expect to be rated at double A or triple A, depending on the composition of the portfolio. This high rating implies that it is unlikely for the deal to suffer any loss.

Investment strategies

Several investment strategies exploit single-tranche CDOs:

- Leverage strategies: enhancing yield through leverage provided by tranching.
- Market view strategies: expressing a long or short view on the market using the appropriate tranches.
- Correlation strategies: expressing a view on implied correlation (equivalently, expressing a view on tranche technicals).
- Relative value strategies: taking a view on the relative cheapness of old versus new CDX tranches, five-year versus ten-year CDX tranche spreads, and so on.
- Micro/macro hedging strategies: hedging individual default (micro) risk and/or market-spread (macro) risk.

Leverage strategies

Single-tranche CDOs that are referenced on CDX index products allow investors to separate their views on credit fundamentals (defaults) from their views on market and liquidity risk (spreads) and allow investors to take directional investment decision positions on defaults and spreads separately. Single-tranche trades are structured to be superior in terms of carry, leverage and convexity to outright long or short market positions on the CDX index or a portfolio of individual names (Table 9.4).

Table 9.4		Leverage strategies using single-tranche CDOs	
Strategy	Sample trade	Motivation	Investors
Long position (sell protection) in mezzanine or senior tranche of CDX IG or customized portfolio.	Investors sell protection on $10m Sep 12, 7–10% CDX IG tranche	Investors who look for a buy-and-hold investment can obtain enhanced yield through leverage and express a bullish view	Portfolio manager, CDO investors
	Tranche spread (mid): 207.5 CDX IG spread (mid): 184.5bp Date: 12 April 2007		

- **Short position in senior tranche**. Investors who are bearish on overall market spread movements driven by global factors can take a short position (buy protection) in the senior CDX tranche. For example, buying protection on the 7–10 per cent CDX IG tranche because this tranche requires a lower premium for protection per unit of spread risk than junior tranches or an outright short with the CDX IG index. This position offers leverage and positive convexity relative to a short on the CDX IG index, and provides a low carry protection against the spread back-up.

- **Long position in equity tranche**. Investors who are bearish on the credit quality of a portfolio of names or about default rates in the market as a whole can go long (sell protection) the 0–3 per cent tranche. This trade offers bullish investors a leveraged and positive convex position with a high carry. Of course, this trade is exposed to defaults and to spread widening. Depending on their fundamental views, investors can hedge certain individual credits in the reference portfolio by buying default protection on those names and reducing the idiosyncratic risk of the trade. After partially hedging against defaults, investors should still be left with a significant positive carry on the trade.

- **Carry or delta-neutral combination of short senior tranche and long equity tranche**. Investors who are bearish on the possibility of spread sell-off and bullish on credit quality can combine a long position in the equity tranche with a short position in the senior tranche to pay for the negative carry. This carry-neutral trade captures the effect of positive convexity for senior and junior tranches and generates gains in the case of larger spread moves. A short senior and long equity tranche positive can also be combined into a delta-neutral trade. Compared with directional trades, this delta-neutral combination generates lower, but still positive, gains in spread sell-off and spread rally scenarios.

These are summarized in Table 9.5.

Market view strategies with single-tranche CDOs Table 9.5

Strategy	Sample trade	Motivation	Investors
Short position (buy protection) in senior 7–10% CDX IG tranche	Investor buys protection on $10m Sep 2012 7–10% CDX IG tranche. Tranche spread (mid): 207.5bp CDX IG spread (mid): 184.5bp Date: 12 Apr 2007	Investor who wants to protect against spread back-up can execute this leveraged, low-carry, positively convex position	Portfolio managers, bearish investors who worry about a reversal in the corporate spread rally

Strategy	Sample trade	Motivation	Investors
Long position (sell protection) in equity 0–3% CDX IG tranche	Investor sells protection on $10 million Sep 09 0–3% CDX IG tranche Tranche spread (mid): 89bp upfront + 500bp running CDX IG spread (mid): 184.5bp Date: 12 Apr 2007	Investors who are bullish about default rates and want to enter into a leveraged, high-carry position	Credit-savvy hedge funds.
Carry- or delta-neutral combination of short position (buy protection) in 7–10% CDX IG tranche and long position (sell protection) in 0–3% CDX IG tranche	Delta-neutral trade: Investor buys protection on $28.2m Sep 2012 7–10% IG CDX tranche Investor sells protection on $10m Sep 12 0–3% CDX IG tranche 7–10% tranche spread (mid): 207.5bp 0–3% tranche spread (mid): 89bp upfront + 500bp running CDX IG spread (mid): 184.5bp Date: 12 Apr 2007	Investors who are bearish on spreads and bullish on credit quality can structure carry-neutral or delta-neutral position and maintain positive convexity	Hedge funds and investors express view on global macro risk

Correlation strategies

Using a single-tranche synthetic CDO, investors can express their views on the implied correlation of tranches because tranches can have an opposite reaction to changes in correlation. Investors can choose the tranche subordination and size according to their views on correlation. Note that the implied correlation is primarily a market-based factor, driven by the demand and supply of protection for each individual tranche. In most cases, correlation traders delta-hedge their positions against the spread risk. Name-specific spread risk (micro spread risk) can be delta-hedged with the single-name credit default swaps, and market-spread risk (macro-spread risk) can be hedged by the appropriate position in the CDX index. In addition, correlation traders can also hedge a portion of the default risk with a set of selected single-name credit default swaps. Therefore, these trades allow correlation traders to take a view on market demand and supply for STCDOs without taking on credit risk. See Table 9.6.

Single-tranche CDOs: correlation strategies (price levels historical)

Table 9.6

Strategy	Sample trade	Motivation	Investors
Long correlation trade: short position (buy protection) in senior tranche or long position (sell protection) in equity tranche. Delta-hedge with single single-name CDS or CDX IG index	Investor buys protection on $10m Sep 2012 7–10% CDX IG tranche Investor sells protection on $47.3m Sep 2012 CDX IG Tranche spread (mid): 215bp IG CDX spread (mid): 109bp Date: 12 Apr 2007	Investors who want to have long correlation exposure and expect implied correlation to increase. Positive carry	Correlation traders (hedge funds, bank proprietary desks and broker/dealers) with a positive view on implied correlation
Short correlation trade: long position (sell protection) in senior tranche	Investor sells protection on $10m Sep 2012 7–10% CDX IG tranche Investor buys protection on $47.3 million Sep 2012 IG CDX IG index Tranche spread (mid): 215bp IG CDX spread (mid): 109bp Date: 12 Apr 2007	Investors who want to have short correlation exposure and expect implied correlation to decrease	Correlation traders (hedge funds, bank proprietary desks and broker/dealers) with a negative view on implied correlation
Correlation-insensitive trade: long (sell protection) or short (buy protection) position in junior mezzanine tranche	Investor sells or buys protection on $10m Sep 2012 3–7% CDX IG tranche Tranche spread (mid): 295bp CDX IG spread (mid): 54.5bp Date 12 April 2007	Investors who are uncertain about correlation levels and don't want to take correlation risk, but want to invest in single-tranche CDOs to get leverage or take a directional market view position	Investors who don't want to take exposure to changes in correlation

Short position in senior tranche or long position in equity tranche (long correlation)

Investors who prefer to be long correlation can set up such a position by going short the senior tranche (buying protection) or going long the equity tranche (selling protection). A rise in senior tranche implied correlation would imply that increased demand for protection was pushing senior tranche spreads wider and, all else being equal, making the trade profitable. A rise in equity tranche implied correlation would imply that increased supply of protection was pushing equity tranche spreads tighter and, all else being equal, making the trade profitable.

Long or short position in junior mezzanine tranche (correlation insensitive)

If investors are uncertain about default correlation levels and do not wish to take correlation risk, they can invest (sell protection) in the tranche on the capital structure that is correlation insensitive. Typically, this tranche would be the junior mezzanine (second-loss tranche), but the exact attachment point and size depend on the characteristics of the collateral pool. Proactive investors can achieve a similar correlation-neutral position by investing in a more junior and a more senior tranche below and above the correlation inflection point. These two tranches have opposite sensitivities to the correlation, and the investors can earn a higher spread with this position than investing in the correlation-insensitive mezzanine tranche alone. Although at origination the specific tranche can be correlation-insensitive, with time the correlation sensitivity will change.

Relative value strategies

Relative value strategies of single-tranche CDOs are summarized in Table 9.6.

Long/short position in on-the-run CDX IG tranches v. short/long position in matching off-the-run CDX IG tranches

The rolls of the indices provide a set of relative value trade opportunities in the single-tranche market. With the two-sided market in on-the-run and off-the-run CDX IG tranches, investors can compare matching tranches referenced to similar underlying portfolios. Investors can focus on the implied correlation of new and old CDX IG single tranches and look for relative value opportunities at the same leveraged level in the capital structure.

Long/short position in 5-year CDX IG tranches v. short/long position in 10-year CDX IG tranches

Expecting that liquidity in the market for ten-year IG CDX tranches will improve, investors should be able to execute relative-value trade strategies based on the comparison between the five- and ten-year IG CDX tranches referenced to the same portfolio. Implied correlation skew surface should be an indicative cheap/rich measure for individual tranches.

Long/short position 3–100% CDX IG tranche with short/long position in CDX IG index v. short/long position in 0–3% CDXIG tranche

Investors can combine a 3–100 per cent CDX IG tranche and delta-hedge it with the IG CDX index to replicate synthetically the equity 0–3 per cent tranche of the CDX IG index. Comparing the obtained spread premium with the market spread for the traded equity 0–3 per cent equity tranche of the CDX IG index allows investors to enter into a relative value trade or execute the directional view by using a cheaper way to access the equity part of the CDX IG capital structure.

Micro/macro hedging strategies

Micro/macro hedging strategies of single-tranche CDOs are summarized in Table 9.7.

Single-tranche CDOs: relative value strategies — **Table 9.7**

Strategy	Sample trade	Motivation	Investors
Short position (buy protection) in equity tranche on a customized portfolio of names	Investor buys protection on 0–3% tranche of a customized portfolio Investor sells protection to the same counterparty on individual CDS names (exchange the deltas)	Cheaper way to hedge against default risk than buying protection on each individual name	Portfolio managers and bank loan portfolios
Short position (buy protection) in equity tranche on a customized portfolio of names and long protection (sell protection) in CDX IG tranche	Investor buys protection on 0–3% tranche of a customized portfolio Investor sells protection on Sep 2012 7–10% CDX IG tranche	Portfolio managers with a positive view on macro risk can compensate the cost of hedging by going long CDX IG tranche	Portfolio managers or buy-and-hold investors who are not subject to mark-to-market accounting treatment

Strategy	Sample trade	Motivation	Investors
Short position (buy protection) in senior CDX IG tranche	Investor buys protection on $10 million Sep 2012 7–10% IG CDX tranche	Investors who already hedged the most risky names against default and want to hedge against market-wide spread widening. This strategy is more efficient hedged than a short CDX IG position	Portfolio managers or buy-and-hold investors with strong fundamental approach to portfolio selection
	Tranche spread (mid): 215bp		
	IG CDX spread (mid):109bp		
	Date: 12 April 2007		
Long position (sell protection) in senior IG CDX tranche	Investor sells protection on $10m Sep 2012 7–10% IG tranche	Portfolio managers who have bought default protection in single-name CDS market and want to protect their hedging portfolio against mark-to-market risk	Bank loan portfolio managers
	Tranche spread (mid): 215bp		
	IG CDX spread (mid): 109bp		
	Date: 12 Apr 2007		

Short position in equity tranche

A short position (buying protection) in an equity tranche on a customized portfolio of names is an efficient way to hedge against default risk. Investors select names from their portfolio that, in their view, have high risk of default and the protection on the first-loss tranche of their portfolio. Usually, investors sell protection to the same counterparty on individual CDS names ('exchange the delta'). Buying protection on the equity tranche of a customized portfolio is a cheaper way to hedge against default than buying protection on each individual name. In addition, investors who are comfortable with a certain number of defaults being unhedged can buy protection on the second-loss tranche. The higher attachment point of the tranche can substantially lower the cost of carry.

Short position in equity tranche and long position in mezzanine tranche

Hedging against default using individual credit default swaps or a short position in the equity tranche can be an expensive strategy. Investors who are less sensitive to market-spread widening or who have a positive view on the general macro risk factors but worry about defaults in their portfolio can compensate for their hedging cost by going long a senior tranche on the CDX IG index. The premium received on their senior tranche protection should lower the cost of protection on the equity tranche.

Short position in senior tranche

Certain investors are searching to protect themselves against general market-spread widening in their portfolios, especially if they have already hedged the most risky names against default or they trust in their selection of credits based on their fundamental view. For such investors, hedging with the CDX IG index is not the most efficient solution, because the outright market short does not separate default and spread risk protection. A more efficient hedging strategy is to put on a short position (buy protection) in the senior tranche that has the highest Credit01-to-carry ratio. The 7–10 per cent CDX IG tranche may provide investors with the most suitable hedge, after taking into account the liquidity component of traded CDX IG tranches.

See Chapter 10 for tranche sensitivities, but CDO risk measures are defined as:

- Credit spread sensitivity is equivalent to delta.
- Credit spread convexity is equivalent to gamma.
- Default sensitivity can equate to omega.
- Correlation sensitivity can be termed as rho.
- Time-decay sensitivity is equivalent to theta.

Long positions in mezzanine or senior tranche

A long position in mezzanine and senior CDX IG tranches is a leveraged position on market-wide spread movements. If investors, such as bank loan portfolio managers, have bought protection in the single-name CDS market against defaults in their portfolios, this hedging portfolio is exposed to mark-to-market risk driven primarily by macro factors. If investors want to protect against mark-to-market risk in their hedging portfolios, then a long position in the mezzanine or senior CDX IG tranche can provide the solution. Because the junior tranches take on relatively more default risk than the senior tranches, they are much less suitable for hedging purposes. In addition, a long position in the CDX IG index is a less efficient hedge against market-wide spread moves, because the index spread is affected as much by the systematic market risk as by the credit-specific events.

CSO TRADE OPPORTUNITIES

Figures 9.7 to 9.9 show some CSO trade opportunities initiated from a bank's perspective. More detailed trades are discussed later.

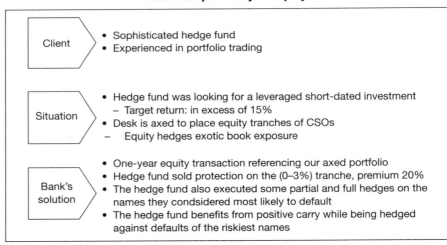

Figure 9.7

Managed CSO example

Client
- Large insurance company in France
- Small group of portfolio managers within the company transact

Situation
- Investment policy: matching assets with liabilities
- Over-exposed to BBB, but needs the yield
- Indifferent to liquidity and experienced in traditional securitization (MBS)

Bank's solution
- Single-tranche CSO with substitution rights – client wants portfolio management
- Meet client's yield target with highest possible rating
- Notes placed: €50m AA at 190bp, €50m AAA at 110bp

Figure 9.8

CSO example: one-year equity

Client
- Sophisticated hedge fund
- Experienced in portfolio trading

Situation
- Hedge fund was looking for a leveraged short-dated investment
  - Target return: in excess of 15%
- Desk is axed to place equity tranches of CSOs
  - Equity hedges exotic book exposure

Bank's solution
- One-year equity transaction referencing our axed portfolio
- Hedge fund sold protection on the (0–3%) tranche, premium 20%
- The hedge fund also executed some partial and full hedges on the names they condsidered most likely to default
- The hedge fund benefits from positive carry while being hedged against defaults of the riskiest names

A CSO has the following features from a bank dealer's perspective:
- Dealer buys/sells default protection on a specific tranche of the reference portfolio from or in the market.
- The dealer must use different hedging techniques from those used for traditional synthetic CDOs because the liabilities are not fully placed.

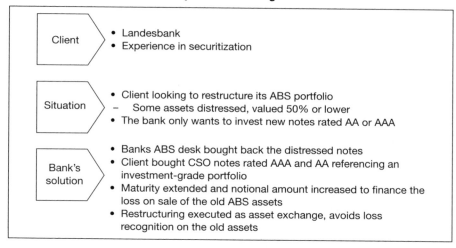

CSO example: restructuring resolution

Figure 9.9

Client
- Landesbank
- Experience in securitization

Situation
- Client looking to restructure its ABS portfolio
  - Some assets distressed, valued 50% or lower
- The bank only wants to invest new notes rated AA or AAA

Bank's solution
- Banks ABS desk bought back the distressed notes
- Client bought CSO notes rated AAA and AA referencing an investment-grade portfolio
- Maturity extended and notional amount increased to finance the loss on sale of the old ABS assets
- Restructuring executed as asset exchange, avoids loss recognition on the old assets

- Dealers hedge these products against movements in underlying risk factors. The simplest approach is to classify the risk factors into two main categories: macro and idiosyncratic.

- Macro risks are correlated changes that affect all names in the portfolio.

- Idiosyncratic risks are uncorrelated changes that affect only one name in the portfolio.

- Dealers view single-tranche CSOs as correlation products.

- Senior tranches are exposed to correlated macro movements.

- Junior tranches are exposed to idiosyncratic risk.

SYNTHETIC CDO STRUCTURES

Attachment and detachment points

It is important to understand the terminology of attachment and detachment points to follow the mechanics of synthetic CDOs. An attachment point, expressed as a percentage or an absolute value, defines the level of losses in the reference pool of assets that needs to occur before a particular tranche starts to experience losses. A detachment point, also expressed as a percentage or an absolute value, defines a level of losses in the reference pool of assets that needs to occur for a complete loss of principal for the tranche. The size of each tranche (width) is the difference between the attachment and detachment points for that tranche and defines the maximum loss that the tranche will experience.

Figure 9.10 illustrates a possible capital structure of a hypothetical synthetic CDO with high-yield, unsecured corporate risk exposure. The numbers in parentheses are tranche widths. The equity tranche has an attachment point of 0 per cent and detachment point of 10 per cent. The first 10 per cent of the credit losses from the underlying portfolio are absorbed by the equity tranche. Similarly, the super-senior tranche has an attachment point of 30 per cent and a detachment point of 100 per cent. All portfolio credit losses exceeding 30 per cent are borne by the super senior tranche. If the portfolio experiences losses equal to 15 per cent, the equity and the BB tranche would be wiped out and the BBB tranche would lose half of its notional.

| Figure 9.10 | Capital structure of a hypothetical synthetic CDO |

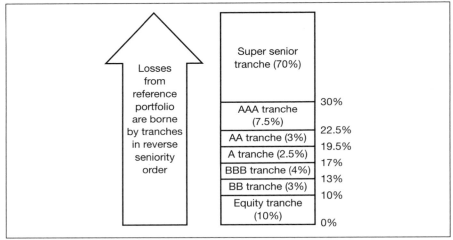

Source: Credit Hedge Ltd

Why synthetic CDOs?

It is no coincidence that the surge in investor interest in synthetic CDOs has coincided with exploding trading volumes in credit default swaps and standardized index tranches. The application of credit derivative technology has led investors with a wide range of interests to explore synthetic CDOs. This section outlines some of the motivations for synthetic CDOs over their cash counterparts.

Funding gap and the super senior tranches

The larger the funding gap, the higher the potential return to the equity tranches for a given level of leverage. Expressed differently, a higher funding gap would enable a transaction to be structured with lower leverage for a given level of target returns for the equity tranches. The larger funding gap of synthetic CDOs is primarily caused by the so-called unfunded super-senior tranches, which receive a lower spread than the spread paid to Aaa/AAA note tranches of cash CDOs. This lowers the average funding cost for the CDO (the weighted average spread paid to non-equity tranches). In essence, synthetic CDOs enable investors to capture risk premiums efficiently, resulting in a ratings arbitrage.

Increased flexibility and customization

Relative to cash CDOs, synthetic CDOs provide increased flexibility. Synthetic technology makes it possible to customize risk exposures, with respect to currency, cashflow, tenor and size of exposure. Since there is no need for the SPV to identify and acquire a specific asset, the maturity of the transaction is not constrained by the maturity of the pool of assets. With the increased liquidity of credit default swaps across different maturities, it is possible to customize synthetic CDOs to shorter maturities, an option typically not available with cash CDOs. It is possible to structure the CDO liabilities such that the tranche coupon payment dates exactly match the premium receipt dates on the underlying CDS transactions. There is always a significantly lower ramp-up period and therefore lower carry costs. The increased flexibility brings higher efficiencies and lower costs.

Range of permissible assets

Synthetic CDOs enable managers to gain exposure to a wide range of assets and strategies. For example, it is possible to structure CDOs to have long and short risk exposures, whereas cash CDOs are typically long only.

Efficiency of unfunded liabilities

Considering that there is not always a funded portion of a synthetic CDO, several sponsoring financial institutions find unfunded liabilities cheaper, easier and faster to execute.

Taxonomy of synthetic CDOS

The innate flexibility of synthetic structures implies a wide variety of synthetic CDO types depending upon the motivation, funding, underlying risk exposure, collateral management strategies and liability structures. This section illustrates some of the categories of synthetic CDOs and discusses the unique issues involved with each of them.

Balance sheet versus arbitrage

Obtaining economic and/or capital relief was the original motivation for development of synthetic CDOs. Transactions so motivated are balance-sheet synthetic CDOs in which a financial institution, typically a bank, uses a credit default swap to remove credit exposure to a portfolio of credit-risky assets from its balance sheet while retaining its ownership of the assets. This allows the sponsoring financial institution to maintain lending relationships with the entities issuing the credit-risky assets and at the same time achieve capital relief and efficient credit risk management. The portfolio underlying such a transaction is typically static with few substitution privileges.

In contrast, arbitrage synthetic CDOs, whose evolution followed that of the balance sheet genre, are designed to take advantage of the difference between the spread received from selling protection on individual reference assets/entities and the spread paid to investors on buying protection on a tranched basis. Unlike balance-sheet CDOs, the credit-risky assets are not on the sponsoring institution's balance sheet. As with several cash collateral bond obligations (CBOs), excess spread plays an important role in arbitrage synthetic CDOs, often used to offset losses or to hedge against future losses and in some cases returned to the investors of equity tranches.

Single-traunch CDOs are an increasingly popular type of arbitrage CDO. The prevalence of bespoke portfolios looking for an effective risk management vehicle is probably the motivation behind structures that allow the investor to customize the credit risk exposure to assume or lay off by picking the reference pool as well as the attachment and detachment points.

Static v. managed

The underlying portfolio in arbitrage synthetic CDOs can be static or managed. In a static portfolio, the reference pool of entities is fixed at deal inception. In a managed transaction, changes can be made to the reference portfolio by a designated collateral manager within a broad framework of trading guidelines and restrictions. The trading guidelines and restrictions are designed to ensure the collateral manager maintains the risk and returns of the portfolio according to a predetermined level of credit quality, diversification and risk management. There is a wide variation in the nature and scope of the trading guidelines. In some cases the guidelines permit the manager to have long and short risk buckets allowing for the acquisition as well as hedging of credit risk, subject to constraints.

In dealing with the trading guidelines, investors and rating agencies have to contend with a dilemma. In general, trading out of a deteriorating credit may be thought of as a prudent risk management measure. However, trading out of a deteriorating credit also implies having to make termination payments and incur losses because of trading. These transactions treat such losses as subordination erosion without replenishing the notional amount of the underlying portfolio. However, some transactions allow for the replenishment of notional traded out, which introduces the potential of adverse credit selection that misaligns the interest and debt tranches. Rating agencies impose maximum spread per reference credit limits to address the potential for such adverse selection, which is not unlike the limits in cash CDOs on the purchase of deeply discounted securities.

Another approach to this issue is through the excess spread mechanism. In many cases, the structure allows the excess spread to cushion the tranches from trading losses. Trading profits are used to supplement the excess spread. Trapping the excess spread until maturity or allowing the leaking out of the excess spread only as long as the deal is performing satisfactorily are some other mechanisms used to address adverse selection issues. In many cases, the trading ceases at some predefined point of the CDO life cycle or when trading losses reach a predefined level.

Rating agencies review trading guidelines by focusing on isolating trading losses so that losses to investors in rated tranches come from credit events or risk management of credit risk in the underlying portfolio and not because of discretionary trading. Typically, the portfolios in single tranche CDOs are static.

Funded v. unfunded

Unfunded portfolio credit default swaps are the most basic synthetic CDOs (Figure 9.11). The protection buyer enters into a CDS on a specific portfolio of reference entities with the SPV, which in turn obtains protection by entering into CDS on a tranched basis with the investors, the ultimate sellers of protection. The CDS with investor(s) in each tranche defines the attachment and detachment points and the credit events. As seller of protection, each tranche receives a fixed spread applied to the tranche size. As losses occur, the sellers of protection make loss payments to the SPV in the reverse order of seniority, passed on to the protection buyer.

The structure of the funded synthetic CDO is more complicated (Figure 9.12). In funded tranches, the CDO investors pays the notional amount of the tranche at the deal's inception and losses due to any credit events result in principal writedown. Throughout the life of the transaction, the investor receives Libor/Euribor plus a spread, which reflects the riskiness of the tranche. The amounts paid by the tranche investors (the proceeds of issuance) are invested in eligible collateral; typically, either GICs issued by highly rated issuance companies or highly rated short-term securities. The maturity dates of the GICs are set to match the maturity dates of the funded notes. Premium income from the CDS written by the SPV and interest on income received by investing the proceeds in eligible collateral form the source of income to the SPV. This is then used to pay interest to the funded note holders and premiums to the unfunded tranches.

Figure 9.11

Structure of a typical unfunded sythentic CDO

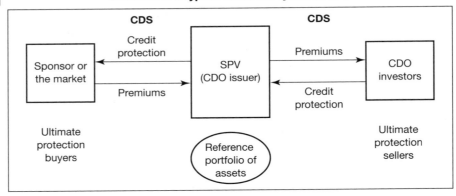

Figure 9.12

Structure of a typical funded synthetic CDO

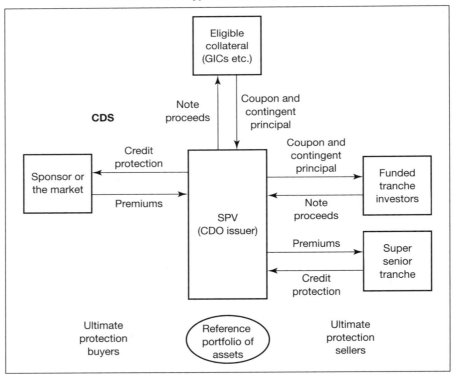

In practice, most funded synthetic CDOs are partially funded, in that only part of the CDO capital structure is represented by the funded tranches. Super-senior and equity tranches are typically unfunded.

Rating agency approaches to synthetic CDOs

While not all synthetic CDOs are necessarily rated, ratings are important benchmarks for assessing investments in CDO tranches. This section provides an overview of the methodologies used by the three major rating agencies, Fitch, Moody's and Standard & Poor's. In general, their approaches involve attributing default probabilities to each reference entity in the reference pool of assets and assumptions regarding the correlation of default probabilities and recovery rates. Correlation is usually formally incorporated into rating agency models. The three agencies have developed distinct methodologies for rating synthetic CDOs. For each agency, the basic framework for cash and synthetic CDOs is similar. However, certain stress factors and haircuts are applied to analysing synthetic CDOs to take the unique features of credit default swaps into consideration. It is important to point out that analytical models are only part of the rating agencies' analyses and each agency relies on other qualitative considerations such as deal documentation, legal assessment and evaluation of all parties involved to arrive at a rating for each tranche.

Moody's

A Moody's rating represents an opinion on the expected loss for each tranche, expressed as the difference between the present value of the expected payments and the promised payments. For a long time, Moody's used variations of the binomial expansion technique (BET), first developed in the context of cash CDOs, for rating synthetic CDOs. Then, Moody's introduced a Monte Carlo simulation model called CDO ROM for rating synthetic CDOs, marking a departure from the earlier approach.

The BET approach maps the reference portfolio of assets into a hypothetical portfolio of assets of N uncorrelated, homogeneous assets with identical default probabilities and equal par values for calculating expected loss distributions. The number N in the hypothetical portfolio is the 'diversity score', which is a measure of portfolio diversification (the higher the diversity score, the more diversified the reference portfolio). The formula for calculating the diversity score incorporates obligor and industry concentrations in the reference portfolio as well as default correlations across industry. The model calculates expected losses stemming from defaults in the hypothetical portfolio, going from no defaults to N defaults and assigning a probability to each default scenario. Calculating probability-weighted losses for each CDO tranche results in the expected loss for that tranche, which is then mapped into a specific rating.

Moody's refined the BET approach by the use of the multiple binomial variation for rating synthetic CDOs, which divides the reference pool of assets into sub-pools and models default behaviour of each sub-pool with its own binomial analysis. CDS ROM uses Monte Carlo simulation techniques to model the default behaviour of the assets in the reference portfolio and explicitly incorporates both intra- and inter-industry correlation. The model also simulates correlated recoveries to take into account systematic variation in recoveries.

Moody's addresses the soft credit events by applying a stress factor to the default probabilities used to model transactions. A stress factor of 12.5 per cent is applied to transactions using the 1999 ISDA definitions and includes the restructuring credit event without any supplements. A stress factor of 5 per cent is used for transactions that use the 2003 ISDA definitions or if all the supplements are applied to the 1999 definitions (see Chapter 4).

Recovery rate haircuts are applied to take consideration of the cheapest-to-delivery option embedded in the settlement of credit default swaps upon a credit event. Moody's applies a haircut of 5 per cent and 10 per cent, respectively, for investment-grade and below-investment-grade assets, if there is no restructuring, or modified restructuring, with restructuring maturity limitations. A stress factor of 12.5 per cent is applied for transactions using the 1999 ISDA definitions and includes the restructuring credit event without any other documentation supplements in the final documentation terms.

Standard & Poor's (S&P)

The S&P approach is based on the CDO Evaluator. Introduced in 2001, it was the first rating agency to apply Monte Carlo simulation methods to CDOs. The S&P approach is different from the Moody's approach in that the rating addresses the first dollar loss for a given rating category as opposed to mapping expected losses into a specific rating category. The simulation takes into account individual asset default probabilities based on its rating and pair-wise correlation between the assets in the reference portfolio. The model draws a large number of multivariate normally distributed numbers, which are then compared with a default threshold based on the asset's default probability and maturity to decide whether an asset defaults. The model produces a correlation-adjusted probability distribution of potential, aggregated default rates for the collateral pool of assets. As such, it may be seen as an estimate of the distribution of aggregate defaults and losses at different levels.

Correlations in the Evaluator model are based on historically observed defaults, with asset correlation calibrated to default correlation. S&P classifies corporate industries at local, regional and global levels and gives an additional credit for geographically diverse portfolios. While explicitly incorporating intra-industry correlation, the S&P model currently treats inter-industry correlation as being zero.

To account for the unique features of CDs, S&P applies haircuts to the base-case recovery assumptions used in the CDO Evaluator. A haircut of 5 per cent is applied to the base-case recovery assumption to address the cheapest-to-deliver option. Likewise, a haircut of 2.5 per cent each is applied to account for the specified currency feature, if consent required loans are deliverable and the period between the credit event notification date and value date is deemed too short (S&P prefers transactions to have the longest possible valuation period, with 45 days as the minimum). A haircut of 10 per cent is applied when a transaction allows for the so-called old restructuring as a credit event (1999 ISDA definitions without any supplements). A 21 per cent haircut is applied in transactions where the deliverable obligation is denominated in a currency other than the floating payment currency. All the haircuts discussed are mutually exclusive.

Fitch

Fitch's ratings are based on its Monte Carlo simulation platform Vector, which was introduced in 2003. Like S&P, the Fitch approach also addresses the probability of a first dollar loss. The model determines CDO portfolio default distributions on the basis of Monte Carlo simulations using individual asset default rates and asset correlations as the key inputs. The default rates are derived from a matrix that provides default rates by rating and maturity based on historically realized defaults. Pair-wise correlations are based on estimates of intra- and inter-industry as well as geographical correlations of equity returns. The underlying statistical model for estimating correlations is a factor model that expresses the return of the equity security of a firm as a function of statistically determined factor and company-specific idiosyncratic risk. Using this approach, average factor loading and average idiosyncratic risk exposure are computed for each industry-geographic region grouping and used to derive asset correlations.

ANALYTICAL CHALLENGES IN MODELLING SYNTHETIC CDOS

While synthetic CDOs are significantly simpler than their cash counterparts in terms of valuation because of a simpler waterfall, cashflow diversion rules and optional redemption potential, they still pose analytical challenges. While this is true both under a risk-neutral valuation framework as well as objective or historical probabilities, the challenge is best understood juxtaposed against the neutral value framework.

The application of Gaussian copular models for analysing correlation defaults in standardized credit index tranches has become an industry benchmark in much the same way as the Black–Scholes model has been for equity option pricing (for details, see Chapter 6).

Key point	**Specialized cases**

In fact, standardized credit index tranches can be thought of as specialized cases of synthetic CDOs. The differences stem mainly from two sources. First, the underlying portfolios can be managed or static asset pools with a CDS index and, second, there is an additional layer of counterparty credit risk with synthetic CDOs.

Portfolios that allow trading pose analytical challenges for valuation and risk management of synthetic CDOs. With a static portfolio knowledge of the credit portfolio of reference entities in the underlying portfolio, the default correlation between each credit, the CDO capital structure and the cashflow waterfall structure of the transaction are sufficient to make a reasonable determination of the credit risk and return for a given tranche. With managed portfolios, since the underlying reference entities may be changing, the portfolio is more complicated.

How does an analyst determine the credit quality of reference portfolios or calibrate appropriate correlation levels when the construction of the portfolio is unknown?

One approach is always to assume the manager will trade at the limits of the trading constraints. For example, if there is a maximum spread constraint, assume that the manager will always trade at that spread level. While some may consider this a prudent approach, it may not adequately reflect the risks and returns faced by an investor in a given tranche; also, it has the effect of treating all managers with the same brush stroke. In a similar way, correlation can be implied from observed prices of standard index tranches. Estimating the same non-standard synthetic CDO tranches with managed underlying portfolios imposes an additional layer of constraints.

There are two layers of counterparty credit risk with synthetic CDOs. The SPV enters into a CDS with the sponsoring financial institution or the market in general and purchases credit protection from investors in funded and unfunded tranches. This introduces credit risk in transactions outside the credit risk contained within the reference portfolio assets to the CDS counterparties. With funded tranches, there is also credit risk associated with the eligible collateral investments.

THE ABCs OF CDOs-SQUARED

A CDO-squared, sometimes denoted as CDO^2 or CDO2, is a type of collateralized debt obligation where the underlying portfolio includes tranches of other CDOs. CDOs-squared, particularly of the synthetic type, have become an important segment of the global CDO market.

Types of CDO-squared

A cash CDO-squared is a CDO backed by a collateral portfolio consisting of tranches of existing cash CDOs. On the other hand, a synthetic CDO-squared involves a portfolio of credit default swaps (CDS) and has a two-layer structure of credit risk. In most synthetic CDOs-squared, the underlying CDOs are created for the sole purpose of being included in the CDO-squared. Because of its synthetic nature, these underlying CDOs are simply conceptual and used to calculate cashflows and values of the CDO-squared. Therefore, a synthetic CDO-squared may be viewed as a complex derivative instrument, while its cash counterpart is simply a repackaging of existing CDOs.

More recently, hybrid deals have begun to appear in the market. In these deals, a small portion of the reference portfolio is synthetic CDOs and the rest is cash or synthetic assets, such as ABS, RMBS or CMBS. However, given the typical high credit quality of those structured finance assets, most of the risk in hybrid deals stems from the CDO-squared part.

Synthetic CDOs-squared first appeared in Europe and the market segment experienced great growth in the US in 2004. According to S&P, the number of US synthetic CDO-squared deals jumped from just one in 2003 to twenty-seven in the third quarter of 2004, with issuance volume of $2.6b. By volume, CDOs-squared accounted for about 20 per cent of all synthetic issuance and 4 per cent of all CDO issuance in the US in 2007.

Structure of a CDO-squared

A typical synthetic CDO-squared references a portfolio (sometimes called the 'master' or 'outer' CDO) consisting of other synthetic CDO tranches (sometimes called 'inner' CDOs). The underlying CDO tranches may have similar size and subordination, referencing similar portfolios.

A CDO-squared usually comes with subordination, in addition to the subordination in the underlying CDO tranches. In Figure 9.13, the lower shaded boxes represent the underlying CDO tranches, which collectively form the 'master' CDO portfolio. The dotted box is the CDO-squared tranche. Tranches at the 'inner' and 'master' CDO levels come with separate attachment points (AP) and detachment points (DP), which define tranche sizes and subordination. Also, the inner CDO portfolios often include some of the same reference credits. The degree of this 'overlap' is important in determining the risk profile of the CDO-squared.

| Figure 9.13 | Importance of default location to a CDO-squared |

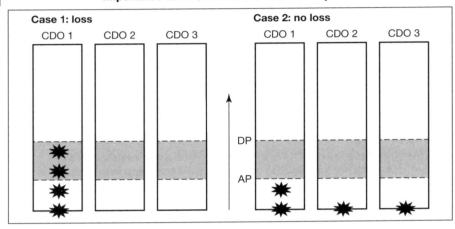

Rationale for CDOs-squared

There are two reasons for using the double-layer structure. One is the higher degree of diversity achieved by including underlying CDOs that already reference many corporate names. While a one-layer CDO typically references 50–100 corporate credits, a CDO-squared tends to include between five and ten such one-layer CDOs. Another benefit of a CDO-squared is relatively larger spreads available for investors. Given the double-layer structure, CDOs-squared are often perceived as having an added protection against losses, because tranches in underlying CDOs and the CDO-squared are protected by subordination at each level. However, higher spread levels achieved in the CDO-squared reflect the complexity and the unique characteristics of the instrument.

CDO-squared mechanics

In a CDO-squared, losses are filtered through the double layer of CDOs in the following manner:

(1) Reference credit defaults in the underlying ('inner') CDO portfolios.

(2) The corresponding inner CDO tranches suffer losses or lose part of their subordination, depending on the amount of losses.

(3) If one or more of the inner CDO tranches suffer losses in (2), the losses flow into the master CDO portfolio.

(4) The tranche of the master CDO suffers losses or loses part of its subordination, depending on the amount of losses in the master CDO portfolio.

As an illustration of the deal structure, consider a CDO-squared created from three underlying CDO tranches. Suppose each underlying CDO includes ten reference credits, equally weighted. For now, assume there are no overlaps, so the deal as a whole is exposed to thirty individual reference credits. Each underlying CDO tranche can withstand two defaults before getting hit with losses, but two additional defaults would wipe out the entire tranche.

Losses at the underlying CDO tranche level would flow into the master CDO portfolio, which in this example consists of the three underlying CDO tranches. In other words, the master CDO is exposed to credit risk of up to six defaults. Also, the CDO-squared tranche is typically protected by its own cushion of subordination. Assuming that the CDO-squared has its own subordination sufficient to absorb one default, the tranche suffers losses only if more than one default flows into the CDO-squared portfolio, *after* one or more of the underlying CDOs has suffered more than two defaults.

Level of losses

Key point

Interestingly, the amount of losses in a CDO-squared tranche depends on not only how many defaults occur but also *where* they occur (i.e. location of default in underlying CDOs). In the above example, four defaults that are *evenly spread across* the three underlying CDOs will *not* cause any losses to the underlying CDO tranches (see case 2 in Figure 9.13).

In such a case, one underlying CDO suffers two defaults and the other two suffer one default each, but losses do not reach any of the three tranches. In contrast, if all four of the defaults occur in just one CDO, it would wipe out that CDO tranche (Case 1 in Figure 9.13). Furthermore, two additional defaults that flow into the master CDO portfolio exhaust the subordination at the master CDO level, causing losses to the CDO-squared.

This scenario highlights one difference between a CDO-squared and a regular CDO. In a regular CDO, only the *number* of defaults in the underlying portfolio determines tranche losses. In a CDO-squared, however, we need to identify exactly *where* defaults occur before we can identify whether or not losses have reached the CDO-squared tranche. A CDO-squared is very sensitive to the *shape* of loss distributions of the underlying CDO tranches. The shape of loss distribution reveals the degree of 'tail risk', or the likelihood of extreme outcomes.

In a CDO-squared, credit risk in the underlying CDO tranches is already 'tranched' and another round of tranching is made at the master CDO level. Accordingly, the double-layer structure amplifies the sensitivity of a tranche to various parameters, such as default probability and subordination. An obvious question for an investor would be, then, whether to stay with a regular CDO that has a similar structure to the underlying CDOs discussed above, or pick a CDO-squared that comes with a complex structure but offers a larger spread.

Understanding tranche sensitivity 10

Having introduced the market standard correlation model in Chapter 7, we can now discuss how to calculate relative sensitivity measures based on this model, in the typical language of option 'Greeks' (see Table 10.1). The inclusion of tranches in portfolios has enabled investors to express credit views with very different risk and return profiles. For example, it is now possible to separate default risk from spread risk, and to take credit positions that become long when spreads are falling and short when spreads are rising. This precision, necessary for the implementation of such sophisticated strategies, emanates directly from the differences in sensitivities of tranches.

Table 10.1	Summary of Greeks	

Greek	What does it measure?
Delta (δ)	Tranche price sensitivity to changes in underlying portfolio spreads, measured as a ratio of tranche PV01 to index PV01 (PV10% is used also sometimes)
M – Gamma ($m - \gamma$)	Tranche price sensitivity of a delta-neutral position to parallel shifts in spreads of underlying names. It represents a form of convexity (M = Market)
I – Gamma ($I - \gamma$)	Tranche price sensitivity of a delta-neutral position to jump-to-default risk or changes in spread distribution of the underlying portfolios. It represents a form of convexity to moves in a single credit while all others remain constant (I = idiosyncratic risk)
Rho (ρ)	Change in tranche value due to changes in default correlation
Theta (θ)	Change in tranche value due to the passage of time

While the concepts come from the world of equity derivatives, where option sensitivity or 'Greeks' are well documented and understood, the Greeks for tranches of credit portfolios have a distinct flavour. Table 10.1 gives definitions of various Greeks for structured credit. This chapter explores how tranches can be viewed as options on defaults and then delves deeper into the Greeks. The approach taken is an intuitive one, as opposed to a mathematical one. Note that although the focus is on standardized tranches for simplicity, the discussion holds for similar synthetic CDO tranches.

TRANCHES AS OPTIONS ON DEFAULT

One way of thinking about tranches is to view them as options on default losses on the underlying portfolio/index. This perspective helps develop a feel for the sensitivity of tranches to various variables, such as time, spread changes and default exposure. Expected losses for an index can be easily estimated from its spread level, which serves as a benchmark for the tranches of the index.

For example, a spread level of 50bp on the investment-grade CDX five-year index implies losses of about 2.5 per cent for five years of the portfolio (ignoring discounting and lost premiums in case of defaults), in a risk-neutral sense.

2.5% (over 5 years) = 5 years × 50bp (per annum)

Therefore, the 0–3 per cent tranche is expected to lose some notional due to defaults and can be viewed as having a positive mark-to-market value: it is 'in-the-money'. By the same argument, more senior tranches are out-of-the-money.

Interestingly, as the index spread widens, expected losses increase and senior tranches could expect some notional loss, depending on the increase in spreads. Consequently, the subordination level that separates in-the-money and out-of-the-money tranches could change.

For example, assume that the index widens to 100bp, translating to roughly 5 per cent losses. Now the mezzanine tranche, 3–7 per cent, is also expected to lose some notional due to defaults. In other words, the tranche is now in-the-money. This implies that while the mezzanine tranche behaves more like senior tranches at low spread levels, it would act more like an equity tranche as spreads widen significantly.

Each index tranch has a different capital structure, implying that the subordination level that separates in-the-money and out-of-the-money tranches may be different.

For example, the 0–10 per cent and 10–15 per cent tranches in High-Yield CDX are in-the-money (i.e. the index level implies that defaults would penetrate these tranches), implying that they behave more like an equity tranche, while the next tranche, 15–25 per cent, behaves more like the investment-grade mezzanine tranche. Similarly, the mezzanine investment-grade 3–7 per cent five-year tranche is out-of-the-money, while it is in-the-money for the ten-year index, again implying markedly distinct sensitivities.

For the same reason, as time passes and spreads roll down the credit curve, tranches could move from in-the-money and their Greeks would also change. Again, the intuition about how in-the-money and out-of-the-money tranches behave makes the process of projecting changes in tranche sensitivity more approachable.

SENSITIVITY TO SPREAD CHANGES ('DELTA')

As the spread of the underlying index changes, the effect on different tranches varies. Overall, it is consistent with the index directionally, i.e. spreads widen; a short protection position in any of the tranches would lose money. Conversely, as spreads tighten, a short protection position would see a positive mark-to-market (Figure 10.1).

Key point

Estimating change

For spread movements, one can estimate the change using tranche delta, which is the ratio of change in the tranche value to change in the index for a given spread change.

While it is usually calculated as the ratio of PV01s, some participants also use PV10%. (PV01 is the change in the mark-to-market for a 1bp move in each of the underlying credits in the portfolio. PV10% is the change in mark-to-market for a 10 per cent increase.) Tranches with higher deltas would move more than tranches with lower deltas. Furthermore, tranches with deltas less than 1× would move less than the index, while tranches with deltas higher than 1× would move more than the index.

However, for bigger moves in spread, the delta-based calculation is only approximate because the influence of tranche convexity becomes more meaningful, which will be discussed later in this chapter.

Figure 10.1

Spread sensitivity

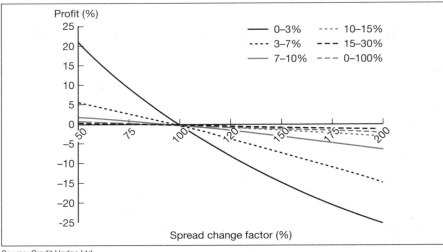

Source: Credit Hedge Ltd

Broadly speaking, junior tranches have higher deltas than senior tranches, assuming both are quoted on the basis of a running premium.

Given that junior tranches take losses before senior tranches, wider spreads make them proportionally more likely to be affected by the increased likelihood of defaults implied by wider spreads. In other words, the 'default PV' (PV of expected default losses) rises faster than the index for junior tranches, but slower than the index for senior tranches, bringing the average default PV for tranches in line with index default PV. Additionally, as expected losses rise, the likelihood of lost premiums due to lower notional outstanding (as a result of defaults) also rises, which accentuates the negative effect of rising spreads.

Impact of upfront payments

However, the presence of upfront payments for tranches lowers their deltas, compared with the same tranches without an upfront payment. Currently, the equity tranche for the investment-grade CDX index and the first two tranches for the higher-yield CDX index trade with upfront premiums (see Chapter 4).

Why does an upfront payment lower the delta of a tranche? The answer lies in understanding how rising spreads affect the present value of expected premiums (premium PV) and default PV. An upfront payment with no running coupon implies that as spreads widen, the tranche value is affected only by higher expected defaults and lower expected premiums, since the protection seller has already collected all of the premiums. On the other hand, an all-running contract will have both negative impacts – higher expected defaults and lower expected premiums due to more defaults making it more sensitive.

'I – GAMMA': SENSITIVITY TO SPREAD DISTRIBUTION CHANGES

While the effect of overall spread changes on tranches is more or less obvious, the effect of changes in distribution of the underlying spreads, especially when the overall portfolio averages remain unchanged, is subtle and worth exploring because such moves are more common than big swings in the indices.

Tight trading names moving wider generally affect senior tranches, while wide or even average credits moving significantly wider alter junior mezzanine and first-loss tranches, depending on the size of the move. A good example of this was the reshaping of the risk profile of the investment grade in October 2004 because of stress in the insurance sector, especially with Marsh & McLennan, the US broker.

Thus the shape of the risk distribution within the portfolio influences the pricing of tranches (see Figure 10.3). It should be fairly intuitive to recognize that the length and thickness of the right tail (distribution tail) influence the pricing of subordinate tranches, meaning that the bigger the tail, the riskier the equity and mezzanine tranches. Similarly, the shape of the middle to left side of the distribution should influence the more senior notes.

Figure 10.2   **Insurance moves to the right, affecting both senior and subordinate tranches**

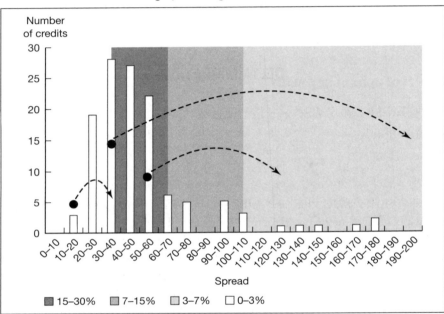

Figure 10.3   **Tranche pricing effect: two opposing examples**

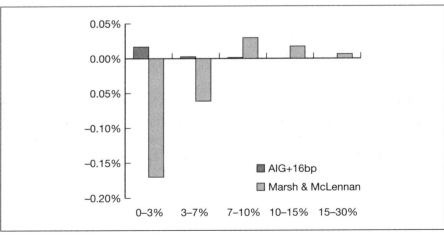

Source: Credit Hedge Ltd

As credit risk increases (shifts from left to right), senior tranches should become riskier.

Two credits in the insurance sector serve as useful examples. The move in the default swap premium for American Insurance Group (from 18bp to 34bp) increased risk in 15–30 per cent type tranches, while reducing risk in super-seniors (30–40 per cent). On the other hand, Marsh & McLennan (which widened from 30bp to above 250bp) was clearly a right tail event, shifting risk from 150–30 per cent type tranches to 0–3 per cent (hypothetically, since it was not a part of the index). Taking this analysis one step forward, the hypothetical pricing effects on tranches can be seen in Figure 10.3.

DELTA MIGRATION

Broadly speaking, tranche deltas are affected by:

- index spreads;
- passage of time;
- changes in correlation.

Consequently, trades that are delta-neutral at inception can easily become delta-positive or negative, depending on these factors.

Understanding these sensitivities can help fine-tune investment strategies to achieve a desired delta under different scenarios. For example, it is possible to construct trades that become delta-positive when spreads tighten and delta-negative when spreads widen, resulting in a more desirable payoff. Similarly, suppose an investor believes that spreads are too tight and will widen in the near future but start tightening down the road, say next year. It is possible to implement a tranche combination that starts out delta-negative but becomes more delta-positive as time passes.

How does index level affect tranche deltas? Figure 10.4 shows how deltas change with spread movements.

Way of thinking   **Key point**

The intuitive way to think about delta sensitivity to spread changes is that the deltas for in-the-money tranches decrease with spread increases, while deltas for out-of-the-money tranches increase with spread increases.

Figure 10.4

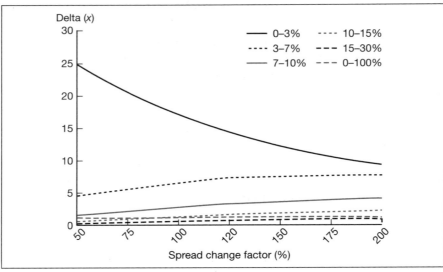

Source: Credit Hedge Ltd

Additionally, one has to bear in mind that the more senior tranches start becoming in-the-money after a certain level of spread increase. This point is easier to see in the delta sensitivity pattern for ten-year investment-grade CDX tranches, as shown in Figure 10.5. Another point worth noting is that beyond a certain level of spread widening, the equity tranche delta declines rapidly. This is because expected losses far exceed the tranche notional, and the influence of any increase in expected losses is marginal.

Figure 10.5

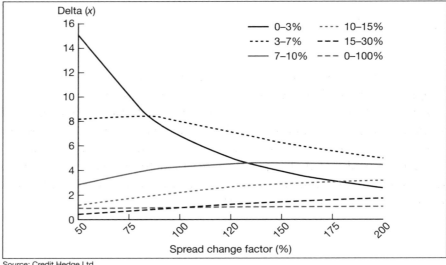

Source: Credit Hedge Ltd

How do tranche deltas change as time elapses? Figure 10.6 shows how tranche deltas migrate as the index approaches maturity. For simplification, it is assumed that the credit curves for the underlying portfolio and tranche base correlation remain unchanged. Once again, it is more intuitive to think of the results in terms of tranches being options on defaults.

Deltas for tranches that are in-the-money rise as time passes, while deltas for out-of-the-money tranches decline over time.

Furthermore, since it is assumed that spreads roll down the curve, senior tranches get more and more out-of-the money over time (assuming there are no defaults).

Another way to understand this delta migration pattern is to look at delta sensitivity to spread movements (Figure 10.4). As we roll down the curve index, spread declines result in rising delta for equity tranches and falling delta for more senior tranches.

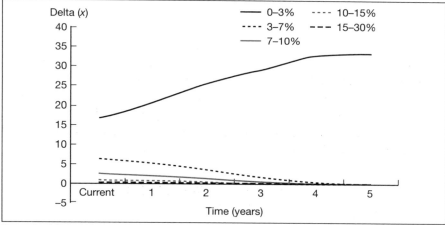

Delta sensitivity over time for 5-year IG CDX — Figure 10.6

Source: Credit Hedge Ltd

Now that the delta migration pattern over time is understood, it possible to design strategies with desired spread sensitivities over time.

For example, by combining delta-neutral notional amounts of equity and senior tranches, a bank can put together a trade that becomes delta-positive as spreads ride down the curve, resulting in a positive mark-to-market. Similarly, a bank can design positions with a delta mismatch initially, so that the position becomes delta-negative or positive for an expected spread move or passage of time (see Figure 10.7).

Figure 10.7	Delta migration over time

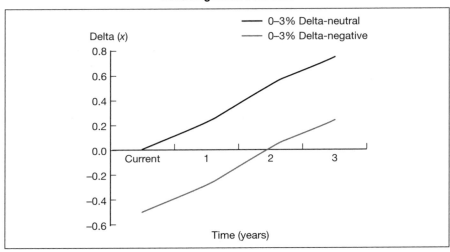

Source: Credit Hedge Ltd

'M – GAMMA': CONVEXITY

As discussed earlier, for wide spread moves, the relationship between tranche value and index value does not remain linear. The difference between linear approximation (using deltas) and the actual movement in market value is captured by a tranche's convexity or gamma.

Gamma is typically measured as a ratio of PV100 to $100 \times \text{PV01}$, i.e. the ratio of tranche mark-to-market for a 100bp move in underlying spreads to 100 times PV01 of the tranche.

The easiest way to observe the materiality of convexity is to plot the profit of a delta-neutral transaction of tranches, as done for the five-year DJ CDX tranches in Figure 10.8. As mentioned earlier, tranches that are in-the-money are positively convex, while out-of-the-money tranches are typically negatively convex (from the perspective of the protection seller).

In other words, a delta-neutral short protection position in a five-year IG equity tranche would have a positive mark-to-market for large changes in spreads, while a delta-neutral 7–10 per cent tranche of the same index would have negative mark-to-market.

Figure 10.9 shows the convexity characteristics of ten-year IG tranches, where both 0–3 per cent and 3–7 per cent tranches are convex. To illustrate this, Figure 10.10 shows the convexity attributes of the 3–7 per cent five-year and ten-year tranches.

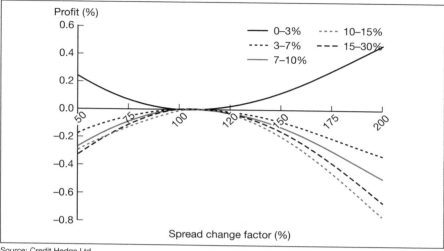

Five-year IG: tranche covexity (delta-neutral)

Source: Credit Hedge Ltd

Clearly, the 3–7 per cent tranche is negatively convex (and out-of-the-money, given current spread levels) for five-year DJ CDX, but is convex (and in-the-money) for ten-year maturity.

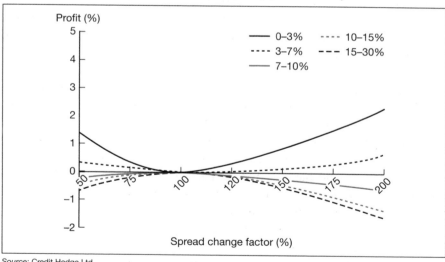

Ten-year IG: tranche convexity (delta-neutral)

Source: Credit Hedge Ltd

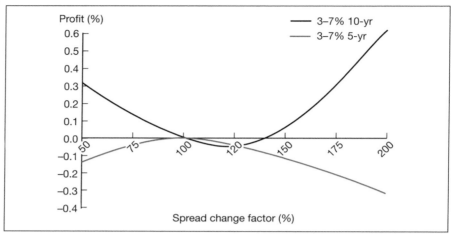

Source: Credit Hedge Ltd

While trading tranches of different underlying indices, for example ten-year tranches versus five-year tranches, convexity can be hard to measure, as the underlying indices are different and have convexity differences themselves.

In addition, curve shape changes are also important. For example, a steepening of the 5s–10s credit curve would affect ten-year tranches but not the five-year tranches.

JUMP-TO-DEFAULT SENSITIVITY

While higher default sensitivity for junior tranches and lower for senior tranches is intuitive, given their relative positions in the capital structure, comparing sensitivities across maturities and indices provides valuable insight into how defaults affect different tranches.

For example, one default shaves 14 per cent in value from a five-year investment-grade equity tranche, but only 7 per cent from a ten-year tranche and 2 per cent from a five-year, high-yield equity tranche.

Figure 10.11 summarizes the average effect of one default on various tranches, assuming a 40 per cent recovery for investment grade and a 35 per cent recovery for high-yield. Figure 10.12 shows the same impact on a delta-neutral basis, i.e. assuming that protection was bought on the index to offset the tranche's spread sensitivity.

Loss caused by default (% of notional)

Figure 10.11

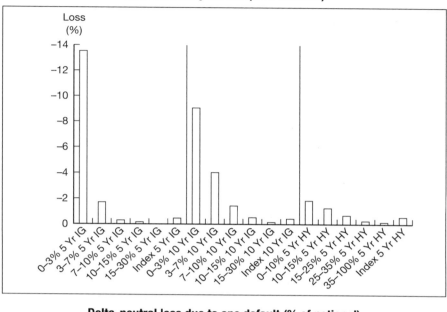

Delta-neutral loss due to one default (% of notional)

Figure 10.12

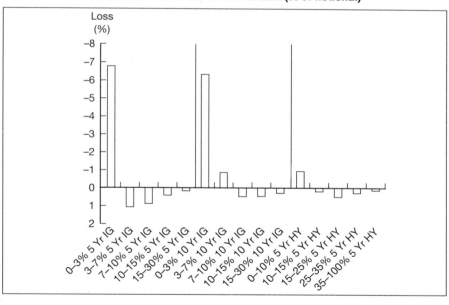

Tranche thickness, the expected number of defaults for the index and the presence of an upfront payment are important variables to watch for in assessing default sensitivity.

A thicker tranche, e.g. high-yield equity versus investment-grade equity, implies lower sensitivity to a default. Similarly, if the index is expected to have a large number of defaults, a single default has a smaller effect.

A tranche with upfront payment has lower default sensitivity, compared with the same tranche without such a payment, much like spread sensitivity.

Again, the reason for lower sensitivity is that, because of an upfront payment, the protection writer does not lose premium after a default, while in the absence of an upfront payment, the running premium would decline proportionally to the amount of tranche notional lost through defaults.

Of the three equity tranches mentioned, the five-year, high-yield equity tranche is the thickest, has the highest number of expected defaults (given that the high-yield index trades much wider), and has all of its premium paid upfront. As a result, it has significantly lower sensitivity to defaults compared with the investment-grade equity tranches.

How can it be determined if a tranche has more default risk or spread risk? Delta-neutral default sensitivity, as shown in Figure 10.12, helps define the subordination level in the capital structure where tranches change from being net default-sensitive to net spread-sensitive.

For example, the mezzanine tranche (3–7 per cent) of five-year investment grade is net spread-sensitive (i.e. the delta-neutral protection writer would have a positive mark-to-market in the case of a default), while the ten-year mezzanine tranche is net default-sensitive.

The distinction between net default and spread sensitivities of tranche can be used to construct trades that are more efficient in expressing a bank's credit views. For example, a combination of long equity and short mezzanine in a delta-neutral ratio effectively expresses a credit view that is constructive on default risk but not on spread levels.

'THETA': TIME DECAY

As a credit default swap approaches maturity, the spread is bound to converge to zero because credit protection provided by a CDS eventually becomes worthless if a default does not occur. Furthermore, the rate of decline in the value of protection is determined by the slope of the credit curve.

An upward-sloping credit curve implies that a larger number of defaults are expected to occur towards the end of the index maturity. For example, the early 2008 high-yield DJ CDX curve implied that about one-third of the total expected defaults in the next five years were projected to occur during the fifth year. Assuming no defaults occurred during the first year and spreads roll down the curve, essentially these defaults disappear, implying a substantial gain for the protection writer.

Key point	Effect of leverage

Since junior tranches are levered investments on defaults, their value (to protection buyers) declines much faster than the index.

Figure 10.13 shows the total returns of DJ CDX IG five-year tranches for different time horizons, from the perspective of the protection seller. The value of protection declines precipitously initially, assuming a static credit curve (i.e. spreads ride down the curve with the passage of time), and decelerates towards maturity. On an absolute basis, tranches with higher than 1 × delta lose value faster than the index, while senior tranches with lower than 1 × delta lose value slower than the index.

Time decay for 5-year IG

Figure 10.13

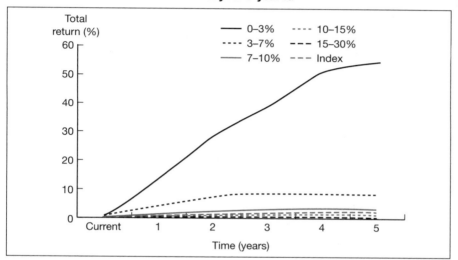

However, when a tranche's time decay relative to itself is analysed over time (i.e. how much of the total value is realized every year), it can be seen that equity tranche value decays slower than the index while all other tranches decay faster than the index, in the case of investment-grade five-year tranches.

More importantly, about half of the total return is realized within the first year for tranches other than the equity tranche (assuming static base correlation and credit curves). See Figure 10.14.

'RHO': SENSITIVITY TO CORRELATION CHANGES

As we discussed in earlier chapters, junior tranches are long correlation; senior tranches are short correlation; and mezzanine tranches are relatively insensitive.

In other words, higher correlation is better for junior tranches and worse for senior tranches (from the perspective of the protection sellers).

Figure 10.14

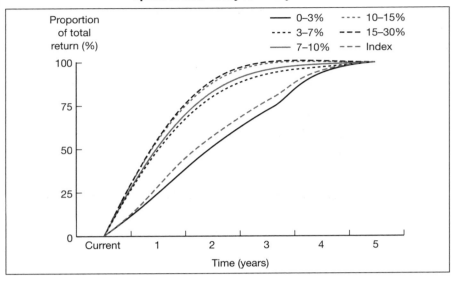

Speed of time decay for five-year IG

Since premium is the compensation for taking default risk, the par premium for an equity tranche decreases with rising correlation while it falls for senior tranches.

Figure 10.15 shows the sensitivity of five-year, investment-grade tranches to parallel shifts in the base correlation curve. For example, the +5% scenario assumes that the equity tranche's correlation increases 5 per cent and the base correlation skew curve remains unchanged. Thus for all tranches, the attachment and detachment point correlations change by the same amount.

Figure 10.15

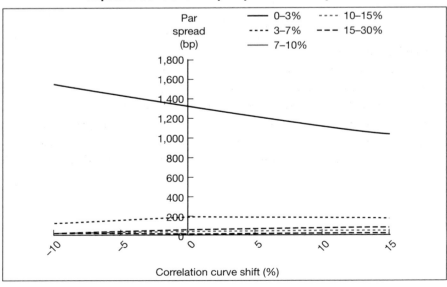

Impact of correlation on par spreads for five-year IG

Because base correlation considers all tranches as a portfolio of two equity tranches, as the skew (the difference between the implied correlation for attachment and detachment points) increases, the par decreases, just like the equity tranche.

It is important to note that correlation sensitivity of tranches changes as the underlying index spread moves. Figure 10.16 analyses the mark-to-market effect of a 1 per cent increase in correlation for five-year, investment-grade tranches at different spread levels. As shown, senior tranches are relatively insensitive to correlation for small changes in spread but become significantly more sensitive as the index widens.

Correlation sensitivity changes with changes in spreads for five-year IG   Figure 10.16

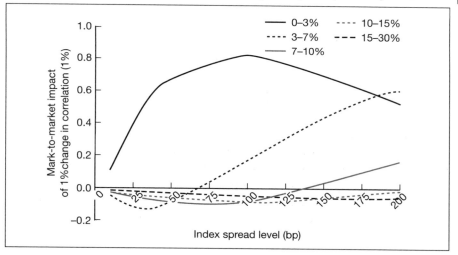

The converse is true for the equity tranche: it is rather sensitive to small changes in the index, but beyond a certain point of widening, correlation sensitivity declines.

To isolate correlation changes, it is assumed that the base correlation skew does not change. However, given a large number of ratings-based investors in very senior tranches, these tranches have a non-zero floor on price.

In other words, when spreads fall to very low levels, the pricing on very senior tranches is very resilient. Consequently, base correlation skew tends to rise as spreads fall to very low levels and to flatten as spreads increase.

CONCLUSION

This chapter has discussed tranche Greeks from a conceptual perspective. Thinking of tranches as options on defaults helps to develop intuition for the various sensitivities. Spread sensitivity (delta) declines higher up the capital structure; however, upfront payments tend to decrease this sensitivity. Furthermore, tranche deltas themselves are not constant, and change with changes in the index and over time. In-the-money tranches have favourable convexity for protection sellers, while convexity in out-of-the-money tranches favour buyers of protection. Time decay for tranches is very rapid in the first few years and decelerates materially as they approach maturity. Finally, subordinate tranches benefit from rising correlation, while senior tranches lose value. Mezzanine tranches are relatively insensitive.

11

Innovation, the credit crisis and the future

INNOVATION OUTSTRIPS RISK MANAGEMENT

Credit default swaps are becoming the most important instrument I've seen in decades.

Alan Greenspan

When credit default swaps appeared in the early 1990s, they were used primarily by banks to hedge the default risks they faced in their loan portfolios. But by the late 1990s the use of these swaps had spread to the larger credit market, and two Deutsche Bank researchers could write that 'credit derivatives are no longer an exotic corner of the bond market but must now be considered a market in its own right'.

In discussing the role of credit derivatives in the US, Alan Greenspan, then the chairman of the Federal Reserve Board, in a speech in September 2002 stated:

> More generally, such instruments appear to have effectively spread losses from defaults by Enron, Global Crossing, Railtrack and WordCom, and Swissair in recent months from financial institutions with largely short-term leverage to insurance firms, pension funds, or others with diffuse long-term liabilities or no liabilities at all. In particular, the still relatively small but rapid growing market in credit derivatives has to date functioned well, with payouts proceeding smoothly for the most part. Obviously, this market is still too new to have been tested in a widespread down-cycle for credit. But so far, so good.

That statement above was made in 2002. By 2008, credit derivative products had moved on from just flow CDS to more structured credit products such as synthetic CDOs, and credit derivatives were tested in a 'widespread down cycle'. Risk management and prudent regulation need to catch up.

> I believe it is fair to say that the creation of new, innovative financial products outstripped banks' risk-management capabilities.
>
> *Donald Kohn, Federal Reserve vice-chairman (April 2008)*

SUBPRIME MORTGAGE CRISIS OF 2007

The subprime mortgage financial crisis of 2007 was a sharp rise in home foreclosures that started in the US during the autumn of 2006 and became a global financial crisis within a year.

The crisis began with the bursting of the housing bubble in the US and high default rates on 'subprime', adjustable rate, and other mortgage loans made to higher-risk borrowers with lower income or a poor credit history. The share of subprime mortgages to total originations increased from 9 per cent in 1996 to 20 per cent in 2006. Furthermore, loan incentives including 'interest only' repayment terms and low initial teaser rates (which later reset to higher, floating rates) encouraged borrowers to take up mortgages believing they would be able to refinance at more favourable terms later. While US housing prices continued to increase in 1996–2006, refinancing was available. However, once housing prices started to drop moderately in 2006–07 in many parts of the US, refinancing became more difficult. Defaults and foreclosure activity increased sharply. By October 2007, 16 per cent of subprime loans with adjustable rate mortgages were 90 days delinquent or in foreclosure proceedings, roughly triple the rate of 2005. By January 2008, this number had increased to 21 per cent. During 2007, nearly 1.3 million US homes were subject to foreclosure activity, up 79 per cent on 2006. As of 22 December 2007, one estimate said subprime defaults would reach $200–$300bn.

The mortgage lenders that retained credit risk (the risk of payment default) were the first to be affected, as borrowers became unable or unwilling to make payments. Banks and other financial institutions reported losses of about $130bn by January 2008. Using a securitization, many mortgage lenders had passed the rights to the mortgage payments and related credit/default risk to third-party investors via mortgage-backed securities (MBS). Individual and institutional investors holding MBS faced significant losses, as the value of the underlying mortgage assets and payment streams declined and became difficult to predict.

In addition, certain legal entities designed to isolate this risk from the originating lenders, for example collateralized debt obligations (CDO) and structured investment vehicles (SIV), held substantial amounts of MBS. As the value of payments into these entities declined, their value also declined, forcing the urgent sale of MBS in some instances.

The widespread dispersion of credit risk and the unclear effect on large banks, MBS, CDOs, and SIVs led banks to reduce their loans to each other or make them at higher interest rates. Similarly, the ability of corporations to obtain funds through the issuance of commercial paper was restricted. This aspect of the crisis is consistent with a credit crunch. The liquidity concerns drove central banks around the world to provide funds to member banks to encourage the lending of funds to worthy borrowers and to reinvigorate the commercial paper markets.

The combination of credit risk and liquidity risk caused several big corporations and hedge funds to shut down or file for bankruptcy. Stock market declines among both depository and non-depository financial corporations were dramatic. Many hedge funds and other institutional investors holding MBS also incurred significant losses.

With interest rates on a large number of subprime mortgages due to rise during 2008, US legislators and the Treasury took action. A programme to limit or defer interest rate adjustments was implemented. In addition, lenders and borrowers facing defaults were encouraged to cooperate to enable borrowers to stay in their homes. Restrictions on lending practices were also considered. Many lenders stopped or sharply curtailed subprime lending.

The crisis held back economic growth because significant losses from subprime loans reduced the willingness of banks to loan funds to other financial institutions and to consumers. Such loans increase investment by businesses and consumer spending, which drive the economy. A separate but related element was the downturn in the housing market, where a surplus supply of homes resulted in a decline in construction and housing prices in many areas. This put further pressure on growth. The risks to the broader economy created by the financial market crisis and housing market downturn were primary factors in the 22 January 2008 decision by the US Federal reserve to cut interest rates and for Congress to implement an economic stimulus package. Both actions are designed to stimulate growth and inspire confidence in the financial markets.

Let us take a detailed look at the events leading up to the subprime crisis of 2007. I will then follow this up with an analysis of these events.

The unfolding of the subprime crisis of 2007

22 February 2007   HSBC fires the head of its US mortgage lending business as the bank is forced to set aside provisions of $10.5bn to cover non-performing loans

8 March 2007   DR Horton, the biggest US housebuilder, warns of huge losses from subprime fallout

12 March 2007   Shares in New Century Financial, one of the biggest subprime lenders in the US, are suspended amid fears it might be heading for bankruptcy

13 March 2007   Wall Street is hit by subprime fears

16 March 2007   US-based subprime firm Accredited Home Lenders Holding says it is selling $2.7bn of its subprime loan book at a heavy discount to generate cash for its business

2 April 2007   US home sales fall sharply

New Century Financial files for Chapter 11 bankruptcy protection after it is forced by its backers to repurchase bad loans worth billions of dollars. The company says it will have to cut 3,200 jobs, more than half of its workforce, as a result.

17 April 2007	US government-backed lenders Fannie Mae and Freddie Mac try to tackle the subprime crisis
3 May 2007	GMAC reports a loss of $305m in the first three months of the year because of charges taken at its housing finance unit
	Swiss bank UBS closes its US subprime lending arm, Dillon Read Capital Management, after losses in the first three months of the year amounting to $124m
21 May 2007	Business economists forecast US economic slowdown because of the crisis
22 June 2007	Investment bank Bear Stearns reveals it has spent $3.2bn bailing out two of its funds exposed to the subprime market. The rescue is the largest by a bank in almost a decade
29 June 2007	Bear Stearns fires its head of asset management and hires Jeffrey Lane, vice-chairman at Lehman Brothers, to find out what went wrong at its hedge funds
4 July 2007	The UK's Financial Services Authority (FSA) says it will take action against five brokers selling subprime mortgages, claiming they offered loans to people who should not have been given them
18 July 2007	Bear Stearns tells investors they will get little, if any, money back from the two hedge funds that the lender was forced to rescue
19 July 2007	US Federal Reserve chairman Ben Bernanke cuts growths forecasts for 2007 and 2008, blaming problems in the US housing market. His remarks shake the global stock markets
	JPMorgan Chase reports it is reserving $1.53bn to write off bad debts
20 July 2007	Bernanke warns that the crisis in the US subprime lending market could cost up to $100bn
24 July 2007	Rising defaults on subprime loans hit profits at Countrywide, the largest mortgage lender in the US
26 July 2007	Bear Stearns seizes assets from one of its problem-hit hedge funds as it tried to stem losses. Its stock falls 4.2 per cent in five sessions, its worst weekly decline in almost five years
27 July 2007	Worries about the crisis hammer global stock markets and the main US Dow Jones stock index slips
31 July 2007	Bear Stearns stops clients withdrawing cash from a third fund, saying it has been overwhelmed by redemption requests. The lender also files for bankruptcy protection for the two funds it had to rescue ▶

3 August 2007	Shares fall heavily on fears of subprime losses and the global credit crunch
9 August 2007	Short-term credit markets freeze up after French bank BNP Paribas suspends three investment funds worth €2bn, citing problems in the US subprime mortgage sector. BNP said it could not value the assets in the fund, because the market had disappeared. The European Central Bank pumps €95bn into the eurozone banking system to ease the subprime credit crunch. The US Federal Reserve and the Bank of Japan take similar steps
	NIBC announces losses of €137m from asset-backed securities in the first half of the year. The bank says 'severe instability in the US credit fixed income markets' had been a factor behind the fall
10 August 2007	Global stock markets are under intense pressure over subprime fears
	The ECB provides an extra €61bn of funds for banks. The US Federal Reserve says it would provide as much overnight money as would be needed to combat the credit crunch
13 August 2007	Wall Street investment bank Goldman Sachs says it will pump $3bn into a hedge fund hit by the credit crunch to help shore up its value
	The European Central Bank pumps €47.7bn into the money markets, its third cash injection in as many working days. Central banks in the US and Japan also top up their injections
15 August 2007	Shares in US largest mortgage lender Countrywide plunge on fears it will go bankrupt
16 August 2007	Countrywide draws on its entire $11.5bn credit line as the liquidity crisis looms
	Australian mortgage lender Rams admits to liquidity problems
17 August 2007	The US Federal Reserve cuts the interest rate at which it lends to banks (the discount rate) by half a percentage point to help banks deal with credit problems
	BNP Paribas says subprime losses in hedge funds will not affect quarterly profits
20 August 2007	Countrywide Financial, the biggest US mortgage firm, begins cutting staff as it tries to weather the credit crunch
	US mortgage lender Thornburg sells $20.5bn of assets and reduces its borrowings amid a tough market for home loans. The firm says this will enable it to meet its financing obligations and continue mortgage lending operations
	UK subprime lenders tighten up lending terms

21 August 2007	US home repossessions rise 93 per cent compared with a year earlier as subprime borrowers default
	US credit card and banking firm Capital One cuts 1,900 jobs and takes a $860m charge in closing a wholesale mortgage unit as the subprime crisis bites
23 August 2007	Shares slump after leading subprime lender Countrywide warns that the mortgage slump is getting worse. Countrywide gets a $2bn cash injection from Bank of America
	Leading US and European banks borrow $2bn from the Federal Reserve
28 August 2007	German regional bank Sachsen Landesbank is rapidly sold to Germany's biggest regional bank, Landesbank Baden-Wuerttemberg. It came close to collapsing under its exposure to subprime debt. It received a €17bn lifeline
30 August 2007	German chancellor Angela Merkel criticizes credit ratings agencies for not spotting problems in the market
31 August 2007	US president George W. Bush, flanked by Treasury secretary Hank Paulson and Federal Reserve chief Ben Bernanke, pledges to ease the subprime lending crisis
3 September 2007	German regional lender IKB records a $1bn loss as a result of exposure to the US subprime market
4 September	Bank of China reveals $9bn in subprime losses but the Chinese government says its foreign exchange reserves will not be affected
	Overnight bank lending dries up as banks fear defaults from each other
6 September 2007	ECB injects fresh cash into markets as credit fears intensify. Total intervention has now reached €250bn
11 September	ECB president Jean-Claude Trichet blames rating agencies for the subprime crisis but says the EU economy is sound
	US Treasury secretary Hank Paulson says mortgage lenders are to blame for the subprime crisis
13 September 2007	The BBC reveals that UK mortgage lender Northern Rock had asked for and been granted emergency financial support from the Bank of England, in the latter's role as lender of last resort
14 September 2007	Shares in Northern Rock plummet
15 September 2007	Thousands of depositors queue outside Northern Rock branches and try to get their money out ▶

18 September 2007 The US Federal Reserve cuts interest rates to 4.75 per cent from 5.25 per cent to try to energize financial markets

Savers return to Northern Rock after the government guarantees all savings

19 September 2007 The Bank of England makes a U-turn in its treatment of banks struggling to deal with the credit crunch and announces that it will inject £10bn into the money markets

20 September 2007 Deutsche Bank boss Josef Ackermann warns of losses from subprime exposure

Bank of England governor Mervyn King defends his role in Northern Rock crisis to House of Commons Treasury Select Committee

US Federal Reserve chairman Ben Bernanke says the losses from the subprime mortgage crisis are higher than expected

Goldman Sachs makes a profit by betting that mortgage-backed securities will fall despite $1.5bn exposure

1 October 2007 Swiss bank UBS reveals losses of $3.4bn in its fixed income and rates division, and in its mortgage-backed securities business, while Citigroup admits $3.1bn in losses

5 October 2007 Investment bank Merrill Lynch reveals $5.6bn subprime loss

14 October 2007 US banks holding secret talks at US Treasury float idea of a super-fund to revive the frozen credit markets

15 October 2007 Citigroup writes down additional $5.9bn on exposure to the US subprime market

Japanese bank Nomura announced the closure of its US mortgage-backed securities business and takes a $621m hit

16 October 2007 US Federal Reserve chairman warns that the subprime crisis and housing slump will be a significant drag on the US economy

Confidence among US home builders falls to record low

17 October 2007 More falls in US house building

IMF warns that credit crunch will hit world growth

30 October 2007 Merrill Lynch takes a $7.9bn hit following exposure to bad debt. Its chief executive, Stan O'Neal, resigns

31 October 2007 Federal Reserve cuts interest rates again to boost markets

Deutsche Bank reveals a €2.16bn writedown on bad debts

1 November 2007 Credit Suisse reveals a $1bn writedown on bad debts

5 November 2007 Banking giant Citigroup announces fresh losses of between $8bn and $11bn because of exposure to the US subprime market. Chief executive and chairman Charles Prince resigns

8 November 2007   Morgan Stanley unveils a $3.7bn loss from its US subprime mortgage exposure

BNP Paribas (after temporarily freezing hedge funds with $2.1bn in assets under management in August) reveals it has written down €301m because of credit problems, including $197m related to US subprime and home builder lending

9 November 2007   Fourth-largest US lender Wachovia reports a $1.1bn loss due to decline in value of its mortgage debt plus $600m to cover loan losses

12 November 2007   The three biggest US banks – Citigroup, Bank of America and JPMorgan Chase – agree a $75bn superfund to restore confidence to credit markets

13 November 2007   Bank of America writes off $3bn in subprime losses

14 November 2007   HSBC raises its subprime bad debt provision by $1.4bn to $3.4bn

Bank of England says the credit crunch caused by subprime lending will lead to a sharp slowdown in UK growth

Mizuho, Japan's second-largest bank, sees a 17 per cent drop in first-half net profits and cuts its full-year operating profit forecast by 13 per cent, largely as a result of subprime-related losses at its securities arm

15 November 2007   Barclays says it has written down £1.3bn in subprime losses

US House of Representatives passes the Predatory Lending and Mortgage Protection Act

16 November 2007   Goldman Sachs forecasts subprime losses for the financial sector at $400bn

The chief executive of Northern Rock, Adam Applegarth, resigns

19 November 2007   Swiss Re expects to lose $1bn on insurance a client took out against any fall in the value of its mortgage debt

20 November 2007   US mortgage guarantor Freddie Mac sets aside $1.2bn to cover bad loans and reports a $2bn loss

US Federal Reserve cuts its 2008 growth forecast citing credit and housing market woes

UK buy-to-let mortgage lender Paragon sees its shares fall nearly 40 per cent after revealing funding difficulties

Construction of US homes in October remains sharply lower than a year earlier

22 November 2007   UK lender Kensington Mortgages withdraws its subprime mortgages because of market conditions ▶

27 November 2007 US mortgage guarantor Freddie Mac is selling $6bn of shares to cover bad debt losses

US house prices dropped sharply in the third quarter, falling at their biggest rate in 21 years

Citigroup agrees to sell shares worth $7.5bn to an investment fund owned by Abu Dhabi

29 November 2007 The US lowers its 2008 economic growth forecast amid housing and credit market problems

30 November 2007 US construction spending falls sharply, led by a large fall in the building of homes

Morgan Stanley co-president Zoe Cruz is to retire, seen as a casualty of the subprime crisis

3 December 2007 Credit agency Moody's widens its debt review, having already earmarked $116bn of debt for downgrading

4 December 2007 US mortgage lender Fannie Mae is to issue $7bn of shares to cover losses linked to the housing market

Canada cuts interest rates for the first time since April 2004 amid credit fears

6 December 2007 US president George W. Bush outlines plans to protect more than a million homeowners hit by the housing slump

Royal Bank of Scotland warns it will write off about £1.25bn because of exposure to the US subprime market

The Bank of England cuts UK interest rates for the first time since 2005, amid signs that the economy is slowing down

The European Central Bank keeps interest rates in the euro-zone at 4 per cent

10 December 2007 UBS reports a further $10bn writedown caused by bad debts in the US housing market

Lloyds TSB reveals that bad debt linked to the US subprime mortgage crisis will cost it £200m

11 December 2007 US Federal Reserve cuts interest rates for a third time to 4.25 per cent to ease the credit crunch

13 December 2007 World central banks agree coordinated action to inject at least $100bn into short-term inter-bank credit markets to restore confidence

14 December 2007 Citigroup takes $49bn worth of subprime debts back on its balance sheets; effectively closing seven structured investment vehicles that had relied on money market funding

17 December 2007	US Federal Reserve makes $20bn available to commercial banks at auction to help ease the credit crunch
	Former US Federal Reserve chairman Alan Greenspan urges the government to give direct aid to homeowners hit by the subprime crisis
18 December 2007	US Federal Reserve tightens rules on subprime lending, requiring mortgage companies to check more carefully on customers' income and give full disclosure of the cost of the loan
	ECB lends European commercial banks $500bn over the Christmas period to help ease the credit crisis
	Bank of England makes £10bn available to UK banks to ease credit crunch
19 December 2007	Morgan Stanley writes off $9.4bn in subprime losses and sells a 9.9 per cent stake in the company to the Chinese state investment company CIC for $5bn to rebuild its capital
4 January 2008	US unemployment rises sharply as job report sparks fall in stock market
7 January 2008	US president George W. Bush admits that the credit crunch could hinder the US economy in 2008, but says it is still fundamentally strong
	Economists urge US government action to ease looming economic slowdown as a result of credit crunch
9 January 2008	Bear Stearns boss James Cayne steps down after the firm reveals $1.9bn in subprime losses, the largest in its history
	World Bank says world economic growth will slow in 2008 because of the credit crunch, but strong performance in China and India will cushion the effect
11 January 2008	UBS warns that it still does not know its total losses from the subprime crisis and says it could make a loss in 2007 when it reports its full results
	Federal Reserve says the outlook for the US economy is deteriorating among continuing worries about the crisis
	Countrywide, which pioneered subprime mortgages, is bought by Bank of America for $4bn after its shares plunge 48 per cent
15 January 2008	Citigroup reports a $9.8bn loss for the fourth quarter and writes down $18bn in subprime losses. It also announces investments by Kuwait and Saudi Arabia
	UBS says the crisis has cost it about $13.5bn in total

▶

16 January 2008	JPMorgan Chase says its earnings for the last three months of 2007 fell 34 per cent as a result of its exposure to bad US mortgage loans. The bank said it had to cut the value of investments linked to the US mortgage market by $1.3bn
	US bank Wells Fargo reports a 38 per cent decline in net income to $1.36bn for its last three months of 2007
17 January 2008	Merrill Lynch unveils a $7.8bn loss for 2007, crippled by exposure to risky investments in the US housing market. The loss includes a massive $14.1bn writedown on failed investments related to subprime mortgages
18 January 2008	Ambac Financial Group is the first monoline insurer to be downgraded, as Fitch reduces its rating from AAA to AA. Because of the nature of monoline insurance, this event signalled a simultaneous downgrade of bonds from over US100,000 municipalities and institutions totalling more than $500bn
22 January 2008	Bank of America and Wachovia, the second and fourth-largest US banks, say quarterly profits were nearly wiped out by more than $10bn of writedowns and credit losses
	Ambac Financial Group reports a quarterly loss of $3.3bn after suffering record writedowns
24 January 2008	French bank Société Generalé reports it has uncovered a fraud by one of its traders, which will cost it €4.9bn
	Fitch Ratings cuts Société Generale's credit rating by one notch to AA–
25 January 2008	US legislators agree on a $150bn economic stimulus package that will offer tax rebates to boost growth
7 March 2008	CDX Broad Credit index five-year touches a record 185bp, having been at about 60bp in July 2007

CREDIT CRISIS EVENTS IN CONTEXT

Substantially lower risk tolerance among investors

Risk tolerance among investors received considerable blows. Poor sentiment among investors was fuelled by bad news concerning the US housing market and problems at hedge funds. Coinciding with this, rating agencies lowered the credit ratings of a number of investment products based on subprime (high risk) mortgages in the US. Declining risk tolerance among investors began to become apparent in mid-July. The S&P 500 index fell more than 5 per cent in the last two weeks of July and lost another 5 per cent in the first two weeks of August.

Revealing markets   **Key point**

The deteriorating sentiment had been revealed on the bond and CDS markets. The premium that investors demanded for credit risk rose sharply within a month.

These developments were accompanied by a sharp increase in volatility in all markets. International money markets were also faced in early August with a decreasing willingness among investors to provide loans to investment vehicles that (possibly) included subprime mortgages as underlying assets. The central banks had to come to the rescue and provide additional (temporary) liquidity to prevent an acute crisis.

From easy money...

To understand the underlying causes of the crisis on the financial markets, we must first go back to the original reason for the turmoil, i.e. the development of the subprime mortgage market in the US and the easy provision of loans by US financial institutions in the preceding years. The period 2002–04 was characterized by extremely low money market interest rates as a result of the accommodative monetary policy of the US Federal Reserve (and, to a lesser degree, the ECB).

The US central bank recognized a potential danger for deflation in 2003 and numerous parties at that time thought that low policy interest rates during that period were justified to prevent the economy sliding into a similar depression to that in which the Japanese economy had been languishing since the early 1990s. The combination of low interest rates and rising house prices led many people to take out a second and sometimes a third mortgage. 'Exotic' mortgages that only paid off interest or were adjustable rate became commonplace. Many mortgage providers offered loans with extremely low entry interest rates (sometimes for several years).

Speculative buying also abounded as people exploited rising house prices. Many consumers bought a house with borrowed money in the hope of being able to resell it in the short term. On the expectation of continuous increases in house prices, this made sense to them. This went hand in hand with the whirlwind growth of subprime mortgages. This growth was connected to the fact that many US families with a poor credit score were still eligible for a loan via the subprime segment of the mortgage market. The mortgage providers did, however, demand a higher interest rate as compensation for the greater risk of default. This was bound to lead to problems, in part due to the insufficient level of supervision. In some cases, loans were even extended to people who could not afford to take out a loan because they did not have any form of income. What's more, strong competition among subprime lenders is likely to have compelled mortgage lenders to take greater risks.

...via financial innovation...

Another development intertwined with the above developments was financial innovation. Mortgage lenders (and other financial institutions) increasingly securitized parts of their mortgage portfolio. In other words, the mortgages were pooled and resold in packages – tranches. Each tranche has its own rating (risk category). The tranche with the most risky rating takes the first loss from bankruptcies/delinquencies in the pool of mortgages and consequently pays out the highest premium. This premium is the credit risk premium, or credit spread, that the investor demands to compensate for bearing the mortgage risk.

The tranches were resold to other parties, including financial institutions, hedge funds and investors, and as a result the risks and returns were transferred to these parties. Reselling mortgages gives banks the advantage of removing the mortgages from the balance sheet. One of the driving forces behind this was to improve their solvency benchmarks in connection with increasingly stringent regulations (such as the BIS regulations). This was done by placing them in special vehicles or structured investment vehicles (SIVs). The SIVs (or conduits) are usually financed by money market loans that have the backing of the underlying assets, asset-backed commercial paper (ABCP).

The investors, normally money market funds, were attracted by ABCP because of the asset backing. Often, banks guaranteed the funding of the SIV, which means that banks would need to provide liquidity in case investors were not willing to invest in ABCP. Securitization also takes place with assets such as corporate loans and credit card loans.

...to tight money

When the US economy began recovering in 2004 and inflation started rising in tandem, the Federal Reserve decided to implement a policy of interest rate increases, which drove up the policy interest rate to 5.25 per cent in the summer of 2006. Some households were already having trouble making their house payments in the early part of this period, but rising interest rates meant that more and more families were finding it increasingly difficult to pay their mortgages.

This was not a unique phenomenon. Rises in the (real) interest rate had led to families experiencing payment difficulties before. However, in this instance, the homeowners who had initially enjoyed low entry interest rates were hit harder than the rest. In addition, a dangerous situation had emerged in which a growing supply of houses had been stimulated for years by speculative buying and the ease of the subprime market. So this time the increased interest rate led to a reduced demand for houses, slumping house prices, which in turn once again resulted in lower demand. This affected primarily the speculative buyers and created a downward spiral of increasing payment problems, forced house sales and falling house prices.

Decreasing value

The crisis in the housing market has two effects on the parties that purchased tranches with subprime mortgages as underlying assets. First, the tranches are worth less because of delinquencies; some people could no longer pay their mortgages.

Second, the market value of the tranches falls because investors are demanding higher credit spreads. The value of an asset falls when the expected future stream of cashflows are discounted at higher discount rates. In this case, the credit spreads, which have been fixed in the beginning, now need to be discounted at higher discount rates.

Increasing credit spreads

The subprime mortgage crisis had an effect on credit spreads in general. Credit spreads fell to historically low levels in the first half of 2007, which could be partially explained by both the good fundamentals at that time and considerable investor demand in their search for yield.

However, the spreads reached a level that could not be maintained. Yet, ample liquidity and the considerable demand for these kinds of investments by investors in pursuit of higher returns managed to delay a 'healthy correction' to these spreads. The developments in the US mortgage market and a general risk reconsideration among investors, however, caused the process to be accelerated and the spreads consequently widened considerably. Market players realized that the fundamental outlook was deteriorating and that credit spreads were too low.

The fact that the demand for risky debt had come to a standstill due to the problems in the housing market served to reinforce the effect on the widening of credit spreads. As stated above, the market value of risky debt fell because investors demanded a higher risk premium than was previously agreed. Therefore, investors who held credit risk in their books of any form, for example corporate bonds, mortgage loans or structured credit, suffered a mark-to-market loss.

Slumping stock market

While credit spreads were rising, share prices were falling. The problems on the subprime mortgages market primarily hit the share prices of financials because they had direct exposure to the mortgage market.

However, investors feared that the problems would have repercussions on the economy as a whole and so the share prices of other sectors were affected.

Moreover, uncertainty regarding the consequences and the volatility on the markets led investors to reduce their positions in risky investments, such as shares. Another related factor was that hedge funds in particular had invested with borrowed money based on strategies that prospered in years when markets had shown low volatility. However, these strategies did not hold up in these extremely volatile markets and the process of reversing the leverage turned out to stir up the turbulence and worsen the situation. This also caused many investors to lose their confidence in hedge funds, which in turn once again led to redemptions and forced selling.

Reversing carry trade

As stated above, hedge funds often invested with borrowed money. As US and European central banks raised interest rates and the Bank of Japan conversely kept interest rates low, it paid to borrow in cheap yen, borrowings that were then exchanged into other currencies.

Low Japanese interest rates and good returns on investments denominated in other currencies, including deposits, shares and corporate bonds, made these 'carry trades' profitable. To some extent, the borrowings were hedged with forwards and options, but positions had been left open to pick up extra return.

Once returns began deteriorating, many of these positions had to be reversed, either by choice or force. As a result, a strengthening of the yen is likely against the euro, US dollar, Brazilian real and the New Zealand dollar. The yen carry trade also plays an important role in the contagion to other financial markets of what started as a subprime mortgage and credit crisis.

As investors in the mortgage and credit markets unwind their positions, this leads to a strengthening of the yen. In turn, the strengthening affects yen borrowers in general, for example hedge funds investing in equity markets, who see profits erode because of the loss made on the exchange rate. As a result, positions in other financial markets are unwound as well.

Investors seek a safe haven

Under the situations witnessed in early 2008, investor sought safety by switching out of high-risk investments (shares, corporate bonds) into government bonds (particularly short-term bonds that have limited duration exposure).

Such flows were clearly visible in financial markets in March 2008. This placed considerable downward pressure on interest rates, particularly in the US. For example, the yield on five-year US treasury notes fell by more than 90 basis points since it peaked at 5.25 per cent in mid-June (the yield on its German counterpart, the Bobl, plummeted by 50bp).

The fact that the flows sought exposure to short-term rates also meant a steeper interest rate curve in the US. This was, incidentally, less the case in the eurozone because market thinking there was that it was much less likely that the ECB would genuinely move to lower interest rates, while there was growing speculation that the US could lower the interest rate by as much as 50bp in the near term.

Volatility and mark-to-market

The tremendous volatility of the markets also caused problems when valuing positions. Many financial players such as investment banks use derivatives markets to hedge their exposures when they enter into transactions with other market players such as banks and investors. But the turbulence in the markets increased to the point that it proved difficult to hedge positions.

Moreover, volatility led to unwanted exposure for existing positions. Additionally, this caused problems relating to the pricing of financial instruments: in some cases parties could not, or were reluctant to, issue a valuation of these instruments and as a result in some cases the market came to a standstill. More stringent accounting and reporting regulations and the securitization of (originally) non-transferable loans created a situation in which more financial assets had to be continually valued at the 'current market price' or marked-to-market, rather than on the basis of more stable forms of valuation (such as 'cost price' or 'long-term valuation'). This resulted in investors being confronted with large fluctuations in the valuation of their assets (especially with markets being so volatile). In some cases, when there is a solvency problem or if investors want to pull out of investment funds en masse, investment funds (such as hedge funds) can be forced to sell assets. Falling market prices may then exert additional downward price pressure due to this forced selling.

Liquidity crisis

The financial markets were confronted with an acute liquidity shortage in the money market on Thursday, 9 August 2007, which involved primarily the dollar market but soon spread to euro markets. The most plausible explanation is that the collective banks were faced with an increased liquidity demand from the SIVs in which securitized loans had been placed.

It was revealed that these vehicles were encountering difficulties raising the required financing on the dollar money market (via commercial paper) because investors decided to stop providing funds to parties with uncertain exposure in the subprime market.

Key point	**No distinction**
	In short, investors were no longer able to make a distinction between those with and without exposures. Also, possible downgrades kept investors from investing in ABCP, as most investors have clearly defined investment criteria. Instead, investors primarily bought Treasury bills.

The vehicles in many cases turned to their sponsors (the banks) to step in as guarantors and provide them with liquidity. This consequently created an acute liquidity shortage in dollars among the banks. Also, banks were uncertain about which counterparties had subprime exposure, and to what extent. Therefore, they we reluctant to provide liquidity to any counterparty, even if there was no reason for doubt. This primarily hurt low-creditworthy guarantors of SIVs (conduits) and non-guaranteed SIVs.

Central banks meet most urgent need

The liquidity crisis caused the overnight money market rates (both in dollars and euros) to rise sharply, even at times to levels significantly above the official interest rates of the central banks.

The ECB was the first to inject temporary extra liquidity into the financial system and other large central banks followed suit. For example, the ECB injected €95bn on 9 August. It did this to promote market stability and to push money market rates back down to their original levels. Attempts to achieve these two objectives were only partly successful. It is, coincidentally, a misconception that the banks received the money from the central bank; they were required to provide collateral (in the form of, for example, government bonds) in exchange and the funding was also for an extremely short period. This, however, did not solve the problem. Banks still did not have full information about which counterparties had subprime exposure, and to what extent – the market lacked 'transparency'.

ACTION TAKEN

- The case for government intervention: smooth stock adjustment process and lower risk of fire sales; against: moral hazard, slow recovery.

- US Federal Reserve cut rates by 100bp in the second half of 2007. This was followed by an aggressive 75bp emergency rate cut on 22 January 2008, on emerging risks of an equity market meltdown.

- Subprime rescue plan by US Treasury (five-year freeze on mortgage rates that are scheduled to reset between January 2008 and July 2010 for sub-prime borrowers who were not more than 60 days behind and had a credit score below a certain level).

- US tax-cut plan worth $150bn (most individuals to receive $600–$1,200 tax rebates; cut in corporate taxes).

- MLEC, or 'super-SIV' initiative proposed but not seen as viable; recapi-talization of banks by sovereign wealth funds.

- Rescue plan for monoline insurers in US (monoline sector was said to have guaranteed $127bn of CDO exposures linked to subprime); poten-tial takeovers by other financial institutions.

SUBPRIME CREDIT CRUNCH: A SUMMARY

The subprime mortgage situation had its roots in the failure of market-based restraints on the riskiness of loans that lenders could make. Before securitiza-tion, subprime mortgage lenders retained the loans that they originated and, therefore, cared deeply about credit quality. Following the rise of securitiza-tion, bond insurers constrained subprime lenders from making unreasonably risky loans. The bond insurers did so through their pricing decisions and through limits on their appetite for risk. Later, sophisticated investors from the mainstream MBS area started taking credit exposure to subprime mort-gage ABS by purchasing subordinate tranches from uninsured deals. Like the bond insurers, they were experts in mortgage credit risk and that expertise was reflected in their risk appetite and pricing behaviour.

However, starting in 2004, CDOs and CDO investors became the domi-nant class of agents pricing credit risk on subprime mortgage loans. Their assessments of risk were based on a different approach from that of the bond insurers and traditional investors whom they replaced.

The CDOs essentially drove bond insurers and the traditional subordi-nate investors out of the market. The departure of the bond insurers and the traditional subordinate investors left a void, because the CDOs were less discriminating and selective in allowing high-risk loans to be included in securitizations. In the absence of restraints, lenders started originating unreasonably risky loans in late 2005 and continued to do so in 2007.

High levels of defaults and foreclosures have an effect far beyond the borrowers and their families. Communities suffer dislocations and the result can be great enough to become a political issue. Market-based restraints on lending practices are not sufficient to prevent a repeat of the 2007 crisis.

Accordingly, policy action to provide a better framework of restraints through legislation or regulation is an appropriate measure to prevent a repeat of the subprime problem.

SUBPRIME AND CREDIT CRUNCH DEBATE

Having examined the subprime crisis and credit crunch, I would like to conclude this primer on structured credit products on a positive note by looking at possible ways risk management by banks and other users of structured credit products can improve and catch up with the innovation in the structured credit markets. I have posed some simple questions within the context of the current subprime crisis, and provided some answers.

ECB and Fed and interbank lending

Why did the ECB and Fed flood the money markets with liquidity in August 2007?

Interbank lending was seizing up. Overnight interest rates shot up above the target levels of the central banks. Rates spiked to 4.6 per cent in Europe against an official rate of 4 per cent and 6 per cent in the US, against an official rate of 5.25 per cent.

Why wouldn't banks lend to each other?

Banks didn't know who was creditworthy. They didn't want to end up losing money by popping it into an unsound institution.

What triggered this?

The situation had been building up for weeks. The final straw was the fear that the banks might be on the hook of emergency back-up loans needed to bail out the commercial paper (CP) market. Most of these loans were put in place on the assumption that they would never be called upon. The problem was that investors in the CP market seemed to have gone on a buyers' strike. Suddenly, the banks faced demands to pay those loans.

CP financing of mortgage-backed securities

Why did CP buyers go on strike?

A lot of the commercial paper was used to finance asset-backed securities. Some of these were for subprime mortgages in the US. Many of these mortgages were given to people with no income, no jobs, no assets (so-called Ninja mortgages). CP is only as safe as the houses it was secured against – and in many cases this turned out to be not very safe.

But hadn't we known about subprime problems for months?

Yes. They have been exposed by falling house prices. One consequence: if you grabbed a delinquent's home, the collateral might not be good enough to pay back the loan.

Why would anybody make a Ninja mortgage?

Banks thought they were protected for two reasons. First, US house prices were rising. So, if worst came to worst, the lenders could just grab the house, sell it and recoup the loan. Second, the banks didn't hang on to the loans. They just packaged the loans up and sold them off to somebody else, taking a cut. The risk was cleverly sliced and diced, allowing many of the securities to be dressed up as credits rated at triple A.

The credit crunch

So why was there a credit crunch?

Because of the game of pass-the-parcel, it had not been clear who was holding the toxic paper. In August 2007, though, blow-ups in different parts of the world rammed home how widespread the problem was. Three, in particular, spooked the markets: Bear Stearns in the US, IKB in Germany and BNP Paribas in France. What's more, another important market – lending to leveraged buyouts (LBOs) – had frozen.

Bad loans and unrealistic ratings

How could these mortgages get triple-A?

The likely-to-go-bad loans were put into pools with lots of other mortgages. Then the risks and returns on these pools were divided into tranches. The riskiest slices were called 'equity'. Whenever a mortgage in the pool runs into difficulties, the 'equity' tranche takes the first hit. It's only if all the equity gets wiped out that the next tranche steps up to the plate and has to take a hit. It's a bit like the lines of soldiers in a Napoleonic battle. Those at the back don't tend to get killed unless those in front are massacred first. The last ones in the line of fire are the triple-A tranche.

Bear Sterns

What happened to Bear Stearns?

The US investment bank sponsored two hedge funds partly invested in subprime paper. Most of the cash came from outside investors. They were then leveraged up by borrowing from other banks. When the subprime crisis hit, investors tried to take out their cash, but Bear closed the funds. The lenders also demanded more collateral – a so-called margin call – and asked Bear to pump in cash itself. Initially, it refused. But the investment bank was eventually prevailed upon to provide a $1.6bn credit line to the least risky fund. The creditors seized the assets of the other fund.

Why did this unnerve the market?

It suggested Bear had liquidity problems. It undermined confidence in the whole 'mark-to-model' method for valuing asset-backed securities.

The problem with mark-to-market

And mark-to-model?

For an asset that is traded frequently, financial institutions (such as banks and hedge funds) value it by looking at the market price. That's called mark-to-market. But some of these mortgage-security tranches were not traded – or only infrequently. So they were valued by reference to mathematical models that estimated how many mortgages were going to go sour. It's a bit like calculating how many soldiers in the back row are going to get killed by analysing old battles in the Napoleonic wars.

What's wrong with this?

It ignores liquidity. It's all very well to have an asset that is theoretically worth, say, 95 per cent of what you paid for it. But if you have to sell it in a hurry, because you are subject to a margin call, it's only worth as much as somebody is prepared to pay.

Leveraged buyouts (LBOs)

What have LBOs got to do with this?

Although it is a different market, financing techniques were similar. What's more, the market for supplying credit to LBOs got gummed up just after Bear's funds ran into difficulties. Some of the same institutions were involved, so there was a double blow to confidence.

How does LBO financing work?

Initially, the debt is supplied by banks. They syndicate the debt on to others in the market.

What is the effect on the LBO market?

Some banks faced difficulties in syndicating the debt, for two deals in particular: Chrysler and Alliance Boots. This made banks reluctant. There was also a knock-on effect on equity markets because LBOs had been one of the factors boosting share prices.

Conduits

How does IKB fit into this?

The German bank set up an off-balance-sheet 'conduit' called Rhineland Funding. This invested in asset-backed securities, including some that owned bits of subprime mortgages. It funded itself with commercial paper – a huge $19bn worth. The problem was that banks that had provided CP back-up credit lines were worried that the CP market would seize up as soon as investors realized how exposed Rhineland was to these assets. The banks would then be called on to step into the breach. One of the banks, Deutsche Bank, alerted the German regulators. The result was that the CP market did indeed freeze up, causing problems for other entities funding themselves in the market.

Why was this any different from Bear?

There were two new worries. First, the virus was not contained in the US: it had crossed the Atlantic. Second, Rhineland's troubles focused attention on risks in the CP market, which had been considered a virtually risk-free investment.

How can lending to a conduit such as Rhineland be considered risk-free?

First, back-up loans meant banks would provide liquidity if the CP market failed. Second, sponsors (like IKB) put in 'credit enhancement' contracts, which mean they take the first hit if there are any losses.

Does this mean the risk rebounds on financial institutions?

That is why a problem that started with subprime mortgages in the US might infect other financial institutions.

Hedge funds

What happened to BNP Paribas?

It had three money market funds. Part of these were invested in instruments with exposure to the subprime market. When it found it couldn't get a value for these assets, it suspended redemptions.

The variation is that these BNP funds were 'money market' funds, which are supposed to be even less risky than conduits, let alone hedge funds. Money market funds are viewed as pretty much the same as cash. Investors expected to be able to pull their cash out whenever they needed it.

What is the role of hedge funds?

When asset prices fall, some investors want to take out their capital. The hedge fund then has to sell assets – driving prices down further. Financial institutions that lend them money then ask them to cut their leverage by making a margin call – as they did with Bear Stearns. That forces them to sell yet more assets. Other hedge funds come under pressure to sell – giving the vicious spiral a further twist. This is why big high-profile 'quant' hedge funds like Renaissance Equity Hedge Fund, Goldman Alpha and Man's AHL faced difficult times.

Why should this spread contagion beyond subprime?

Hedge funds that need cash quickly don't sell subprime assets because they'd get fire-sale prices. Instead, they sell other assets, such as shares.

And the financial institutions?

They are exposed to credit market woes in four ways: via trading losses on credit instruments they are holding on their own books; via CP back-up loans; via stuck loans to big LBOs; and through lending to hedge funds. Investment banks' equities businesses might suffer if stock markets fall. And their advisory businesses have fewer M&A opportunities.

How does this exposure spread contagion?

Financial institutions will become more risk-averse across the board. They won't just stop funding LBOs and subprime debt. They could become less keen to fund hedge funds, conduits and other special purpose vehicles. That could have a further knock-on effect. Eventually, financially sound companies may start to find it hard to roll over existing debt programmes or raise new finance, forcing them to delay investment. And banks could become more wary about lending to each other. That is why central banks put liquidity in the market.

The upshot of the credit crunch

What was the result of it all?
Even after a year of woes, no-one really knew what the situation was. Banks and other financial institutions don't disclose detailed risk positions to the market because other market players could then use that information to trade against them.

HOW REGULATORS AND BANKS IMPROVE RISK MANAGEMENT

The credit crunch unveiled two fundamental problems with financial regulations. First, 'mark-to-market' requirements had forced sales of assets by some investors who thought they were good value. These sales pushed prices lower, forcing other investors who mark to market to sell.

Mark-to-market and related mechanisms such as stop losses and value-at-risk are supposed to be good risk management, but in a crisis, they are a source of risk. The solution is to avoid forcing investors to sell because of short-term price volatility if that volatility is not a risk because they have long-term liabilities or funding. To protect against fraud, non-market pricing should be carried out by third parties and should be accompanied by greater transparency on asset quality. Regulators are moving towards this approach.

Financial markets are regulated because they are prone to systematic failure. The biggest source of systematic failure is the economic cycle. Markets are poor at judging risk through the cycle, so you might think contra-cyclical measures would be at the heart of regulation. However, regulation is blind and deaf to the cycle.

Regulatory capital should rise and fall with asset prices. This would ensure that when market optimism is at its peak, just before a crash, bank capital is strong. As it stands, at the peak of market optimism, financial institutions think their capital is strong because their market-sensitivity risk measures tell them risk is low. The credit crisis showed them this was not the case.

Notes and references

Chapter 2

1 Mashall R, Naldi M. Extreme Events and Default Baskets: Working Paper, Columbia Graduate School of Business et Quantitative Credit Research. Lehman Brothers Inc; 2002

Chapter 3

1 Black, Fischer and Scholes MS. Merton's 1974 model in: The pricing of options and corporate liabilities – Journal of Political Economy; 1973. pp. 81, 637–54

2 Jarrow and Turnbull. Pricing derivatives on financial securities subject to credit risk; 1995. pp. 53–85, vol.50

3 O'Kane and Turnbull. Valuation and Risk-Management of Credit Default Swaps; 2003. Lehman Brothers

4 Altman, Altman. High Yield Bond and Default Study, Salomon Smith Barney – U.S, Fixed Income High Yield Report; 2002.

5 Hull and White. The general Hull-White model and supercalibration; 2001; Financial Analysts Journal. pp. 6, 34–43. Valuing Credit Default Swaps 1: No Counterparty Default Risk. pp. 26–36; The general Hull-White model and supercalibration. Financial Analysts Journal; 2001. pp. 6, 57

6 Credit metrics is a methodology that quantifies credit risk. Refer to www.creditriskresource.com/papers/paper_125.pdf in portfolios of traditional credit products (loans, commitments to lend, financial letters of credit), fixed income instruments, and market-driven instruments subject to counterparty default (swaps, forwards, etc.)

7 Egert B, Backé P, and Zumer T, Credit growth in Central and Eastern Europe: new (over)shooting stars: European Central Bank (ECB); Working papers published in 2006 www.ecb.int/pub/scientific/wps/date/html/wps2006.en.html

See also:

Merton RC, (1974). On the pricing of corporate debt: the risk structure of interest rates, Journal of Finance; 1990. pp. 29, 449–470.

O'Kane and Turnbull (2003); O'Kane (2001); Credit Derivatives Explained, Lehman Brothers; 2001

O'Kane and Schloegl, Modelling Credit: Theory and Practice; 2001

Nicolo' A, and Pelizzon L, Credit derivatives and bank credit supply, Staff Reports Federal Reserve; 2006

www.federalreserve.gov

Chapter 4

1 On 12 January 2007, the International Swaps and Derivatives Association (ISDA) published the 2006 ISDA Definitions. The definitions are intended for use in confirmations of individual transactions governed by an ISDA Master Agreement and are an update of the 2000 ISDA Definitions (including the Annex to the 2000 Definitions).

The 2006 Definitions are intended to provide the basic framework for the documentation of privately negotiated interest rate and currency derivative transactions but may also be used in documenting other types of privately negotiated derivative transactions.

www.isda.org/publications/isda2000def-annex-sup.html

2 The Bank for International Settlements (BIS) is an international organization of central banks which *'fosters international monetary and financial cooperation and serves as a bank for central banks.'* BIS carries out its work through subcommittees, the secretariats it hosts, and through its annual General Meeting of all members. It also provides banking services, but only to central banks, or to international organizations like itself.

www.bis.org/publ/bcbs122.pdf

Chapter 6

1 For an excellent discussion of the different approaches to compound correlation, see:

O'Kane D, and Livesey M. Base Correlation Explained, Lehman Brothers Quantitative Credit Research; 2004. pp. 3–20

For a discussion of base correlation, see:

Roy R, and Shelton D. Trading Credit Tranches; Citigroup, Global Structured Credit Strategy. London; 2004

2 Rajan A, Mcdermott G, and Roy R. The Structured Credit Handbook, Hoboken, N.J., John Wiley & Sons; 2007

3 Duffie, Time To Adapt Copula Methods For Modelling Credit Risk Correlation; 2004, (Risk 77)

See also:

Mashal R, Naldi M, and Tejwani G. The Implications of Implied Correlation; 2004. (Risk 66–8)

Chapter 9

1 Andersen L, Sidenius J, and Basu S. All your hedges in one basket, Risk; 2003. pp. 67–72

See also:

Gibson M. Understanding the risk the risk of synthetic CDOs. Trading Risk Analysis Section, Division of Research and Statistics. Federal Reserve Board; 2004

Li D. On default correlation: a copular function approach. Working paper – Risk Metrics Group; 2000

Mina J, Stern E. Examples and application of closed-form CDO pricing. RiskMetrics Journal; 2003. pp. 5–24

Chapter 10

For further reference on correlation structures, see:

Rajan A, Mcdermott G and Roy R. The Structured Credit Handbook, Hoboken, N.J., John Wiley & Sons; 2007

Further references

Hull JC. Options, Futures and Other Derivatives. 7th ed. Pearson Education, London; 2008

Hull JC and White A. Valuing credit default swaps II: modelling default correlations – Journal of Derivatives 8; 2001. pp. 12–22

Hull JC and White A. The valuation of credit default swap options: working paper, University of Toronto; 2003

Finger C. Conditional approaches for CreditMetrics portfolio distributions – RiskMetrics Group, New York; 1999

Finger C, A comparison of stochastic default rate models. RiskMetrics Group, New York; 2000

Fitch Ratings – Default correlation and its effect on portfolios of credit risk Structured Finance, Credit Products Special Report; 2003

Glossary

Asset-backed commercial paper (ABCP) Commercial paper collateralized by loans, lease, receivables or asset-backed securities

Asset-backed security (ABS) A type of bond or note that is based on pools of assets, or collateralized by the cashflows from a specified pool of underlying assets. Assets are pooled to make otherwise minor and uneconomical investments worthwhile, while also reducing risk by diversifying the underlying assets. Securitization makes these assets available for investment to a broader set of investors. These asset pools can be made of any type of receivable, from the common, like credit card payments, car loans, and mortgages, to esoteric cashflows such as aircraft leases, royalty payments and movie revenues. Typically, the securitized assets might be highly illiquid and private in nature

Call (put) option A financial contract that gives the buyer the right, but not the obligation, to buy (sell) a financial instrument at a set price on or before a given date

Capital-to-risk-weighted assets ratio A measure that represents an institution's capacity to cope with credit risk. It is often calculated as a ratio of categories of capital to assets, which are weighted for riskiness

Carry trade A leveraged transaction in which borrowed funds are used to take a position in which the expected return exceeds the cost of the borrowed funds. The 'cost of carry' or 'carry' is the difference between the yield on the investment and the financing cost (e.g. in a 'positive carry' the yield exceeds the financing cost)

Cash securitization The creation of securities from a pool of assets and receivables that are placed under the legal control of investors through a special intermediary created for this purpose. This compares with a 'synthetic' securitization where the generic securities are created out of derivative instruments

Collateralized debt obligation (CDO) In financial markets, CDOs are a type of asset-backed security and structured credit product. CDOs gain exposure to the credit of a portfolio of fixed income assets and divide the credit risk among different tranches: senior tranches (rated AAA), mezzanine tranches (AA to BB), and equity tranches (unrated). Losses are applied in reverse order of seniority and so junior tranches offer higher coupons (interest rates) to compensate for the added risk. CDOs serve as an important funding vehicle for portfolio investments in credit-risky fixed-income assets

Collateralized loan obligation (CLO) A structured vehicle backed by whole commercial loans, revolving credit facilities, letters of credit, or other asset-backed securities

Commercial paper A private unsecured promissory note with short maturity. It need not be registered with the US Securities and Exchange Commission provided the maturity is within 270 days, and is typically rolled over such that new issues finance maturing ones

Credit default swap (CDS) A default-triggered credit derivative. Most CDS default settlements are 'physical', whereby the protection seller buys a defaulted reference asset from the protection buyer at its face value. 'Cash' settlement involves a net payment to the protection buyer equal to the difference between the reference asset face value and the price of the defaulted asset

Credit derivative A financial contract under which an agent buys or sells risk protection against the credit risk associated with a specific reference entity (or specific entities). For a periodic fee, the protection seller agrees to make a contingent payment to the buyer on the occurrence of a credit event

Credit-linked note (CLN) A security that is bundled with an embedded credit default swap and is intended to transfer a specific credit risk to investors. CLNs are usually backed by highly rated collateral

Credit spread The spread between benchmark securities and other debt securities that are comparable in all respects except for credit quality (e.g. the difference between yields on US treasuries and those on single A-rated corporate bonds of a certain term to maturity)

Derivatives Financial contracts whose value derives from underlying securities prices, interest rates, foreign exchange rates, commodity prices, and market or other indices

Expected default frequency An estimate of a firm's probability of default over a specific time horizon constructed using balance sheet and equity price data according to a Merton-type model

Hedge funds Investment pools, typically organized as private partnerships and often resident offshore for tax and regulatory purposes. These funds face few restrictions on their portfolio and transactions. Consequently, they are free to use a variety of investment techniques, including short positions, transactions in derivatives and leverage, to raise returns and cushion risk

Hedging Offsetting risk exposure by taking an opposite position in the same or a similar risk, for example by buying derivatives contracts

Implied volatility The expected volatility of a security's price as implied by the price of options or swaptions (options to enter into swaps) traded on that security. Implied volatility is computed as the expected standard deviation that must be imputed to investors to satisfy risk-neutral arbitrage conditions, and is calculated with the use of an options pricing model such as

Black–Scholes. A rise in implied volatility suggests the market is willing to pay more to insure against the risk of higher volatility, and hence implied volatility is sometimes used as a measure of risk appetite (with higher risk appetite being associated with lower implied volatility). One of the most widely quoted measures of implied volatility is the VIX, an index of implied volatility on the S&P 500 index of US stocks

Institutional investor A bank, insurance company, pension fund, mutual fund, hedge fund, brokerage, or other financial group that takes large investments from clients or invests on its own behalf

Interest rate swap An agreement between counterparties to exchange periodic interest payments on some predetermined dollar principal, which is called the notional principal amount. For example, one party will make fixed-rate and receive variable-rate interest payments

Intermediation The process of transferring funds from the ultimate source to the ultimate user. A financial institution, such as a bank, intermediates credit when it obtains money from depositors or other lenders and on-lends it to borrowers

Investment-grade obligation A bond or loan is considered investment grade if it is assigned a credit rating in the top four categories. S&P and Fitch classify investment-grade obligations as BBB– or higher, and Moody's classifies investment grade bonds as Baa3 or higher

Large complex financial institution (LCFI) A financial institution operating in many sectors and often with an international scope

Leverage The proportion of debt to equity. Leverage can be built up by borrowing (on-balance-sheet leverage, commonly measured by debt-to-equity ratios) or by using off-balance-sheet transactions

Leveraged buy-out (LBO) Acquisition of a company using a significant level of borrowing (through bonds or loans) to meet the cost of acquisition. Usually, the assets of the company being acquired are used as collateral for the loans

Leveraged loans Bank loans that are rated below investment grade (BB+ and lower by S&P or Fitch, and Baa1 and lower by Moody's) to firms with a sizeable debt-to-EBITDA ratio, or trade at wide spreads over Libor (e.g. more than 150 basis points)

Libor London Interbank Offered Rate

Mark-to-market (MTM) The valuation of a position or portfolio by reference to the most recent price at which a financial instrument can be bought or sold in normal volumes. The mark-to-market value might equal the current market value (as opposed to historic accounting or book value) or the present value of expected future cashflows

Mezzanine capital Unsecured, high-yield, subordinated debt, or preferred stock that represents a claim on a company's assets that is senior only to that of a company's shareholders

Monoline insurance Monoline insurers guarantee the timely repayment of bond principal and interest when an issuer defaults. Insured securities range from municipal bonds and structured finance bonds to collateralized debt obligations (CDOs) domestically and abroad

Mortgage-backed security (MBS) A security that derives its cashflows from principal and interest payments on pooled mortgage loans. MBSs can be backed by residential mortgage loans (RMBS) or loans on commercial properties (CMBS)

Nonperforming loans Loans that are in default or close to being in default (i.e. typically past due for 90 days or more)

Payment-in-kind toggle note A note (or loan) feature that gives the borrower the option to defer the interest due on existing debt or to make payment using new debt, and in the process pay an effectively higher interest rate

Primary market The market in which a newly issued security is first offered/sold to investors

Private equity Shares in companies that are not listed on a public stock exchange

Private equity funds Pools of capital invested by private equity partnerships. Investments can include leveraged buyouts, as well as mezzanine and venture capital. In addition to the sponsoring private equity firm, other qualified investors can include pension funds, financial institutions and wealthy individuals

Put (call) option A financial contract that gives the buyer the right, but not the obligation, to sell (buy) a financial instrument at a set price on or before a given date

Risk aversion The degree to which an investor who, when faced with two investments with the same expected return but different risk, prefers the one with the lower risk. That is, it measures an investor's aversion to uncertain outcomes or payoffs

Risk premium The extra expected return on an asset that investors demand in exchange for accepting the risk associated with the asset

Secondary markets Markets in which securities are traded after they are initially offered/sold in the primary market

Securitization The creation of securities from a pool of pre-existing assets and receivables that are placed under the legal control of investors through a special intermediary created for this purpose (a 'special-purpose vehicle' [SPV] or 'special-purpose entity' [SPE]). With a 'synthetic' securitization the securities are created out of a portfolio of derivative instruments

Structured investment vehicle (SIV) A legal entity, whose assets consist of asset-backed securities and various types of loans and receivables. An SIV's liabilities are usually tranched and include debt that matures in less than one year and must be rolled over

Security arbitrage conduit A conduit (a vehicle that issues ABCP only) that is formed specifically for the purpose of investing in assets using relatively cheap financing. The mix of assets can change over time

Sovereign wealth fund (SWF) A special investment fund created/owned by government to hold assets for long-term purposes; it is typically funded from reserves or other foreign currency sources and predominantly owns, or has significant ownership of, foreign currency claims on non-residents

Spread See 'credit spread' (the word credit is sometimes omitted). Other definitions include (1) the gap between bid and ask prices of a financial instrument; and (2) the difference between the price at which an underwriter buys an issue from the issuer and the price at which the underwriter sells it to the public

Sub-investment-grade obligation An obligation rated below investment grade, sometimes referred to as 'high-yield' or 'junk'

Subprime mortgages Mortgages to borrowers with impaired or limited credit histories, who typically have low credit scores

Swaps An agreement between counterparties to exchange periodic interest payments based on different references on a predetermined notional amount. For example, in an interest rate swap, one party will make fixed-rate and receive variable-rate interest payments

Syndicated loans Large loans made jointly by a group of banks to one borrower. Usually, one lead bank takes a small percentage of the loan and partitions (syndicates) the rest to other banks

Value-at-risk (VaR) An estimate of the loss, over a given horizon, that is statistically unlikely to be exceeded at a given probability

Yield curve A chart that plots the yield to maturity at a specific point in time for debt securities having equal credit risk but different maturity dates

Index

ABCP *see* asset-backed commercial
    paper (ABCP)
ABS *see* asset-backed securities (ABS)
accounting standards 87–8
Accredited Home Lenders Holding
    236
ACT/360 day count convention 109
Ambac Financial Group 244
American Insurance Group 221
Argentina default 11
asset-backed commercial paper (ABCP)
    246, 250
asset-backed securities (ABS) 5, 152, 160
Association of Credit Portfolio
    Managers 82
attachment/detachment points 133,
    191, 201–2, 212
Australian Prudential Regulation
    Authority (APRA) 92, 93, 95

back-of-the-envelope value 53
BAKred 92, 93
Bank of America 241, 244
Bank of China 239
Bank of England 240, 241, 242, 243
Bank of International Settlements (BIS)
    6, 89–90
Bank of Japan 248
bank regulation
    asset mismatches 93–4
    Bank of International Settlements
        (BIS) 89–90
    basket structures 92–3
    credit derivatives business 6–7, 6f, 41
    funded credit derivatives 91–2
    maturity mismatches 94–5
    unfunded credit derivatives 90–1
bankruptcy 27, 85, 87
    see also credit events

barbelling 171
Barclays 241
Basel Accord 6, 90
Basel Committee 88–9, 90–1, 94
basis drivers (CDS)
    accrued interest differentials 72
    arbitrage opportunities 68
    bond trading above par 72
    bond trading below par 69
    cheapest-to-deliver option 69
    counterparty default risk 71–2
    coupon specificities 73
    demand for protection 70–1
    fundamental determinants 69, 71–2,
        73
    funding issues 71
    issuance patterns 71
    negative basis factors 71–2
    positive basis factors 69–71
    positive/negative/undecided basis
        67–8, 73–4
    premia floored at zero 69
    profit realization 69
    relative liquidity 73–4
    restructuring clause 69
    risk factors 68
    shorting the cash market 70
    synthetic CDO issuance 72
    technical determinants 70–1, 72, 73–4
basis trades 76
basket default swaps
    default correlation 29, 31, 33
    hedging 33–5
    leveraging 33
    second-to-default (STD) baskets 30,
        32–3
    valuation pricing model 30
        see also first-to-default (FTD) baskets

Bear Sterns 12, 237, 243, 253, 254, 256
Bernoulli probability 120–21
binomial expansion technique (BET)
    207–8
BIS *see* Bank of International
    Settlements (BIS)
BISTRO (Broad Index Secured Trust
    Offering), case study 189–90
Black-Scholes model 50, 125
Bloomberg web pages 99, 103
BNP Paribas 238, 241, 253, 256
Bond Market Association (BMA) 88
bond spreads
    asset swap spreads 64–6
    CDS-bond basis 65–7
    fixed-rate bonds 63–4
    I-spread 64
    market asset swap spread 65
    option-adjusted spread (OAS) 65
    par asset swaps 64
    Z-spread 64
Bush, George W. 239, 242, 243

Calpine 69
Capital One 239
Capital Requirements Directive (CRD)
    81
cash CDOs (collateralized debt
    obligations)
    à la carte menu 157
    amortization phase 167
    arbitrage transactions 155–6, 158, 165
    asset manager 176
    assets 153–4, 157f
    balance sheet transactions 155–6,
        158, 165
    barbelling 171
    capital structure example 164–5
    cashflow CDO 153
    collateral manager 162
    collateral portfolios 158
    collateral quality tests 172–3, 177–8
    coverage tests 169–70, 171–2
    credit structures 156–7, 157f
    deal summary 176
    debt returns 174–5

debt structure, typical 163
debt tranches 162–3
default/default losses definitions 154
definition of 152n
delayed draw feature 155
diversification 159–60, 175
equity returns 174
excess CCC haircut 171
fixed-rate/floating-rate mismatches
    162
investment-grade 153
investor motivation 158–9
junior notes 161
key features 175
lifecycle 166–7
market compass 152
market value structures 166
monoline reinsurance 162
outstandings 153–4
over-collateralization (O/C) 169,
    170, 171, 177
payment-in-kind provision (PIKing)
    171
performance tests 167, 176–7
preferred shares 161–2
purposes of 155–6, 157f
ramp-up phase 166–7
rating definitions 178
re-REMICs 153
repacks 153
revolving period 166–7
senior debt tranches 155
senior notes 161
special purpose vehicle (SPV) 152n,
    159, 160–1, 162
subordination 155, 168
tranches 154–5, 157f
trigger levels 169–71
trustee 162
variety 153
waterfall mechanism 164, 167, 168f,
    169, 170f, 175
workings of 161
cash settlement 15, 17, 19, 61, 142,
    191
CBO *see* collateralized bond obligation
    (CBO)

CDO (collateralized debt obligation) *see* cash CDOs; squared CDOs; synthetic CDOs

CDS *see* credit default swap (CDS)

CDX/iTraxx *see* credit indices

CFO *see* collateralized fund obligation (CFO)

China Investment Corporation (CIC) 243

Citigroup 240, 241, 242, 243

Classical Asset Pricing Model (CAPM) 114

CLO *see* collateralized loan obligation (CLO)

coefficient of variance 119–20, 120t

collateral synthetic obligation (CSO) 187–8, 200–1

collateralized bond obligation (CBO) 152n, 153

collateralized debt obligation (CDO) *see* cash CDOs; squared CDOs; synthetic CDOs

collateralized fund obligation (CFO) 152n

collateralized loan obligation (CLO) 5, 152n, 153

Collins & Aikman 12

commercial mortgage-backed security (CMBS) 152, 177

commercial paper (CP) 252

Commission Bancaire 93

Conseco 82–3

Constant Proportion Debt Obligation (CPDO) 3

Constant Proportion Portfolio Insurance (CPPI) 3, 9

convergence trades 76

copular functions 122–3, 136, 138–9

Gaussian copula model 122, 125, 130, 131–2, 137, 210

corporate collateralized debt obligations (CDOs) xi–xii

correlation

aggregate correlation 116–7

attachment/detachment points 133

base correlation 123–6

breakeven spread, calculating 134–6

CDO pricing summary 137

combined simulation results 134

compound correlation 125

copular functions 122–3, 130, 131–2, 136, 137, 138–9

correlated *versus* independent assets 114

correlation coefficient 126

correlation missing 136–7

credit indices 125, 137

credit risk portfolio analysis 129

default correlation 119–20, 129–30, 130, 131–6

default time 129–30, 132

diversification 126–7

extreme return 118

implied correlation 115, 117–8, 123–4

loss distribution 31–2, 121–2

loss tranche, valuing 133–4

meaning of 114–5

multivariate distribution 131

portfolio default 127–8

portfolio size, and volatility 119–20, 120t

price correlation 118

single tranche pricing methodology 125

spread correlation 116, 117

structured credit markets, valuation in 120–1

timing correlation 118

trading rules of thumb 138

tranche losses, sample path 133–4

tranched transactions, valuing 132–3

univariate distribution 131

see also 'rho'

counterparty credit charge (CCC) 59–60

counterparty risk 59, 71–2, 210

Countrywide Financial 238, 239, 243

CP market *see* commercial paper (CP)

CPDO *see* Constant Proportion Debt Obligation (CPDO)

CPPI *see* Constant Proportion Portfolio Insurance (CPPI)

credit crunch 10, 12, 235, 253, 257

see also subprime mortgage crisis

credit default swap (CDS)
  arbitrage transactions 56–7
  asset swap spread 28, 62
  basis calculation 24–5
  basis drivers 67–74
  bond basis 74–5, 75f
  bond cashflows 74, 75f
  cash settlement 15, 17, 19, 61
  corporate debt 60–1
  counterparty risk 59–60, 74, 75f
  coupon bonds 54–5
  credit curves 51–2, 55–6, 57–8
  credit deterioration risk, hedging 42
  credit events 14, 15, 16, 61
  credit modelling 44–7
  customizability 20
  default probability, calibrating 52–4
  default swap basis calculation 28
  delivery option 61
  description of 16–17
  digital settlement 17, 19
  versus insurance contract 16
  interpolation assumptions 54
  ISDA standards/definitions 16
  joint defaults, modelling 48–9
  leverage 20
  liquidity 16, 56
  mark-to-market methodologies 50–1
  market segmentation 56
  mechanics of 14–16, 14f
  no-arbitrage assumptions 60, 62
  obligations 56
  option pricing models 50
  par floater bond spread 28
  physical settlement 15, 17–18, 61
  position, valuation of 46–7
  practical credit default swap
      application 26–7
  predicive/theoretical pricing models
      49–50
  premium leg 14
  pricing model 45–6
  principle payments, timing of 74
  protection leg 14–15
  recovery assumption 54–5
  recovery rates 47–9

  reduced-form models 44, 48, 62
  risk measures for 23–4
  short credit 20
  single credit modelling 44–5
  single-name CDS 19, 25, 76–7
  spread levels 62
  spread view 20
  uses of 41
  Wal-Mart example 26
  see also bond spreads
credit derivatives business
  asset managers 9
  bank regulation of 89–95
  bank uses of 6–7, 6f, 41
  corporates 10
  at crossroads xi–xii
  dealers 7–8
  funded versus unfunded 28
  hedge funds 6f, 8–9
  insurance companies 6f, 9
  interdealer brokers 10
  investment banks 6
  market size 3–5, 10–12, 60
  pension funds 9
  protection, buyers and sellers of 6, 6f
  retail investors 9–10
credit events
  baskets 142
  CDS 14, 15, 16, 61
  definitions of 14, 27, 87
  restructuring 83–4
  synthetic CDOs 180–1
  tranched indices 109–10
credit indices 3, 5, 8, 128
  background to 100–2
  DJ CDX EM 99t
  DJ CDX NA HVOL 99t
  DJ CDX NA HY B 99t
  DJ CDX NA HY BB 99t
  DJ CDX NA IG 11, 99t, 100, 103,
      105f, 106, 108, 109
  DJ CDX NA XO 99t
  early indices 102
  examples 101
  global benchmarks 100–1
  HiVol indices 102

index cashflows 99
index maturities 101
iTraxx Asia ex-Japan 99t
iTraxx CJ Japan 99t
iTraxx Europe 99t
iTraxx Europe Crossover 99t
iTraxx Europe HiVol 99t
main indices 98–9
merging of 12
new indices 101, 102
on-the-run index 101
single name *versus* indices basis 102
standardized index trades 101
standardized payment and maturity
    dates 100
start of 11
theoretical *versus* market price 102
trading dynamics 102
Xover indices 102
    see also tranched indices
credit-linked note (CLN) structures 91–2
credit portfolio management 6–7
credit risk, trading of 3
Credit Suisse 240
CreditMetrics 49, 59
CSO *see* collateral synthetic obligation
    (CSO)
curve flatteners 77
curve steepeners 77
curve trades 77

dealers
    licensed index dealers 8t
    market making function 7
    proprietary trading 7
debt service coverage ratio (DSCR) 177
deliverable obligations (CDS) 15, 18
Delphi 12, 69
delta hedging 34
delta migration
    changes over time 222–4
    in-the-money and out-of-the-money
        tranches 222, 224
    index levels 221–2
delta spread changes
    change, estimating 218

junior *versus* senior tranches 219
PV01, and PV01% 218
spread sensitivity 218
upfront payments, impact of 219
Deutsche Bank 7, 240
digital settlement 17, 19
Dillon Read Capital Management 237
diversity scores 172
documentation
    Basel accords 80–1
    Credit Derivatives Definitions 82–3,
        85
    flexibility 80, 89
    ISDA, role of 81
    Long Form Confirmation 82
    restructuring clause 82
    synthetic CDO market 81
documentation and regulations 80–95
DR Horton 236
DTCC DerivServ settlement system 9

Enron 11
European Central Bank (ECB) 238,
    239, 242, 243, 250, 252

Fannie Mae 237, 242
Federal Reserve Board (FRB) (US) 12,
    92, 93, 237, 238, 240, 241, 242,
    243, 246–7
Financial Accounting standard Board
    (FASB) 88
Financial Services Authority (FSA)
    (UK) 92, 93, 95, 237
first-to-default (FTD) baskets
    advantage of 29
    basket default swap mechanics
        142–4
    cash settlement 142
    correlation products 143–4
    credit events 142
    five-name baskets 29–30, 30f, 142,
        143f
    funded baskets 149–50
    investor motivation 144–5, 148–9
    mergers 146–8
    *n*th-to-default basket products 142

first-to-default (FTD) baskets
   (*continued*)
   physical settlement 142
   pricing, and correlation 31–3
   protection, selling 143
   second-through-fifth default baskets
      148–9
Fitch ratings 177, 178, 244
fixed rate payer 16
floating rate payer 16
Freddie Mac 237, 241, 242

Gaussian copula model 122, 125, 130,
      131–2, 137, 210
GMAC 237
Goldman Sachs 238, 240, 241
Greeks, summary of 216
   see also tranche sensitivity,
      understanding
Group of Six (G6) 83
guaranteed investment contract (GIC)
      account 187

HSBC 236, 241

'I-gamma', spread distribution changes
   insurance moves to the right example
      219–21
   tranche pricing effect 220, 220f
IKB Deutsche Industriebank 239, 253,
      255
indices *see* credit indices
innovation
   and risk management 234
   subprime mortgage crisis 245–6
insurance companies 6f, 9
insurance policies 9, 16
interest coverage (I/C) ratio 177
Internal Revenue Service (IRS) (US) 88
International Accounting Standards
      (IAS) 87
International Association of Credit
      Portfolio Managers (IACPM) 88
International Monetary Fund (IMF) 240
International Swaps and Derivatives
      Association (ISDA)

documentation 81–3, 85, 86
   market size survey 3, 5
International Swaps and Derivatives
      Association (ISDA) definitions
      (2003) 5, 11, 12
   bonds and loans procedures 87
   credit events 87
   guarantees 87
   novation provision 87
   reference entity successor tests 83
   restructuring 83–7
iTraxx *see* credit indices

JPMorgan 7, 49
JPMorgan Chase 237, 241, 244
jump-to-default (JTD) sensitivity
   default, delta-neutral loss due to
      226–7, 228
   default, losses cause by 226–7
   net default *versus* spread sensitivities
      228
   tranche thickness 227, 228
   upfront payment, effect of 228

Kensington Mortgagees 241

leveraged buyouts (LBOs) 253, 254–5,
      256
Lloyds TSB 242
loan diversity index (LDI) 178
loan-to-value index (LTV) 177
London Investment Banking
      Association (LIBA) 82, 88
long-only funds 9
loss given default (LGD) 20, 23

'M-gamma', convexity
   mezzanine tranche sensitivity 226
   tranche and index value relationship
      224
   tranche convexity, delta-neutral 224
mark-to-market (MTM) 24
   counterparty risk 59
   credit default swap (CDS) 50–51
   MTM(*t*) 46
   subprime mortgage crisis 249, 254

market makers *see* dealers
Marsh & McLennan 219, 221
Master Liquidity Enhancement Conduit
    (MLEC) initiative 251
mergers 146–8
Merkel, Angela 239
Merrill Lynch 240, 244
Mizuho 241
Mod Mod R 84, 85, 86, 100
Mod R 84, 85–6, 100
monoline reinsurance 162
Monte Carlo simulations 129, 131,
    132, 139, 207
Moody's 119–20, 173, 242
Morgan Stanley 241, 242, 243
mortgage-backed security (MBS) 152,
    177, 235, 252–3
MTM *see* mark-to-market (MTM)
multi binomial variation 208
multivariate distribution 131

negative basis trades 76
New Century Financial 236
NIBC 238
No R 84, 85, 86, 100
Northern Rock 239–40, 241

OECD banks 90, 94
Old R 84, 85
Omni Financial Services 92
option-adjusted spread (OAS) 65
over-collateralization (O/C) 169, 170,
    171, 177
over-the-counter (OTC) derivatives 3, 16

Paragon (UK) 241
payment-in-kind provision (PIKing) 171
physical settlement 15, 17–18, 61, 142
poolwide expected loss (PEL) 176–7,
    178
Predatory Lending and Mortgage
    Protection Act (US) 241
premium, definition of 27
profit and loss (P&L) adjustments 21
PV01 24, 106, 218

quant hedge funds 256

recovery rate haircuts 208
reduced-form models (CDS) 44, 48, 62
reference entity 3, 11, 27
reference portfolio 16
repo market 174
residential mortgage-backed security
    (RMBS) 152
restructuring, ISDA definitions
    cheapest-to-deliver option 84
    credit event, value of 83–4
    hard credit events 85
    Mod Mod R variant 84, 85, 86
    Mod R restrictions 84, 85–6
    No R 84, 85, 86
    Old R 84, 85
    soft credit events 85
'rho', correlation changes
    five-year IG spreads 231
    junior and senior tranches 229–31
    par spreads for five-year IG 230–1
risk management 90–1, 234, 257
Risk Management Association (RMA)
    82, 88
risky cashflows 52, 55
Royal Bank of Scotland 242

Sachsen Landesbank 239
second-to-default (STD) baskets 30,
    32–33
    see also basket default swaps
securities houses 6
settlement
    cash settlement 15, 17, 19, 61, 142,
        191
    definition of 27
    digital settlement 17, 19
    physical settlement 15, 17–18, 61,
        142
single-name credit default swaps 3
single-tranche CDOs (STCDOs) 184
    attachment/detachment points 191
    cash settlement 191
    correlation strategies 194–6
    credit default swaps 191

single-tranche CDOs (STCDOs)
  (*continued*)
  investment strategies 191–9
  leverage strategies 192–3
  micro-macro hedging strategies 197–9
  reference portfolio selection 190
  relative value strategies 196–7
  single tranche cash flows 191
  single tranche ratings 192
SIV *see* structured investment vehicle (SIV)
Société Générale 244
special purpose vehicle (SPV) 152n, 159, 160–1, 162, 185–6, 205–7
spread PV01 (SPV01) 24, 106, 218
SPV *see* special purpose vehicle (SPV)
squared CDOs (collateralized debt obligations)
  attachment/detachment points 212
  default location, importance of 212f
  loss levels 212–13
  numbers of 211
  outer/inner portfolios 211
  rationale for 212
  structure of 211–12
  subordination 211
  types of 211
Standard and Poor's (S&P) 208–9, 245
standards *see* International Swaps and Derivatives Association
STDCOs *see* single-tranche CDOs
stress factor 208
structured credit market 2
structured investment vehicle (SIV) 235, 250
subprime mortgage crisis
  bad loans 253
  carry trade, reversing 248
  CDOs approach 251
  conduits, and IKB 255
  credit crunch 12, 235, 253, 257
  credit/liquidity risks, combination of 235
  credit spreads, increasing 247–8
  economic growth, stunting of 236
  exotic mortgages 245
  financial innovation 245–6

foreclosures, increase in 234–5, 252
government intervention 251
hedge funds 256
house buying, speculative 245–6, 247
interbank lending 252
interest rate adjustments 236, 245, 246–7
investors, lower risk tolerance among 244–5
leveraged buyouts (LBOs) 254–5
liquidity crisis 250
loan riskiness 251
mark-to-market, problem with 249, 254
market volatility, increased 245
MLEC initiative 251
monoline insurers rescue plan, US 251
mortgage-backed securities (MBS) 235, 252–3
mortgage reselling 246, 247
refinancing difficulties 235
stock market slump 248
structured investment vehicles (SIV) 235
tax-cut plan 251
unfolding of 236–44
US Treasury rescue plan 251
Swiss Re 241
synthetic arbitrage CLO 153
synthetic CDOs (collateralized debt obligations) 3, 153
  AAA reference portfolio example 187–8
  attachment/detachment points 201–2
  balance sheet *versus* arbitrage transactions 184, 204
  BISTRO (Broad Index Secured Trust Offering), case study 189–90
  and CDS, mechanics of 180–1
  collateral synthetic obligations (CSOs) 187–8, 200–1
  counterparty credit risk 210
  credit quality, determining 210
  economic advantages of 184–5
  eligible collateral 181
  eligible investments 187

examples of 181–2, 185–7
full capital structure 36–37
funded *versus* unfunded 184, 205–7
investor motivations 183–5, 189–90
market size 35
mechanics of 37
portfolio loss distribution 38–9
rating agency approaches 207–9
relative value investor rationale 185
reputational risks 188
reserve account 187
risk redistribution 35–6, 39, 40–1, 40f
risk/reward profile 188
static *versus* managed 204–5
trading constraints 210
tranche loss distribution 39–40
    see also single-tranche CDOs
    (STCDOs)
Synthetic Tracers 11

'theta' time decay
5-year IG, speed of time decay for
    229, 230f
5-year IG, time decay for 229
leverage, effect of 228
Thornburg 238
trades
    credit curve 22
    negative basis 21
    positive basis 22
    relative value 21
    senior *versus* subordinated 22–3
    trading the credit spread 20
tranche sensitivity, understanding
    convexity ('M-gamma') 224–6
    correlation changes ('rho') 229–31
    delta migration 221–4
    Greeks, summary o 216
    jump-to-default 226–8

precision 216
spread changes ('delta') 218–19
spread distribution changes
    ('I-gamma') 219–21
time decay ('theta') 228–9
tranches, as options on default losses
    217, 232
tranched indices
    accurate indices 110
    benchmark tranches 105–8
    credit default swap indices 98–102
    credit derivative indices 108
    credit event trading example 109–10
    index cashflows, impact of defaults
        on 103–4
    investors 112
    iTraxx/CDX snapshots 111–12
    premium payments trading example
        108–9
    simple instruments 98
    standard default swap indices 104–5
    upfront payment, determining 103
transformers 9

UBS 237, 240, 243–4
univariate distribution 131

Vector, Monte Carlo simulation
    platform 209

Wachovia 241, 244
Wal-Mart 26
weighted average coupon (WAC) 177
weighted average life (WAL) 173
weighted average maturity (WAM) 173
weighted average rating factor (WARF)
    172–3
weighted average spread (WAS) 177
Wells Fargo 244
World Bank 243

FT

FINANCIAL
TIMES

Think big
for
less